# THE
# PURPOSE
## OF THE
# PAST

REFLECTIONS ON THE USES OF HISTORY

## GORDON S. WOOD

THE PENGUIN PRESS

*New York*

2008

THE PENGUIN PRESS
Published by the Penguin Group
Penguin Group (USA) Inc., 375 Hudson Street, New York, New York 10014, U.S.A.
• Penguin Group (Canada), 90 Eglinton Avenue East, Suite 700, Toronto, Ontario
Canada M4P 2Y3 (a division of Pearson Penguin Canada Inc.) • Penguin Books Ltd,
80 Strand, London WC2R ORL, England • Penguin Ireland, 25 St. Stephen's Green,
Dublin 2, Ireland (a division of Penguin Books Ltd) • Penguin Books (Australia),
250 Camberwell Road, Camberwell, Victoria 3124, Australia (a division of Pearson
Australia Group Pty Ltd) • Penguin Books India Pvt Ltd, 11 Community Centre,
Panchsheel Park, New Delhi–110 017, India • Penguin Group (NZ), 67 Apollo Drive,
Rosedale, North Shore 0632, New Zealand (a division of Pearson New Zealand
Ltd) • Penguin Books (South Africa) (Pty) Ltd, 24 Sturdee Avenue, Rosebank,
Johannesburg 2196, South Africa

Penguin Books Ltd, Registered Offices:
80 Strand, London WC2R ORL, England

First published in 2008 by The Penguin Press,
a member of Penguin Group (USA) Inc.

Copyright © Gordon S. Wood, 2008
All rights reserved

Acknowledgments to the original publishers of these essays appear with the
respective selection. The works which appeared in *The New York Review of Books*,
*The New Republic*, and *William & Mary Quarterly* are reprinted with permission
of the respective publisher. The letters by Jackson Lears, John Patrick Diggins,
and Richard K. Matthews were published in *The New York Review of Books* and
reprinted with permission of the publisher. For detailed copyright and permission
information, please see pages 321 to 323.

LIBRARY OF CONGRESS CATALOGING-IN-PUBLICATION DATA
Wood, Gordon S.
The purpose of the past: relections on the uses of history / Gordon S. Wood.
p. cm.
Includes index.
ISBN-13: 978-1-59420-154-7
1. Historiography.   2. Criticism.   I. Title.
D13.2.W66   2008
907.2—dc22        2007030979

Printed in the United States of America
1  3  5  7  9  10  8  6  4  2

DESIGNED BY MARYSARAH QUINN

TO BERNARD BAILYN,

*The Most Inspiring of Historians*

# CONTENTS

THE **PURPOSE** OF THE **PAST**

# INTRODUCTION

T HE REVIEWS COLLECTED in this volume were written over the
past quarter century or so. Like most historians, I have written
reviews of works of history since the beginning of my career over four
decades ago. But nearly all of my early reviews were for academic journals
and usually were short (five hundred words or so) and directed at an in-
sider academic readership. Only in the early 1980s did I begin to write
longer reviews (four thousand words or more) for nonacademic journals,
such as *The New York Review of Books* and *The New Republic.* Although such
long reviews take a considerable amount of time, more time certainly than
the brief reviews written for an academic journal, I have never regretted
writing them. Not only do such lengthy reviews for nonacademic journals
require you to come to terms with the larger implications of the book
under review, but they force you to convey what you say in language that
is intelligible to general readers. Writing reviews for a lay readership is a
marvelously stimulating experience, and all historians ought to try to do
it. If they did, they might make our history books much more readable.
Of course, it also helps to have superb editors like Robert Silvers at *The
New York Review of Books* and Leon Wieseltier at *The New Republic* in addition to the keen editorial eye of my wife, Louise.

Scott Moyers, my scrupulous editor at Penguin, and Andrew Wylie,
my indefatigable agent, suggested that I collect some of these lengthy
reviews in a single volume, especially those of books that revealed par-

ticular approaches to the writing of history. As I looked back over the dozens of lengthy reviews I've written over the past several decades, I realized that in some way I was marking the course of much of the research and writing in American history during this period. Perhaps it might be helpful, we thought, for readers who might not have read the original reviews or had forgotten them to see what has gone on in American history writing over the past twenty-five years, as least as it is represented by some of the books that I reviewed. At the same time, these reviews tend to reveal my own varied responses to what has happened to historiography during this tumultuous period.

During the past several decades we have experienced the culmination of what began over forty years ago—what one historian has called "a historiographical revolution." Since the 1960s new people have entered the profession and new subjects have been opened up for research. Instead of writing about statesmen, generals, diplomats, and elite institutions, historians began concentrating on ordinary folk and marginal people: the poor, the oppressed, and the silent. By the 1970s this new social history of hitherto forgotten people had come to dominate academic history writing. Although some historians continued to write political and institutional histories, most began writing about everything else but politics. In fact, there is scarcely an aspect of human behavior that historians over the past generation have not written about—from divorce to dying, from the consumption of goods to child rearing. Historians began delving into the most private, subjective, and least accessible aspects of the past, including marriage, sexual relations, and child abuse. Social science, especially anthropology and ethnography, enabled some historians to reconstruct from riots, rituals, and other kinds of popular nonverbal behavior in the past the beliefs and attitudes of the masses of ordinary men and women who left no written record. Others used social science to compile quantitative data on economic development, population growth, and rates of marriage and death. The profession turned out more and more complex, technical,

and specialized renditions of the past that fewer and fewer people were reading.

Several indices revealed that the American people were becoming less and less interested in the kind of social history academics were teaching and writing. From 1970–71 to 1985–86, years when there was a boom in student enrollments, the number of history degrees granted by all American colleges and universities declined almost by two-thirds, from 44,663 to 16,413. A drop in membership of the American Historical Association in the 1970s and 1980s was itself a sign of this weakening interest in history. The evidence compiled by Peter Novick in his *That Noble Dream,* published in 1988, reinforced the impression of a decline in academic history writing. Novick argued that the historical profession during the 1970s and 1980s seemed to have lost a unified sense of purpose; without a clear sense any longer of America's role in history, the discipline seemed to be coming apart. "In no other field was there such a widespread sense of disarray; in no other discipline did so many leading figures express dismay and discouragement at the current state of their realm." Many historians tended to see themselves as simply congeries of specialists solving technical problems and talking mostly to one another.

At the same time Novick was reaching his pessimistic conclusions, some historians began reacting against the disarray and calling for a return to narrative, to the kind of storytelling that, presumably, history was always noted for. Still others, however, wanted no part of a return to a traditional grand narrative, which they associated with the sort of history writing that had kept women and minorities out of the national story. They wanted instead to promote multicultural diversity, and discovered they could best do so by transforming social history into cultural history. Social history tended to be structurally descriptive and not ideally suited to the historians' desire to see people in all their variety and distinctiveness. By contrast, cultural history offered a way of penetrating through the large-scale economic and social structures of society into the many

different identities and cultures of people in the society. Although the new cultural history tended to increase the fragmentation and disarray, it soon came to dominate the profession.

By the late 1980s most historians in the United States had stopped compiling computer printouts and invoking Pearson correlation coefficients and had begun concentrating almost exclusively on cultural history, focusing especially on issues of race and gender. By now little else seems to matter. In 2006 the Organization of American Historians sponsored the publication of *The Best American History Essays 2006*. This was a collection of the ten best articles in American history as selected by a group of nine historians (of whom I was one) from over three hundred learned and popular historical journals published between the summers of 2004 and 2005. Seven of the ten best articles that were chosen dealt with issues of either race or gender; the only article I picked, one on Washington's presidency, managed to slip in. History departments appear to have stopped hiring anyone but cultural historians, the assumption being that cultural history is the only kind of history worth doing.

This new cultural history is undergirded by theory, and theory has become increasingly important to historians. Perhaps theory has always been part of historical reconstruction; certainly many of the new social historians have sought to apply theories from sociology, economics, and psychology with varying degrees of rigor. Marx and Freud, of course, had always been important in this respect. But the shift to cultural history seemed to require even more elaborate theories; and following the lead of literary scholars, historians in the 1980s began importing into their cultural history new theories, especially those of French intellectuals, such as Jacques Derrida and Michel Foucault. Implicit in many of these theories, which tended to emphasize the textual construction of reality, was an epistemological skepticism that worked to erode established and conventional ways of doing things. Literary scholars first began using these French theories to break down orthodox canons of literature in order to bring in new writers, new works, and new perspectives.

But the epistemological skepticism and blurring of genres that seem to have made sense for some literary scholars had devastating implications for historians. If historians began doubting that there was an objective past reality that they were trying to recover and began thinking that what they did was simply make up the past and write something that was akin to fiction, then they were not just clearing the ground for new kinds of approaches and subjects but were actually undermining the ground for any sort of historical reconstruction at all. Suddenly, it seemed as if Hayden White's contention, that historians were actually writing forms of fiction, which he had been making for many years, was at last being vindicated. Although few historians were willing to go as far as White, many were eager to make explicit the use of theory in their history writing. Some professors actually began criticizing the dissertations of their students for being "undertheorized."

Many feminist historians in particular were keen to import theory into cultural history. I recall listening to a feminist historian in the 1980s talking about using the ideas of Foucault to get rid of all the male-dominated history and clear the way for a new feminist history. When I observed that this seemed tantamount to using a nuclear weapon that could be subsequently used against the new feminist history itself, she replied, "We'll worry about that later."

Most historians have been much less self-conscious about their use of theory. They are not philosophers, and few of them have bothered to read Derrida or Foucault. Most are meat-and-potatoes practitioners of a craft, and, consequently, they have paid no more attention to the epistemological skepticism of the theorists today than their predecessors in the 1930s paid to the calls for an appreciation of European theories of relativism made by Charles Beard and Carl Becker in their addresses to the American Historical Association. Many historians have absorbed from the theories no more than the desire to write about issues of race and gender. And this desire has led to many stimulating and worthwhile contributions to our understanding of the past. Our knowledge of slavery in America, for ex-

ample, has been greatly amplified over the past forty years; and no one can deny that our appreciation of women's history has been similarly enhanced. But perhaps one less beneficial effect of the new cultural history has been to widen the gap between academic and popular history.

Perhaps the two kinds of history have never coincided, but in the 1950s academic historians such as Richard Hofstadter, Allan Nevins, Eric Goldman, Daniel Boorstin, and C. Vann Woodward certainly wrote history that appealed to both academic and general readers. That is much less true today. Consequently, popular historians who have no academic appointment, such as David McCullough, Walter Isaacson, Ron Chernow, Thomas Fleming, and Stacy Schiff, have successfully moved in to fill the void left by the academic historians preoccupied by issues of race, gender, and multiculturalism.

The result of all this postmodern history, with its talk of "deconstruction," "decentering," "textuality," and "essentialism," has been to make academic history writing almost as esoteric and inward directed as the writing of literary scholars. This is too bad, since history is an endeavor that needs a wide readership to justify itself.

What is the justification of history writing? Why should we study or read history? Some think history teaches lessons, but as I try to point out in chapter 4, in the review of Barbara Tuchman's *The March of Folly* (1984), I don't believe that history teaches a lot of little lessons to guide us in the present and future. It is not, as the eighteenth century thought, "philosophy teaching by example." Yet by disparaging the capacity of history to teach lessons, I don't mean to suggest that studying the past can't teach us anything. If history has nothing to say to us, then it wouldn't make much sense to study or teach it or read about it at all. History is important to us, and knowledge of the past can have a profound effect on our consciousness, on our sense of ourselves. History is a supremely humanistic discipline: it may not teach us particular lessons, but it does tell us how we might live in the world.

Some have said that history for a society is like memory for an individual. Without memory the individual is isolated, cut off from where he has been and who he is. But creating memory for a society, as several of these reviews indicate, is a tricky business; it can have very perverse effects, as some scholars have discovered over the past several decades.

Perhaps there has always been a tension between critical history and memory, between what historians write and what the society chooses to remember. But that tension has become much more conspicuous in recent years. Since the beginning of professional history writing a little over a century ago, critical historians have tried to transform memory, to eliminate its falsehoods, and to make it more accurate. Critical historians want the public to know that George Washington did not cut down his father's cherry tree, that Sojourner Truth did not utter the famous words "A'n't I a woman?" These were myths that people wanted to believe, and presumably it was the responsibility of historians to destroy these myths and to establish the truth of the past as much as possible.

In 1969 the distinguished English historian J. H. Plumb wrote a book titled *The Death of the Past,* which has recently been reissued in a new edition. By "the past," Plumb essentially meant memory or heritage, what he called the "created ideology"—the "mythical, religious, and political interpretations"—with which humans have sought to sanctify their societies, buttress their institutions, and invest their lives and their nations with a sense of destiny. Such memory, such imagined pasts, said Plumb, should never be identified with critical history. "True history," he wrote, was basically "destructive"; "for by its very nature it dissolves those simple, structural generalizations by which our forefathers interpreted the purpose of life in historical terms." Its role was to eliminate those simple generalizations and "to cleanse the story of mankind from those deceiving visions of a purposeful past." During the past generation historical scholarship apparently has fulfilled its destructive role only too well, and not just in America. As the historian Carl Schorske pointed out, "History,

conceived as a continuous nourishing tradition," no longer had the same meaning for society, or at least not for that part of the society that read academic history.

Modern critical history writing in the Western world, says the French historian Pierre Nora, has broken the "ancient bond of identity" with what he calls "memory," which is what Plumb meant by the "past." This "critical history," says Nora, has destroyed what hitherto "we had experienced as self-evident—the equation of memory and history." History has now clearly become the enemy of memory. "History," says Nora, "is perpetually suspicious of memory, and its true mission is to suppress and destroy it." But of course it cannot; memory, or what David Lowenthal has called "heritage," is necessary for any society. Heritage may be a worthless sham, its credos fallacious, even perverse; but, writes Lowenthal, "heritage, no less than history, is essential to knowing and acting." It fosters community, identity, and continuity, and in the end makes possible history itself. "By means of it we tell ourselves who we are, where we came from, and to what we belong." We thus tamper with our heritage, our memory, at our peril.

This confrontation between history and memory may be less direct and less serious than Plumb, Nora, or Lowenthal suggests. Many of the new cultural historians seem not to want to destroy memory as much as reshape it and make it useful to their particular cause, whatever it may be. Many of them have an instrumentalist view of history and see themselves essentially as cultural critics who wish to manipulate the past for the sake of the present. Rather than trying to understand the past on its own terms, these historians want the past to be immediately relevant and useful; they want to use history to empower people in the present, to help them develop self-identity, or to enable them to break free of that past.

In their well-intentioned but often crude efforts to make the past immediately usable, these scholars undermine the integrity and the pastness of the past. So we have some anthropologists claiming that the Iroquois confederation was an important influence on the framing of the

Constitution in 1787. Although there is not a shred of historical evidence for this claim, the fact that it might raise the self-esteem of Native American students is sufficient justification for some scholars that it be taught. Even the distinguished sociologist Nathan Glazer suggests that the myth might be taught to elementary school students, though not to students in junior and senior high schools.

Perhaps we can agree with Glazer that truth is not the only criterion for judging what might be taught in the social sciences, but surely falsehood ought not to be allowed on any grounds. Maybe this sort of useful and presentist approach to the past is inherent in being American. As the perceptive English historian J. R. Pole says, "What one misses [in America] is that sense, inescapable in Europe, of the total, crumbled irrecoverability of the past, of its differentness, of the fact that it is dead."

Even many of those historians who concede the pastness of the past and investigate "the past as a foreign country" do so primarily as anthropologists or social critics, seeing in the strange ideas and behavior of past peoples either alternatives to or object lessons for a present they find oppressive and objectionable. "Their vision of the past turns them toward the future," wrote Nietzsche of such sham historians; they "hope that justice will yet come and happiness is behind the mountain they are climbing. . . . They do not know how unhistorical their thought and actions are in spite of all their history." So these sorts of unhistorical historians ransack the past for examples of harmonious well-knit communities that we today ought to emulate, or they seek out abuses of patriarchal power in the past that we in the present must avoid. Much of the work of these present-minded historians thus does violence to what ought to be the historian's central concern—the authenticity of the past—and commits what the great French historian Marc Bloch called "the most unpardonable of sins"—anachronism.

I am not suggesting that history has no connection to the present; I am not advocating that history become antiquarianism. Quite the contrary. It is natural for historians to want to relate the past to the needs

and problems of the present. Indeed, historical explanation is only possible because we today have different perspectives from those of the historical participants we are writing about. Most new historical investigations
begin with an attempt to understand the historical circumstances that lie
behind a present-day problem or situation. It is not surprising that our
best recent work on the origins and nature of slavery coincided with the
civil rights movement of the 1960s. Or that our recent rich investigations
into the history of women grew out of the women's movement of the past
three or four decades. This is as it should be: the problems and issues of
the present should be the stimulus for our forays into the past. It is natural for us to want to discover the sources, the origins, of our present circumstances.

But the present should not be the criterion for what we find in the past.
Our perceptions and explanations of the past should not be directly
shaped by the issues and problems of our own time. The best and most
serious historians have come to know that, even when their original impulse to write history came from a pressing present problem. The best and
most sophisticated histories of slavery and the best and most sophisticated
histories of women soon broke loose from the immediate demands of the
present and have sought to portray the past in its own context with all its
complexity.

The more we study events and situations in the past, the more complicated and complex we find them to be. The impulse of the best historians is always to penetrate ever more deeply into the circumstances of
the past and to explain the complicated context of past events. The past
in the hands of expert historians becomes a different world, a complicated
world that requires considerable historical imagination to recover with
any degree of accuracy. The complexity that we find in that different
world comes with the realization that the participants were limited by
forces that they did not understand or were even aware of—forces such
as demographic movements, economic developments, or large-scale cul-

tural patterns. The drama, indeed the tragedy, of history comes from our understanding of the tension that existed between the conscious wills and intentions of the participants in the past and the underlying conditions that constrained their actions and shaped their future.

Drew Faust, in her superb book *Mothers of Invention: Women of the Slaveholding South in the American Civil War,* published in 1996, nicely captures this complicated character of history. What she hoped to do in her book, she says, was "to give a sense of how people are shaped and constrained by the world into which they are born, of how their choices are limited by the 'taken for grantedness' of their social universe." Faust writes that she "wanted to show how hard it is to cope with change, to adjust to a new world, even a world that to us seems unquestionably more morally and socially desirable—and to show how people managed not just to accept, but to justify social arrangements we today find abhorrent."

To be able to see the participants of the past in this comprehensive way, to see them in the context of their own time, to describe their blindness and folly with sympathy, to recognize the extent to which they were caught up in changing circumstances over which they had little control, and to realize the degree to which they created results they never intended—to know all this about the past and to be able to relate it without anachronistic distortion to our present is what is meant by having a historical sense.

To possess a historical sense does not mean simply to possess information about the past. It means to have a different consciousness, a historical consciousness, to have incorporated into our minds a mode of understanding that profoundly influences the way we look at the world. History adds another dimension to our view of the world and enriches our experience. Someone with a historical sense sees reality differently: in four dimensions. If it is self-identity that we want, then history deepens and complicates that identity by showing us how it has developed through

time. It tells us how we got to be the way we are. And that historically developed being is not something easily manipulated or transformed.

We have heard a lot over the past several decades about the cultural construction of reality: the so-called postmodern sense that the world is made by us. Historians have little quarrel with this notion of the cultural construction of reality—as long as this is understood as the historical construction of reality. Too often postmodernists think that by demonstrating the cultural construction of reality, they have made it easier for men and women to change that reality at will. If culture and society are made by us, they can be remade to suit our present needs, or so it seems. But anyone with a historical sense knows differently, knows that things are more complicated than that. History, experience, custom—developments through time—give whatever strength and solidity the conventions and values by which we live our lives have. Those conventions and values, however humanly created, are not easily manipulated or transformed. They, of course, have changed and will continue to change, but not necessarily in ways that we intend or want.

Take, for example, our debates over the meaning of the Constitution. Some believe that the Constitution has an absolute original meaning and want us to recover that absolute original meaning in our current interpretation of the Constitution. Others believe that the Constitution means today whatever we want it to mean—that's what they mean by a "living Constitution." Neither of these extreme positions is correct. Historians know that the meaning of the Constitution has changed and will continue to change through time. But they also know that no one is free today to give whatever meaning he or she wants to give to it. In our choice of interpretations we are limited by history: by the conventions, values, and meanings we have inherited from the past. Those who fear that abandoning a timeless absolute standard for interpreting the Constitution will lead to moral and intellectual chaos are wrong. History, experience, and custom are powerful restraints on what we can think and do. We are not

as free from the past as we think we are. Knowing this is to have a historical sense.

I don't want to suggest that this historical sense, this concern for the pastness of the past, implies a lack of interest in the future. In fact, I agree with the historian E. H. Carr that a sense of the future is essential to a sense of the past. In his series of lectures on *What is History?*, published in 1961, Carr pointed out that the writers of classical antiquity had little sense of history because they had little sense of a different future. "Thucydides," he said, "believed that nothing significant had happened in time before the events which he described, and that nothing significant was likely to happen thereafter." For the ancients "history was not going anywhere."

If one believes in a different past, one has to believe in a different future. Without a belief in the future there will be no concern for the past, indeed, no history at all. The writer P. D. James emphasized this point vividly in her curious dark 1992 novel *The Children of Men*, one of the few deviations from her usual Inspector Dalgliesh mysteries. She posits a time twenty-five years in the future when all human males have become sterile and no child can ever be born again. That is, the youngest person alive is twenty-five, and when all the twenty-five-year-olds finally die off, there will be no more humans. James's story is set in England, one of the most historically minded of all cultures. Her hero is an Oxford don, a historian, who discovers that without a future there cannot be much interest in the past. "History, which interprets the past to understand the present and confront the future," he says, "is the least rewarding discipline for a dying species." The historian-hero tries to imagine a world without a living human being—"the great cathedrals and temples, the palaces and the castles, existing throughout the uninhabited centuries, the British Library ... with its carefully preserved manuscripts and books which no one will ever again open or read." Of course, in this doomed world there are still some people who read books about the past, more out of habit

and what a colleague calls "the comfort of culture." All such readers want to do, his colleague tells the hero, "is to escape temporarily into a more agreeable and permanent world. We all do it, dear boy," he says, "only you and I call it scholarship."

I don't think that's what historical scholarship is for most historians. History is not just comfort food for an anxious present. Yet it does offer a way of coming to terms with an anxious present and an unpredictable future. Realizing the extent to which people in the past struggled with circumstances that they scarcely understood is perhaps the most important insight flowing from historical study. To understand the past in all its complexity is to acquire historical wisdom and humility and indeed a tragic sense of life. A tragic sense does not mean a sad or pessimistic sense of life; it means a sense of the limitations of life.

Unlike sociology, political science, psychology, and the other social sciences, which try to breed confidence in managing the future, history tends to inculcate skepticism about our ability to manipulate and control purposefully our destinies. Even the eminent scholars Richard E. Neustadt and Ernest R. May, who in their book, *Thinking in Time* (1986), have tried to show how history might be used by government decision makers, have had to concede that the most that history can teach governmental leaders is prudence and cautiousness. In today's world that may not be such a bad thing.

History that reveals the utter differentness and discontinuity of the past tends to undermine that crude instrumental and presentist use of the past that we Americans have been prone to. We Americans resist this kind of historical consciousness. We do not want to hear about the unusability and pastness of the past or about the limitations within which people in the past were obliged to act. We do not want to learn about the blindness of people in the past or about the inescapable boundaries of our actions. Such a history has no immediate utility and is apt to remind us of our own powerlessness, of our own inability to control events and predict the future.

I don't want to suggest that this kind of historical or tragic sense is necessarily deterministic or fatalistic. We do not have to fall into the pathetic mood of the French Annalist historian Fernand Braudel, who sees the individual "imprisoned within a destiny in which he himself has little hand, fixed in a landscape in which the infinite perspectives of the long term stretch into the distances both behind him and before." A sense of the tragedy of the historical process is not necessarily pessimistic, and it does not deny the individual's responsibility for his or her actions; indeed, by making people aware of the circumstances impinging on and limiting them, a historical sense makes true freedom and moral choice—and wisdom—possible. All the great tragic novelists of the nineteenth century— George Eliot, Thomas Hardy, Henry James—wrote with this kind of deep historical sense.

Yet this kind of historical consciousness, this emphasis on the complexity of human affairs, does have its dangers for our moral life, as Richard Hofstadter pointed out forty years ago. "The great fear that animates the most feverishly committed historians," Hofstadter wrote, "is that our continual rediscovery of the complexity of social interests, the variety of roles and motives of political leaders, the unintended consequences of political actions, the valid interests that have so often been sacrificed in the pursuit of other equally valid interests, may give us not only a keener sense of the structural complexity of our society in the past, but also a sense of the moral complexity of social action that will lead us toward political immobility." Understanding the complexity of human affairs, seeing clearly both sides of all issues, knowing that few things work out the way we intend, may breed in us caution and indecisiveness. Imbued with a strong historical sense, we are apt to become one of Nietzsche's historically minded men who could not "shake himself free from the delicate network of his truth and righteousness for a downright act of will or desire." A sense of history, Neustadt and May admit, can be "an enemy of vision."

Fortunately, however, there seems to be little danger of our becoming

too historically minded in America today. We Americans have such a thin and meager sense of history that we cannot get too much of it. What we need more than anything is a deeper and fuller sense of the historical process, a sense of where we have come from and how we have become what we are. This kind of historical sense will give us the best guide we'll ever have for groping our way into an unpredictable future.

# 1.

# "INFLUENCE" IN HISTORY

*Explaining America: The Federalist*
by Garry Wills (New York: Doubleday, 1981)

*The New York Review of Books*, April 2, 1981

Unhappy the land that needs heroes.

—BERTOLT BRECHT

G ARRY WILLS'S BOOK is ostensibly about *The Federalist*, those eighty-five essays written in 1787–88 to promote the ratification of the newly framed Constitution. But it is really about heroes and great men, and about the distance we have fallen in two hundred years since that near-mythical generation of founders put the country together. Indeed, not since the nineteenth century has the high-minded and noble character of the creation of the Constitution been so celebrated, and with so many different heroes. They include, first, the giants of the Enlightenment, like Montesquieu and Hume, who handed down their great thoughts to ordinary mortals, and then the Founding Fathers themselves, those "extraordinary men," that "privileged few" (as Wills calls them), who had a vision of a new kind of virtuous politics conducted by noble men like themselves. Of these perhaps the most extraordinary were those classical lawgivers and principal authors of *The Federalist*, James

Madison and Alexander Hamilton. Finally, the heroes include Wills himself, armed only with his sharp mind and acerbic prose, doing battle single-
handedly against the ignorance and stupidity of the scholarly world.

Wills's earlier book *Inventing America* raised a storm of controversy,
and this book promises to do the same. It is not as carefully done or as
smoothly written as the earlier work. All the faults of the first book are
here exaggerated, carried to excess: the pugnacious arrogance, the un-
charitable regard for previous scholarship, the use of straw men, the clever
manipulation of evidence, the overrefining of distinctions, the straining
for novelty, the mannered mixing of erudition and colloquialism. The
book gets very technical at times, and it is not easy reading. But there is
also evident in this work the same insightful glossing of words, the same
sensitivity to anachronism, the same lively intelligence. And there is the
same provocative emphasis on Scottish influence.

In his earlier book *Inventing America,* Wills argued that the predomi-
nant influence on Thomas Jefferson and his writing of the Declaration of
Independence was not John Locke and possessive individualism, but rather
the moral sense of the Scottish Enlightenment, particularly Francis
Hutcheson. Wills contended that Jefferson, like the eighteenth-century
Scots, was a moral sentimentalist, not a contractarian; that is, he believed
that society was held together not by legal or contractual ties but by ties
of affection, benevolence, and moral feeling. With the Scots having captured Jefferson's mind so completely, "the question arises," Wills writes in
the preface to this new book, "whether any other political thinkers of our
early national period were influenced by the Scottish Enlightenment."
The answer, he says, is emphatically yes.

It is not Hutcheson this time but David Hume who, Wills writes, decisively influenced the thinking of Madison and Hamilton. Wills has
picked up a connection between the thought of Hume and Madison that
Douglass Adair made many decades ago and has greatly expanded it; in
fact, he has dedicated the book to the memory of Adair, "who saw it first."
The ideas of Hume pervade the book: Wills opens each chapter with a

quotation from Hume and finds in his writings the clues to understanding much of the philosophy of *The Federalist.* Since Hume was opposed to the radical-Whig Commonwealth tradition, which, according to scholars such as Bernard Bailyn, was the shaping force of Revolutionary ideology, this Humean reading of *The Federalist* immediately gives the book an iconoclastic, myth-demolishing character that Wills obviously delights in.

The book is undoubtedly a tour de force. It is shrewd, outlandish, probing, and bizarre all at once. It is such a bundle of brilliance and perversity, intelligence and sophistry, ingenuity and wrongheadedness that one scarcely knows how to disentangle it. Perhaps the problem of assessing intellectual "influence," Scottish or otherwise, is the place to begin.

The problem of influence is central to all intellectual history. It was the issue on which the controversial reception of *Inventing America* turned, and it is bound to be important for this book too. This is unfortunate because it is a false issue. The entire debate over whether Locke or Hutcheson was a more important influence on Jefferson is wrongly framed; the question should never have been posed that way.

Wills was right about Jefferson's being a moral sentimentalist concerned with sociability, but he was wrong in attributing these beliefs to some peculiar Scottish influence. Many Britons, including the colonists, were sentimentalists by 1776, and not simply because they had read Hutcheson. By the third quarter of the eighteenth century, the sociability of people and the existence of some sort of moral sense in each person had become widespread presuppositions of Anglo-American culture. For every book by a great thinker like Shaftesbury, Butler, or Hutcheson on the affections and benevolence, there were dozens of long-forgotten lesser works expounding and expanding on the same themes. These themes were not merely Scottish, or even Anglo-American; they were current throughout Western culture and they flowed from common efforts to deal with a similarly changing social reality. Where do we think the French people's "fraternity" in their Revolutionary trinity came from?

The kinds of distinctions that Wills and his critics have drawn between Locke's or Hutcheson's respective contributions to Anglo-American thought are too precious, too refined, too academic for the dynamic culture of the eighteenth century. Jefferson was scarcely capable of drawing such fine distinctions or of perceiving any antagonism or incompatibility between what Locke and Hutcheson had written. The ideas of both thinkers had been blended and molded to fit the developing circumstances of the eighteenth century, and by 1776 both seemed to someone like Jefferson to be part of a general liberal, enlightened consensus.

Wills can hardly be blamed for casting his books according to intellectual "influences," for much of our intellectual history has been written in these terms: ideas emanating from great thinkers are more or less poured into the empty vessels that apparently are the minds of more ordinary people. But in a complicated culture at least, this is not the way ideas operate at all. Historians such as Herbert G. Gutman and William H. Sewell, Jr., became more aware of the inadequacy of the concept of authorial influence once they began investigating the consciousness of large anonymous groups: workingmen's organizations and other collectivities whose members have ideas without having read any great thinkers.

Intellectual activity in a culture is not a one-way flow between the great minds and passive recipients; it is a discourse, a complex marketplace-like conglomeration of intellectual exchanges involving many participants all trying to manipulate the ideas available to them in order to explain, justify, lay blame for, or otherwise make sense of what is happening around them. Everyone, not just the great minds, participates in this complicated process. The ideas of great thinkers like Hutcheson or Hume are not unique. Indeed, such thinkers were recognized as great in their day precisely because they said more clearly and persuasively what everyone else was trying to say. If such great thinkers had not articulated the shared assumptions of the culture, then, like Giambattista Vico, they would have been ignored. It was not until the more receptive nineteenth

century that anyone paid attention to Vico's great anticipations of anthropology and ethnology that he had written in the early eighteenth century.

Tracing the influence of particular minds or works may be a legitimate endeavor within the confined worlds of art or literature. It may be quite possible to speak of the influence of Giorgione on the young Titian or of Shakespeare's imagery on Keats's poetry. But such techniques of attribution are not applicable, at least not in any meaningful way, to the dynamic consciousness of a whole society. There is no possibility of proving the influence of Locke or Hutcheson on the thought of such a person as Jefferson, even if we find Jefferson quoting one or the other. For the ideas of both Locke and Hutcheson had become so mixed up in the discourse of eighteenth-century culture that by 1776 they could never be separated out and their "influence" measured. Thus when Jefferson later recalled that the Declaration of Independence rested "on the harmonizing sentiments of the day, whether expressed in conversation, in letters, printed essays, or the elementary books of public right, as Aristotle, Cicero, Locke, Sidney, etc.," he showed a far more accurate understanding of how cultural consciousness works than do those who would isolate either Locke's or Hutcheson's influence.

In *Explaining America,* Wills strains to find Scottish influence even more than he did in his earlier book. If Madison refers to "the connections of blood, of friendship, and of acquaintance" among members of a legislature, Wills tells us that such seemingly "odd" talk by Madison can best be explained by Scottish influence, for "it was very prominent in Scottish thinking about politics"—and not, apparently, in English thinking about eighteenth-century politics, despite what Sir Lewis Namier has taught us about the nature of that politics. The "passions were a major concern for Hume," and thus Madison and Hamilton were concerned with them too—that's influence. When Hume wrote that people needed to be governed by sentiments other than Spartan austerity, Wills concludes that such a statement "is probably Hamilton's direct source for the June 18

speech" in the Constitutional Convention—as if Hamilton could not have reached such a familiar conclusion on his own. When Hamilton and Madison refer to the improvements of political science in the eighteenth century, or the civilizing influence of commerce, or to government's resting on opinion, they "must have remembered" these common eighteenth-century propositions from Hume.

It is a relief to find Wills writing that "while accepting Hume's general framework of economic thought, Hamilton did not follow him slavishly on all points." Unfortunately for Wills's argument, however, these points turn out to be the most important ones. Hamilton favored a national bank and a national debt, which Hume opposed. Wills tries to make light of these differences between Hume and Hamilton, even going so far as to say that a national debt had little of the centralizing force that Charles Beard and his followers have attributed to it. He simply misses entirely the immense political significance that the public debt had for eighteenth-century Englishmen.

When Wills gets away from tracing the influence of Hume everywhere, he has some interesting things to say about *The Federalist*. But too often his passion to be original leads him to exaggerate and stretch his arguments. In the first two parts of the book, Wills wants to show how our "stereotypes of Hamilton and Madison are misleading," and he does this largely by creating these stereotypes out of what can only be the dated writings of Vernon Parrington or Claude Bowers. (There are no citations; Wills simply refers vaguely to "most commentaries.") If he can establish, for example, that "we tend to consider Jefferson 'democratic' because of his agrarian ideals, and Hamilton 'aristocratic' because he promoted trade and manufacture," then his own contrary findings will appear all the more novel and astonishing.

Perhaps we can see some of Wills's difficulties in his hopelessly contrived discussion of Hamilton's *Federalist* No. 78. Wills argues that Hamilton in this paper was not defending judicial review as everyone seems to think,

but was actually justifying a kind of legislative supremacy. Wills reaches this startling conclusion only because he does not appreciate the radical changes taking place in American political thought since the Revolution. He seems to assume that the constitutional conventions that created the constitutions were akin to legislatures, and thus the fundamental character of a constitution becomes for him an expression of "legislative supremacy." But the constitutional conventions were not legislatures; they were simply another sort of agent of the people making fundamental law. Many of the Federalists, like Hamilton, had come to think of the people at large as a sovereign entity doling out bits and pieces of their power to various popular agents, including at both the federal and state levels the various houses of representatives, senates, executives, constitutional conventions, and in Hamilton's new and ingenious exploitation of this view, even judges.

In *Federalist* No. 78, Hamilton contended that judges who set aside legislative statutes contrary to a constitution were therefore not really asserting judicial supremacy because they were only applying the more fundamental law of the Constitution "legislated" directly by the people in their constitutional conventions. This, said Hamilton, does not "by any means suppose a superiority of the judicial to the legislative power. It only supposes that the power of the people is superior to both." The sovereign people, in other words, were not fully represented in any single institution of government. They simply had many different agents to carry out many different tasks, including judges with the responsibility of upholding the fundamental law of the constitution. Thus judges, said Hamilton, were only acting as another sort of agent of the people, equal in popular authority to the legislative representatives of the people. It is not to be supposed, he added in a direct and provocative denial of traditional legislative supremacy, "that the constitution could intend to enable the representatives of the people to substitute their *will* to that of their constituents."

However fully we today have come to accept this view of judicial

review, it was for eighteenth-century Anglo-Americans a revolutionary doctrine, implying a wholly new way of seeing the people's relationship to government. In other words, the legislative representatives of the people were not really the people, and their will was not equal to the will of the people, who had many different agents working for them, including judges. In the eighteenth century no Englishman or colonist would ever have suggested that the people's representatives in the House of Commons or in the lower houses of the colonial assemblies were essentially no different in their relationship to the people from judicial magistrates. No wonder then that Robert Yates and other opponents of the Constitution in 1788 had trouble accepting Hamilton's logic that judges appointed by governors for life possessed the same authority of the people as legislative representatives elected annually or biennially by the people. Once a logic similar to Hamilton's became more widely accepted in America, some began thinking that if judges were indeed some sort of representatives of the people, then the people ought to elect them—which, as we know, is precisely what eventually happened in a number of states; indeed, today most states do elect their judges. Wills captures none of this. Despite his wide reading in the great books of the Enlightenment, he simply does not know enough about the particular circumstances of American political thought in the Revolutionary era to get away with all he has attempted.

However, in the long final section of his book, that dealing with Madison's *Federalist* No. 10, the most famous of the papers, Wills's interpretation is right. Against all those political scientists, from Harold Laski to James MacGregor Burns, who have argued that Madison in No. 10 was proposing an "interest-group" or pluralist conception of politics, Wills correctly contends that Madison did not expect public policy or the common good to emerge naturally from the give-and-take of hosts of competing interests. Instead, Madison hoped that in an enlarged national republic these competing factions and interests would, like America's many religious denominations, neutralize themselves. This in turn would

allow enlightened and rational men, men like himself, to promote the public good.

Madison did not expect the new national government to be an integrator and harmonizer of the many different interests in the society; instead, he wanted it to be a "disinterested and dispassionate umpire" in disputes among these different interests and parties. In other words, Madison was not as modern as we often make him out to be. Although Wills does not mention it, Madison even said privately (he would never have dared write it in *The Federalist*) that he really hoped this national government might play the same role now that the British king had been supposed to play in the old empire.

But how did Madison expect the new Constitution to ensure that only rational and disinterested men like himself got into power? Here Wills has put his finger on the central point of the scheme of the Federalists, as the supporters of the Constitution called themselves: its enlarged system of representation would act as a kind of filter, refining and extracting out of the mass only those men, in Madison's words, who possessed "the most attractive merit and most diffusive and established characters." Madison offers us a truly noble vision of virtuous impartial leaders promoting no factious or party interests but only the "permanent and aggregate interests of the community."

Wills loves this vision, but unfortunately he never gets beyond lengthy word glossing and chemical analogies to explain the way this refining process was supposed to work. His discussion, like the book itself, has an airy, disembodied quality, without roots in any particular political or social circumstances. Because Wills has no appreciation of the extent to which Madison believed that most of the problems of American politics in the 1780s were caused by rampaging and faction-ridden state legislatures, he can never make full sense of what Madison was up to. It was not because of something they read in Hume that Madison and other Federalists saw in the elevated and expanded nature of the federal government a solution to the problems of factious majori-

tarianism in the state legislatures of the 1780s—it was instead the Federalists' experience with America's popular politics in the states and their sense of its social base.

The Federalists had become convinced that the factionalism and tyrannies of the state legislatures were owing to the kind of people being elected to them. Ordinary people were electing to the state legislatures too many men like themselves; too many narrow-minded representatives who thought only about the partial interests of their little districts; too many parochial politicians promoting only the paper money concerns of their debtor constituents; too many upstarts like Abraham Yates, a part-time cobbler from Albany, or William Findley, an ex-weaver from western Pennsylvania, who had never been to Princeton or King's College and had no breeding or enlightened vision or concern for the "aggregate interests" of the country. It was just these sorts of men that Madison had in mind when he spoke of keeping out of government "unworthy candidates," "men of factious temper" or "of local prejudice," who "practise with success the vicious arts by which elections are too often carried." The Federalists' diagnosis of the problems of American politics in the 1780s was ultimately social. And their remedy was too.

By expanding the electorate and reducing the number of those elected, the new federal system not only would tend to elevate into national office those who were most cosmopolitan and socially established but would as well tend to exclude from federal positions those localist parvenus who dominated the state legislatures. If the people of a state—New York, for example—had to select only ten men to the federal Congress in contrast to the sixty-six they elected to their state assembly, they were more apt in the case of a few national representatives to ignore obscure ordinary men with local reputations and elect only those who were well bred, well educated, and well known. Election by the people in large districts would inhibit those "vicious arts" of electioneering and would therefore, as Madison's closest ally in the Philadelphia Convention, James Wilson, said, "be most likely to obtain men of intelligence and uprightness." This is why

Wilson and Madison in the Convention always favored the direct election of the president by all the people—not because they were fervent democrats but because such an expanded electorate was more apt to result in the kind of enlightened cosmopolitan ruler they wanted.

There were lots of what we might call social code words flying about in *The Federalist,* but those who were presumably to be excluded from office by the new Constitution knew full well what the Federalists were up to. As one Massachusetts Anti-Federalist bitterly complained in 1788: "Those lawyers and men of learning, and moneyed men, that talk so finely, and gloss over matters so smoothly, to make us poor illiterate people swallow down the pill, expect to get into Congress themselves . . . and get all the power . . . in their own hands, and then they will swallow up all of us little folks." Such egalitarian resentment was frustrated by the Constitution, but its day of release was coming. This social resentment was the other side of Madison's virtuous order of distinguished men—a side that Wills never even suggests existed.

This split between cosmopolitans and localists lay at the heart of politics in the 1780s, and it has continued to do so through much of our history. And others besides the Federalists have tried to exploit it. The Progressive period, for example, was marked by the reforming efforts of cosmopolitan types, often liberal, college-educated professionals and businessmen, to wrest government from the hands of "corrupt" and "undesirable" localist elements. The Progressive reformers often did this by shifting the levels of governmental decision making from wards, towns, and counties to the states and the nation. Commissions of educated "experts" at the state and federal level supplanted parochial politicians and ward bosses who presumably could not see beyond their own neighborhoods. Changing the level of decision making in this way continues to have social implications. Although we Americans do not much like to talk about these social implications, much of our present politics still swirls around this cosmopolitan/localist dichotomy.

In 1913 Charles Beard published his *An Economic Interpretation of the*

*Constitution,* surely the most provocative work of history ever written in America. Since then, Beard has been proved wrong on almost every count: in his simpleminded conception of motivation, in the crudity of his class division, in his use of evidence. But Beard was right in trying to strip the creation of the Constitution of its mythical and heroic character in order to make it a humanly comprehensible matter of earthly political conflict and social interests. Wills would have us forget this Beardian legacy and return to an image of high-minded demigods trying to work a miracle. Wills quite rightly stresses the immense distance of the eighteenth-century world from our own, but we make a serious mistake and unnecessarily denigrate ourselves if we think of the Founding Fathers as heroes, as something other than men like ourselves with interests and social positions to promote.

**AFTERWORD**

This was the first review I wrote for *The New York Review of Books.* Of course, I had previously written many reviews for scholarly journals, but writing for an educated but nonscholarly readership was a new challenge. I was and am a great admirer of Garry Wills's work. And after this initial review, I went on in subsequent years to review several others of his books, usually quite favorably. I believe him to be not only a very imaginative historian but also one of America's premier public intellectuals. Although I had been on a committee that awarded a prize to his earlier book *Inventing America,* I had been troubled by what I believed to be his rather narrow focus on the influence of the Scottish philosopher Francis Hutcheson on the thinking of Thomas Jefferson. Wills's follow-up book on *The Federalist,* the subject of this review, gave me an opportunity to question the whole idea of "influence" in history writing.

I suppose it is inevitable for people who are intellectually inclined to believe that thinkers directly influence one another. Somehow we tend to

believe that if Jefferson had not read John Locke or Francis Hutcheson, he could not have written the Declaration of Independence in the way he did. I have had people show me some late seventeenth- or early eighteenth-century text, by a Catholic philosopher, for example, that resembles something Jefferson wrote, and then as a result of this resemblance claim a profound influence of this text on Jefferson. No doubt Jefferson was influenced by writers whom he read—his last letter, for example, contains an image borrowed directly from Algernon Sidney. But in most cases tracing the source of broadly shared ideas is a fool's errand. Many ideas are so much a part of the general culture that specifying a particular textual influence is impossible. To take an example from our own time: Would someone have had to read Karl Marx or any other particular writer to believe in the opinion that poverty causes crime? Yet surely someday a historian will find a specific textual influence for this widespread notion in our culture.

The concept of "influence" seems most important for literary scholars who are used to tracing the forms and syntax of language from one writer to another. This perhaps is why it is literary scholars who have most used and abused the notion of influence. They certainly are the ones who have claimed that particular authors have had a powerful influence on the contours of early American culture—whether it is Montesquieu, Voltaire, Alexander Pope, or Milton. Indeed, the author of the book *Milton in Early America* said that no single individual exerted such an influence over the first two centuries of American culture as did Milton. "For a moment in history, he commanded an authority rarely granted any person, in any country, at any time." It is exaggerated claims like this that undermine the whole idea of influence.

# 2.

# ANACHRONISM IN HISTORY

*The Vineyard of Liberty.* Volume 1 of
The American Experiment,
by James MacGregor Burns (New York: Knopf, 1982)

*The New York Review of Books.* February 18, 1982

WE AMERICANS, unlike many Europeans, have tended to see our history as the product of conscious intentions and purposeful leadership. We have not usually thought of ourselves as caught up in large impersonal forces sweeping us along to destinies we have not chosen. Which is to say that we generally have not had a tragic vision of our past. But there is in our history one notable exception to this: the Civil War. Of all the great events of American history, only the Civil War has been viewed as tragic. Only such a bloody, fratricidal conflict was awesome enough to seem to be beyond traditional American political management. Yet as unaccustomed as we are to being imprisoned by circumstances, it is not surprising that some of us have been unwilling to see even the Civil War as the result of inexorable forces beyond human control. Consequently, that war has become the only major event in our history that has aroused among historians a continual debate over whether it was inevitable or avoidable. The Civil War has become a kind of test of America's ability to govern its fate.

In 1858 Senator William H. Seward sought to describe the differing

views his fellow Americans had of the crisis between North and South and in doing so anticipated the two major interpretations that subsequent historians would make of the Civil War. Some people, said Seward, think the sectional conflict is "accidental, unnecessary, the work of interested or fanatical agitators, and therefore ephemeral." But Seward believed they were mistaken; the sources of the conflict were deeper than that, and in a memorable phrase he said so: "It is an irrepressible conflict between opposing and enduring forces."

The question of the irrepressibility of the sectional conflict, defined by Seward at the outset, has been around for a long time. Indeed, it lies at the heart of this book by James MacGregor Burns, the first in what will be a three-volume narrative survey of the history of the United States, with the larger title The American Experiment. Burns is a distinguished political scientist, and so he is well aware of the uncontrollable power of those impersonal, circumscribing "forces" that are, as he says at one point, "the product of millions of tiny decisions" by countless individuals. Yet Burns has also hobnobbed with presidents and even run for Congress. He has written prize-winning biographies of FDR and JFK, and he has developed a particular fascination with what he believes is the power of extraordinary political leaders at crucial moments to transcend and transform the impersonal forces of history. The tension between these differing views of the historical process—between irrepressible, deterministic forces and free-acting, controlling political leadership—runs through Burns's volume, and lends interest and drama to what would otherwise be a very old-fashioned political narrative of the history of the United States from the Constitution to the Civil War.

Because Burns is covering such a large span of time and so many events, he necessarily has relied heavily on the work of other historians. He has read widely and has brought together a huge amount of material, and he has told a familiar story with clarity and verve. Virtually all the great political personalities and colorful anecdotes of the period are included—from Benjamin Franklin's closing remarks at the Philadelphia

Convention to President Lincoln's shrewd squelching of opposition within his cabinet. But what makes Burns's conventional political narrative new and provocative is the use he has made of ideas and theories drawn from his influential studies of American politics. He focuses particularly on what he describes as the formal and informal constitutions of the American political system and on the extraordinary quality of political leadership that this peculiarly divided political system requires.

In 1787–88, Burns argues, the Founding Fathers, a small elite of illustrious and respectable leaders, created a structure of government that sought to control political power "by splitting it into pieces and balancing the pieces," not only among the various offices of government but also between the national and the state governments. Above all, the Founding Fathers feared factions and parties, especially of majorities, and aimed to make it difficult for people to combine together politically. In order to govern in such a structure, says Burns, politicians would have to bargain ceaselessly "in a vast system of brokerage and accommodation that would give something to everybody—liberty to the individual, desired laws or appropriations to groups, and governmental balance and stability to the whole." It was an immensely complicated political system that the Constitution created—this calculated system of dispersed power—and it placed on American politicians "an enormously heavy burden of leadership." The system demanded "expert brokers and dexterous improvisers ... masterly transactional leaders" who could operate across the variety of boundaries separating governments.

Out of these demands grew gradually and unintentionally another constitution, an informal one, created not by a tiny elite steeped in political theory but by thousands of popular leaders "experimenting with new ways of gaining office and power." This popular constitution was the party system. Unlike the formal Constitution, it "was spawned outside the establishment, often outside the law, and hence, born a bastard and growing up as a political orphan, it never became quite respectable." Parties, "with their coalition building and other unifying tendencies and machin-

ery," brought dispersed power together and helped to make the formal institutions of government workable. After an abortive start in the 1790s and several decades of fumbling, by the late 1830s a recognizably modern party system was in place: two self-conscious, competing parties of Democrats and Whigs, with hierarchical organizations in nearly every state that reached from the localities to national conventions. This impressive party system had the potential for strong popular majority rule. But, says Burns, it remained a potential, for the system had a number of underlying weaknesses. Not only did the parties lack clear programs and ignore large numbers of people, but most important, they remained very awkwardly related to the formal constitution of government. The question always was: could the parties' tendency to concentrate power overcome the Constitution's tendency to disperse it?

During the antebellum period these two constitutions—the formal institutions of government and the informal party system—existed in an uneasy relationship, just managing time after time by accommodation and compromise to stifle the sectional crises over slavery that threatened to break apart the nation. "Then," writes Burns, "in the 1850s, this system crumbled." Powerful centrifugal forces and growing sectional divisions unsettled the delicate balance between the two constitutions. The Whig Party collapsed, and the Democratic Party gained an abnormal dominance over national and local politics, especially in the South.

Thus the "electoral competition in a diverse and balanced electorate" on which the system depended was destroyed. "The two-party system assumed that within each party moderate and 'extremist' forces would grapple for control, but that the two parties would tend toward the center—and hence toward gradual adjustment and morselization—because of the need to win the support of centrist voters."

But without this two-party competition, the Democrats in 1856 "won an undeserved victory over splintered opposition," which in turn only intensified the rise of extremism. The result by 1860 "revealed in naked outline what had been for some years the actual power configuration—a

four-party or multiparty system, with its inherent weaknesses." In the 1860 election, Lincoln and the Republicans won the presidency with less than 40 percent of the popular vote and precipitated the secession of the Southern states from the Union. It was the greatest failure of the American political process in the nation's history.

Although this is a very ingenious and sophisticated argument, it is actually an updated refinement of the point of view opposed by Seward in 1858: an interpretation of the sectional conflict that stresses its superficial, avoidable character. This interpretation, usually referred to by historians as "revisionist," sees the Civil War resulting essentially from a breakdown in the political process. During the 1930s and 1940s some historians, led by James G. Randall and Avery Craven, argued that the Civil War was actually needless and preventable. The differences between the sections, they said, were not fundamental and the forces making for conflict were not irrepressible. Slavery could have been eliminated gradually and peacefully. All that was needed was astute political management. Instead, these "revisionist" historians argued, blundering politicians exaggerated sectional differences for electoral purposes, blew up the crisis artificially, and eventually undermined the political system's capacity for compromise.

Although Burns rejects any stark version of this revisionist, "blundering generation" explanation of the Civil War, his argument is a subtle variation of it. Not only does he, like other revisionists, focus largely on political behavior and assume that politics and political leadership exist autonomously apart from social circumstances, but he also asks of the antebellum period the same question all revisionists have asked: not what were the North and South quarreling about, but rather, how did the political system contain the quarrel for so long, only to allow it in the 1850s to erupt into war?

Like other revisionists, Burns tends to play down the differences between the North and South. Both sections, he says, were examples of

exploitative capitalism. No doubt Southern slavery was a particular degradation, but Northern "wage slavery" was little better. "Behind the lofty pretensions of each [section] lay an ignoble defense of the elite monopolization of property and profits." Burns thus suggests that the North was as morally flawed as the South: it was too vulnerable to Southern charges of wage slavery to be able to mount a respectable defense. Therefore it was not so much the differences between the sections that brought on the war as it was the weaknesses of political leadership.

The central theme of this book, as of all of Burns's other work, is the nature of political leadership. Although he is writing history, Burns is still the political scientist and has the political problems of our recent past, our present, and our future very much on his mind. His history of the first half of the nineteenth century thus becomes something of a tract for our times.

Time and again Burns suggests that proper leadership might have prevented the Civil War. By the 1850s the society was in disarray; people were divided by a host of issues, not only slavery but also temperance, women's rights, education, banks, immigration, and free land. Liberty was more a source of confusion than a guide to coherent political action. "Serious politicians" faced with this disarray "had to win state and local elections against rivals who could easily outdemagogue them in the emotional politics of the early Fifties." The parties were no help in lessening this emotionalism. "The parties were immobilized because their top leadership was immobilized, and the leaders were immobilized because they were enmeshed in state and local politics." What was needed, says Burns, was some "great national leader," someone who was "equal to the deepening crisis," someone "with the power to appeal to the hearts and minds, to the fundamental wants and needs and aspirations of the people able to apply steady moral and intellectual standards to the issues confronting them." What America required were "transcending leaders" who could "turn the shank of history."

It is not as if we have not had that kind of transcendent leadership at other times in our history. What Burns seems to have in mind for his inspirational leader is someone like FDR, someone "adept in mobilizing the grand nationwide coalitions necessary for effective presidential politics." Henry Clay was a logroller and not that kind of leader. Neither was Daniel Webster; he had a national vision, but he chose to serve commercial and industrial interests "rather than respond to the needs and aspirations of the poor throughout the nation." Yet the Whig Party—with its "positive, creative impetus" and its belief that liberty could be promoted "not only against government, but through government"—at least had the makings of a New Deal, and its collapse, says Burns, was "a pity."

What reveals more than anything else Burns's peculiar conception of leadership and his present-day concerns is his remarkable chapter titled "The Majority That Never Was." This chapter is a severe indictment from a modern perspective of the conditions of blacks, women, Indians, and all the poor in antebellum America. The plight of slaves goes without much saying, but women were almost as much degraded. Most were farm women and "most farm women were still drudges." While their husbands bought steel plows and other tools, "farm wives shared little in labor-saving advances." Even worse off were those women who went into factories; their existence became "almost intolerable" and created among them "mounting unrest."

The immigrant poor, too, were victimized by American conditions. Exploited by ship companies and con men, plunged into squalor, and left struggling for jobs, the newcomers drank and fought and barely survived. But the immigrants were not the only poor in America. There were many others: "marginal New England farmers holding onto their rocky soil, frontier people, impecunious scholars, laborers at the bottom of the pile, and, always, Indians and blacks." All these oppressed poor "were bound together in a great commonality of deprivation—denied good homes and

food and clothes, good health and nutrition and education, and hence damaged in motivation, aspiration, and self-fulfillment."

This is an extraordinary present-minded and hence depressing picture of antebellum society that Burns has drawn. If readers had only this one chapter to go on, they could not help believing that antebellum America was latently revolutionary, and they might well wonder why any European in his right mind would ever have come here. In fact, Burns implies that a nationwide radical movement was fermenting just below the surface. Everywhere among this deprived majority there were "unfulfilled wants and needs" and "widespread feelings of injustice" waiting only to be brought into political consciousness and collective action, "into feelings of entitlement that could then be converted into effective demands on the political system." But this did not happen, and the reason it did not was a "failure of leadership." Would-be leaders were too divided from one another and too separated from the masses, and therefore the revolutionary majority that might have been never arose. "Were there in the United States," Burns asks, "persons of rare potential leadership who might have transcended the differences among the reform and radical groups and built a coalition of the have-nots? We will never know, because such a leader did not arise."

It is hard to imagine a greater misconstruing of the nature of historical writing. Better to put clocks in ancient Rome than to create this kind of anachronism. But then one sometimes forgets that Burns is a political activist for whom writing history is really politics by other means. What he wants for the past and what he wants now is "masterful transforming leadership," leadership that can transcend the mundane circumstances that bind the rest of us ordinary mortals.

Burns is well aware of what historians have said about the powerful "economic and ethnic and religious forces" that limited the capacity of leaders to act in the antebellum period. Yet despite his recognition of these "impersonal forces," he cannot help believing that some heroic

leader might have arisen above these forces and controlled them. Over and over Burns reveals his heroic conception of the historical process. "It is not given," he writes, "to more than a few voyagers in the stream of history to influence its basic direction." Most historical inquiries of the coming of the Civil War have been "inconclusive," he says, because they have "failed to differentiate between the givens of history—the geographical, racial, and economic forces that were inextricable and inseparable from the past—and the somewhat more tractable decision-making situations, where leaders might have decided differently." Perhaps the forces were too powerful for any political system to overcome, "yet European and other political systems had encountered enormously divisive forces and survived." After all, says Burns, "a supreme test of leadership" is the leaders' ability to deal with "the 'impersonal' forces streaming around them."

Americans in the antebellum period simply did not produce that kind of leadership. Even Lincoln was "a perplexed and flawed" leader. Neither he nor Stephen Douglas emerged from their debates in 1858 "as a moral leader, capable of reaching into the minds and hearts of human beings, appealing to their more generous instincts, recognizing their fundamental wants and needs, and mobilizing their hopes and aspirations." The strategic problems facing the nation in 1860 were very great, and "only moral, intellectual, and political leadership of the highest order could have readily solved such strategic problems." Unfortunately, "the Republican party could claim no such leadership." And so the war came.

This is romantic American optimism carried to extremes. Somehow from somewhere some great hero, some Lochinvar, might have ridden in and rescued Americans from their predicament. Thus for Burns the coming of the Civil War cannot be a true tragedy, the kind of tragedy that sees the inescapable boundaries within which people have to act. The "tragedy" that he perceives lies elsewhere, in the fact that neither side saw how like the other it was, that neither side linked liberty "to equality and other principles in a well-considered hierarchy of values," and that neither used government

creatively and positively to cure its ills. In other words, the "tragedy" for Burns lies in the fact that those poor benighted people back then were not more like us—or more like the citizens Burns wants us to be.

## AFTERWORD

Since we can never completely escape, even imaginatively, from our present, some degree of anachronism is inevitable in all history writing. But any good historian needs constantly to worry about the problem of injecting his or her contemporary consciousness back into the past. As Yogi Berra might put it, it is difficult to write history, especially about the past.

James MacGregor Burns wrote and thanked me for my review of his book. He welcomed, he said, such intellectual exchanges and hoped that all of us could learn from one another. Such a generous response to a critical review is rare; it is a sign of Burns's magnanimous temperament. Burns went on in 1985 to publish a second volume of his prospective trilogy, *The American Experiment*. This volume, titled *The Workshop of Democracy*, carried the history of America up to the 1930s; no third volume has yet appeared. Instead, over the past two decades Burns has continued to write engaging pieces on the theme of political leadership and to publish several collaborative works of history with Susan Dunn, including a biography of George Washington.

# 3.

# NARRATIVE HISTORY

*The Glorious Cause: The American Revolution, 1763–1789,*
Volume 3 in the Oxford History of the United States,
by Robert Middlekauff
(New York: Oxford University Press, 1982)

*The New York Review of Books,* August 12, 1982

T HE CALL (or is it a cry?) is coming from many directions: the
discipline of history seems to be in trouble and the remedy lies in
some sort of return to narrative history. Henry Steele Commager, Page
Smith, Eric Foner, Lawrence Stone, and Bernard Bailyn (in his 1981 presidential address to the American Historical Association) have all in different ways suggested that historians are or ought to be doing more of what
they have traditionally done: telling stories. This revival of narrative will
not be easy. Indeed, writing narrative history under conditions that make
it difficult if not well-nigh impossible, says Bailyn, is "the great challenge
of modern historical scholarship."

Narrative history has traditionally meant storytelling: laying out the
events of the past in a chronological linear order, a sequential plotting of
one thing after another with a beginning, a middle, and an end. Such narrative history has usually concentrated on human agency and human responsibility, on individual personalities and on unique public happenings:
the great men, great decisions, and great events that, so to speak, made

headlines in the past. Since politics tends to dominate the headlines, politics has traditionally formed the backbone of this narrative history.

Moreover, narrative history usually has dealt with whole societies—an entire nation or, in diplomatic history, even groups of nations—over long periods of time. Such histories have been big and sweeping, like Victorian novels. Narrative histories of the United States, for example, used to require many volumes: ten from George Bancroft, nine from Henry Adams, eight from James Ford Rhodes, nine from John Bach McMaster, and six from Edward Channing. Though never as popular as our own late twentieth-century fictional saga by John Jakes, these grand multivolume histories were written not for other historians but for the educated public.

Most historians, at least professional academic historians, are not writing this kind of multivolume narrative anymore. Among historians of the United States over the past generation, only James MacGregor Burns and Page Smith are attempting anything resembling the old-fashioned narratives and both of them are very conscious of being mavericks running against the herd of professional historians. Smith, for example, remarked at the beginning of his multivolume history of the United States that "any effort to revive 'old-fashioned' narrative history on a large scale was sure to draw the concentrated fire of all those professional historians whose deity (as well as bread and butter) was monographic history."

Monographic history is the kind of history that most academic historians now write: technical, specialized analyses of particular events or problems in the past. The writing of such historical monographs grew out of the nineteenth-century dream that history might become an objective science, a science that would resemble, if not the natural sciences of physics or chemistry, then at least the social sciences—economics, sociology, anthropology, psychology—that were emerging at the same time as professionally written history. Monographic history was scientific history, and the call for a revival of narrative was essentially a protest against the spread of science in history writing.

There is no denying the importance of the social sciences to the dis-

cipline of history, especially during the 1960s and 1970s. The theories, approaches, and methods of the social sciences have expanded our understanding of the past in a thousand different ways and have virtually revolutionized history writing. Many historians are no longer centrally concerned with the exploits of kings, presidents, or generals. Social science forced historians to ask new questions of the past and even to create new kinds of evidence. It has opened up new fields of history, such as family and demographic history, and has refreshed old ones, such as economic and cultural history.

Nowadays there is scarcely an aspect of human behavior that historians do not write about—from bastardy to dying, from sports to department stores. Under the influence of social science, historians such as Lawrence Stone and Philip Greven have penetrated into the most private, subjective, and least accessible aspects of past life, including marriage, sexual relations, and child rearing. Social science, especially anthropology, has enabled historians such as Natalie Davis and Rhys Isaac to reconstruct from festivals, rituals, and other kinds of popular nonverbal behavior in the past the beliefs and attitudes of the masses of ordinary men and women who left no written record. Other historians, such as Keith Thomas, Alan Macfarlane, and John Demos, have exploited social science to write sympathetically of religious zealotry, of magic, of witchcraft, and of many other subjects that used to be thought of as the irrationalities and superstitions of the past.

By diminishing the role of a few great leaders in determining political and social events, social science has helped to reorder our conception of the historical process. In books like Fernand Braudel's *The Structures of Everyday Life*, we have gained a fuller appreciation of the long-existing and deep-lying conditions that limited and circumscribed human behavior in the past. Most of these conditions—whether collective mentalities, demographic patterns, or economic circumstances—were the aggregate products of human action but not of human intention. Never before have historians been so ready to grasp the central insight of all social science—

that society and culture transcend the particular aims and purposes of individuals, that people make their social and intellectual history but are at the same time bound by what they have made. Faced with such an insight, old-fashioned narrative history, which assigns personal responsibility for what happened in the past to particular people, loses much of its meaning.

Yet as enriching as social science has been to history, the historiography of the 1960s and 1970s, with its preference for the quantifiable, the statistical and structural, writes Emmanuel Le Roy Ladurie, one of the foremost French practitioners of social-science history, "has been obliged to suppress in order to survive. In the last decades it has virtually condemned to death the narrative history of events and individual biography."

This new social-science history is not meant for storytelling but for problem solving. It is less interested in dynamic movement than in structural analysis. The new social historians tend to regard old-fashioned narrative history as superficial: it deals, they believe, only with events that are incidental and anecdotal and not the stuff of science. Only repetitive actions or events—so many births per thousand, so many dollars per bushel—could form the uniformities and regularities that underlie all science, which is why statistics and quantification are so important to the new social history.

"History that is not quantifiable cannot claim to be scientific," says Le Roy Ladurie. Yet because the scientific collecting of masses of data, even with the help of computers, is so difficult, many of the new social historians have confined themselves to the in-depth analyses of small, manageable areas—villages, towns, or parishes. And knowing so much about so little, none of them feels qualified any longer to generalize about society as a whole.

The results of all this for history have been a little short of chaotic. The technical monographs pour from the presses in overwhelming numbers—books, articles, newsletters, research reports, working papers

by the thousands. Historians are becoming more and more specialized, experts on single decades or single subjects, and still they cannot keep up with the profusion of monographs. Most now make no pretense of writing for the educated public; they write for one another, and with all their scientific paraphernalia—the computer printouts, Guttman scales, Lorenz curves, and Pearson correlation coefficients—they can sometimes count their readers on their hands. Since the old political backbone of history has been broken, and nothing has been put in its place, the monographs fly about in hopeless disarray. There is no coherence, there are no central organizing principles, no themes or stories—no narratives—to hold the pieces together. Like some vast protoplasm that divides and subdivides again and again, history seems to be in the process of self-destruction.

Against this background, we can perhaps better appreciate the challenge facing the authors of the multivolume Oxford History of the United States, launched under the general editorship of C. Vann Woodward to provide "an interpretative synthesis of the findings of recent scholarship" in a readable narrative "that will be readily accessible to the educated general public." This, says Woodward, is the aim of each of the volumes in the series. Ten chronological volumes are planned, running from the colonial period up to the present. Apparently, two volumes on broad topics are also intended—one for American diplomatic history, another for American economic history. Since no historian today can command with authority anything but a tiny portion of the mass of available historical information, each volume is to be written by a separate specialist but always with the "unspecialized reader" in mind. In light of the plight of the discipline of history, the aim of the series is a worthy one.

*The Glorious Cause* by Robert Middlekauff, professor of history at the University of California, Berkeley, is the first to be published but, presumably, the third chronologically in the series. It deals with the period 1763 to 1789, generally considered by historians to be the chronological boundaries of the era of the American Revolution. Its beginning and ending

events are the Peace of Paris of 1763, concluding the Seven Years' War between Britain and France, and the beginning of the new federal government in 1789. Middlekauff intends his account of these years to be a narrative. Although he has here and there analyzed events "with the intention of extracting meanings beyond those narration reveals," he has "in the main ... chosen to tell the story of the Revolution in the belief that the process of reconstructing what happened may be made to provide an explanation of events and their importance."

Middlekauff believes that "the narrative form" has a special significance for this particular period of American history: it "allows one to recover much that is central to an understanding of the Revolution and to revive at least a part of the passions and commitments of the people who struggled and fought." The result is not just narrative history but old-fashioned narrative history with a vengeance; it even has a warm patriotic glow. Indeed, so committed is Middlekauff to headline personalities and events, so integral is the narrative form to his interpretation of the Revolutionary era, that ultimately the value of his volume comes to rest on the validity of traditional narrative history itself.

Middlekauff's opening description of the coming of the Revolution sets the tone for the book. There is very little scientific or new social history in his explanation of the Revolution. There are no data matrices or frequency distributions, no charts or graphs. There are not even entries in the index for "economy" or "commerce." Whatever brief mention Middlekauff makes of deep-lying structures or large-scale developments—market growth or demographic expansion—is only incidental and prefatory to his main story, which focuses on the motives and decisions of prominent men—William Pitt, George Grenville, Samuel Adams, and so on—and on the chief events their actions brought about: the Sugar Act, Stamp Act, Tea Party, and so on. In other words, this is essentially a narrative history of surface events, what the French social historians disparagingly call *l'histoire événementielle*.

In Middlekauff's story people are not caught up in long-range forces.

They are free-acting autonomous moral beings whose motives and actions have clearly defined consequences. Revolutions, writes Middlekauff at one point, often "take on the appearance of inevitable, even natural events." But this was not true of the American Revolution. For Middlekauff, contingency was everywhere; indeed, the crucial year of 1767, he writes, seems dominated by "accident and chance." With everything so possible and with individual intention and will so responsible for what happened, Middlekauff finds it easy to lay personal blame for the coming of the Revolution. Much of that blame, he suggests, belongs to the officials of Great Britain.

In chapter after chapter Middlekauff criticizes the British for their ignorance and arrogance toward the colonies. They "did not know the people they were dealing with"; they had "an inability to see that they had a problem." "Years of dominance over the colonies had deadened their sensitivities." The British ministers seemed to have lost their "political senses." "For political tacticians of considerable skill, these ministers made some surprising mistakes. . . . They forgot the need for accommodation and flexibility." They never asked themselves about the colonists' reactions and were never able to see the full extent of their "blundering." Was it reasonable to expect the colonists to pay taxes? Would these taxes impair commerce? "These questions were not really broached in Parliament."

No wonder then that the colonists, those "otherwise sober citizens," became suspicious and fearful of a British conspiracy against their liberty. But it was not just British blundering that created American fears. Middlekauff suggests that the colonists might have been primed to see events in conspiratorial terms by their extreme Protestant heritage. This view, however, tends to slight the fact that most of the Revolutionary leaders were the least emotionally religious of any generation of leaders in our history—Washington, for example, hardly ever mentioned Christ and usually referred to God as "the great disposer of events." Nevertheless, Middlekauff calls them "the Children of the Twice-Born" and uses "the

moral dispositions of a passionate Protestantism" to explain not only the coming of the Revolution but also subsequent events. By 1774, he argues, the combination of this Protestant passion and British blundering made the Revolution at last seem inevitable. Only by that late date was there an "air of near hopelessness" and a feeling among Americans that "nothing would recall Britain to its senses." With ignorance and "ferocity of feeling toward America" on one side, and "a fear of tyranny" and "outrage" on the other, armed conflict was finally bound to come.

For Middlekauff it could not have come too soon. For all along the war is really what he yearns to write about—that is where the narrative action is. To be sure, Middlekauff's account of the coming of the Revolution has its exciting moments, such as the seizure of John Hancock's ship *Liberty*, but much of the story he tells in the early chapters is dense and labored. There are too many monographs to be dealt with, too much information to be conveyed, too many qualifications to be registered for Middlekauff to maintain a fast-paced narrative. Sentences crowd one another, and clauses pile upon clauses. He has to backtrack and repeat himself to get the narrative of events straight, and even then, big events, like the Peace of 1763, are not fully described.

When Middlekauff gets to the events of the war, however, his narrative picks up and his story comes to life. It is almost as if Middlekauff is saying that here, in the marching and maneuvering of troops, the clash of arms, and the heroic actions of soldiers under fire is the real stuff of narrative history writing. From Lexington and Concord in 1775 to Cornwallis's surrender at Yorktown in 1781, Middlekauff takes us through all the major battles in detailed and spirited prose. He tells us where the battles were fought, how the various regiments and companies of the respective armies were positioned, who performed well, and what the consequences of the several commanders' decisions were. Here is a typical example of Middlekauff's preparing us for a battle, in this case the British assault on Bunker Hill:

These thirty-seven companies composed the British right.
Howe gave Pigot the left and thirty-eight companies, including
three companies each of light infantry and grenadiers, the 38th,
43rd, and 47th Regiments, and the 1st Marines. These units on
the left were deployed in three lines just as Howe's division
was. All together the attacking British had 2200 rank and file,
six field pieces, two light 12-pounders, and two howitzers.

Middlekauff has many of these "battle pieces," as John Keegan calls
them. Formal pitched battles lend themselves naturally to narrative treatment: they are comprehensible episodes, each with identifiable leaders
and decisions that can be judged, each with a plotline and consequences
that can be assessed. At least ten of the twenty-six chapters in the book
deal in part or in whole with military events and the waging of war. Rarely
has a single volume purporting to be a general survey of the Revolutionary
period 1763 to 1789 devoted so much attention and space to the war itself.

It is not, however, simply Middlekauff's delight in writing traditional
military history that accounts for his lopsided emphasis on the war. For
the war is central to his overall interpretation of the Revolution. He believes that the Americans' experience in the war, more than anything else,
came to define for them what they called "the glorious cause."

The war was everywhere in America. It went on for eight years, the
longest war in our national history until the one in Vietnam. And it involved the entire society, "for the British spread their armies and their
efforts from one end of the new nation to the other." Although not every
state or community was the scene of a battle, all states and communities
knew what the war meant—some two hundred thousand men carried
arms in the Continental armies and the state militias, and "men from
every part of America died."

In fact, Americans suffered proportionally to their total population
more casualties in the Revolutionary War than in any other war we have
fought (always excepting the Civil War). The army and the society be-

came entangled in unprecedented ways. The problems of procuring supplies, protecting property, identifying friends and enemies, and mobilizing
support were common to both. "To an extraordinary extent for the eighteenth century," writes Middlekauff, "the army was an extension of the
society." The army's cause became the society's cause. The honor, glory,
and sacrifice of the war stimulated the imaginations of Americans and
transformed them. The long struggle against British arms brought
Americans together as a people and created their national feeling. The
war was a searing and inspiring ordeal unlike any experienced by other
generations in American history.

In his account of this "glorious cause," Middlekauff makes no pretense
of writing detached objective history. He has a stake in the outcome of the
Revolutionary War, and he writes about it with mounting, wistful passion.
Seldom these days does a professional historian evoke so much patriotic
feeling as Middlekauff does in this book. He is almost embarrassed by it.
He is at pains to explain that his title is not ironic. He warns us and himself repeatedly that the American revolutionaries were not a perfect people, that we must not take a romantic view of them. Yet they believed that
their cause was a "glorious" one, and Middlekauff says he agrees with
them.

Because Middlekauff puts so much of himself into the war, he has very
little left over for the rest of what happened during the Revolutionary era.
He knows in his head that many historians have seen more in the Revolution
than the war with Great Britain, but his heart is not in anything else. The
result is a strangely skewed account of the period. Events that do not contribute to "the glorious cause" are neglected or omitted. Middlekauff has
almost nothing to say about the original contributions to Western consti-
tutionalism that Americans made during the Revolutionary era. The developments of constitutional conventions, written constitutions, separation
of powers are all ignored.

Anyone who wanted to learn how and why Revolutionary Americans
suddenly broke from English constitutional practice and effectively barred

the subsequent emergence of parliamentary cabinet government in the United States will find no answer in this volume. Middlekauff treats the writing of the Revolutionary state constitutions of 1776—which Jefferson called "the whole object of the present controversy"—in an extraordinarily offhand manner, and then only after he has finished fighting the war. He never considers the Articles of Confederation in their own right, as American's first central government; indeed, he manages to squeeze in a description of them only after he has issued the call in 1787 for the Philadelphia Convention.

Essentially Middlekauff shows no real appreciation of the revolutionary character of the Revolution; he never makes sense of why an English radical like Richard Price thought it was the most important event in the history of the world since the birth of Christ. He mentions Jefferson's revolutionary achievements in Virginia—his abolition of entail, his bill for religious freedom, and his legal reforms—but he never succeeds in relating these to the Revolution as a whole. He sees little of the social and economic consequences of the Revolutionary paper money emissions. In the end, Middlekauff's Revolution remains pretty much a colonial war for independence, albeit an inspiring one.

Most conspicuously lamentable is the short shrift Middlekauff has given to the 1780s and the movement for the federal Constitution. To explain how Americans, ten years after declaring independence from a far-removed and much-feared governmental authority, were prepared to create another such distant and astonishingly powerful government is in many ways even more difficult than explaining the coming of the Revolution itself. A powerful superintending national government like that embodied in the federal Constitution of 1787 was inconceivable to Americans in 1776. Yet Middlekauff makes it appear very natural, a mere matter of solving a few weaknesses that had shown up in the Confederation. Middlekauff's account of the formation of the Constitution virtually sets back scholarship on the issue at least a century. It's as if Charles Beard had never written.

In Middlekauff's view, all the anxiety of the 1780s grew out of the impotence of the central government, the Confederation Congress. "Indeed dissatisfaction with Congress and its works—or lack of works—shaped a movement for constitutional reform in the 1780s." But actually Congress was only part of the problem. By 1787 all American leaders were willing to grant to the Confederation additional powers of taxation and trade regulation. Nationalists like Madison, however, had more on their minds than Congress's lack of power; they were worried as well about the problems of state politics. In fact, the vices flowing from the state legislatures, wrote Madison to Jefferson in 1787, "contributed more to that uneasiness which produced the Convention, and prepared the public mind for a general reform, than those which accrued ... from the inadequacy of the confederation." It was in the states that the Revolution originally was to be tested, and during the 1780s many leaders saw it failing there. Middlekauff misses all this; in fact, he believes the states in the 1780s had solved their problems. "By 1787," he writes, "the constitutional structure of most states seemed secure." Not only is Middlekauff wrong in this, but this error prevents him from grasping the ways in which the federal Constitution was designed to remedy the evils of state politics.

In his brief analysis of the federal Constitution, Middlekauff's misunderstandings build one upon another. He cannot fully comprehend the radical character of Madison's Virginia Plan, and he has no insight whatsoever into the depth of Madison's and other nationalists' fears of lawmaking by the states during the 1780s. So when he comes to consider Madison's proposal for a congressional veto over all state legislation, he can only call it a "near-mad scheme." No matter that the delegates voted for and maintained this "near-mad scheme" in the working plan until halfway through the Convention; no matter that Madison thought such a national veto over state laws was "absolutely necessary" to sound government and despaired of the Constitution when it was finally eliminated.

Because Middlekauff does not appreciate the nationalists' fears of the states, he misinterprets the long acrimonious debate over the nature of

representation in the Senate (whether proportional to population or equal for each state) as simply a struggle between large and small states, and thus misses entirely the passionate desire Madison and other nationalists had to avoid any recognition of state sovereignty in the national government. In the end, Middlekauff has the federal Constitution emerging so naturally that the arguments of its opponents, the Anti-Federalists, can scarcely appear credible, and he thus devotes almost no space to them. John Fiske, writing in 1888 in defense of the Federalists, would have been very pleased.

Does Middlekauff's book fulfill the aim of the Oxford series? It certainly has some good narrative history writing, but it is by no means a summary of recent scholarship on the Revolutionary era. It is a very special story, stimulating in places, but much too idiosyncratic and oddly proportioned to be considered the most reliable general history of the period. Indeed, so peculiar and so personal is Middlekauff's story of the era that it raises fundamental questions about the nature of narrative history writing. It is not simply that his narrative tends to focus on surface events; the problem is more serious than that. Precisely because Middlekauff has been so patently selective in the events he has stressed and neglected, his story of the Revolution plays into the hands of all those who, like Hayden White, argue that historical narrative is just another form of fiction.

No doubt there is always a constructed character to all history writing, but this fabricated character seems particularly evident in narrative history. The past, after all, is not a series of stories waiting to be told, as has become more and more apparent in the twentieth century. Jean-Paul Sartre in his novel *Nausea* had his character Roquentin, who is a historian, suddenly recognize that life is not a story. "Nothing happens while you live," Roquentin realizes. "The scenery changes, people come in and go out, that's all."

> There are no beginnings and no endings. Events simply tack on to one another in an interminable, monotonous addition. . . .

> But everything changes when you tell about life; it's a change
> no one notices: the proof is that people talk about true stories.
> As if there could possibly be true stories; things happen one
> way and we tell about them in the opposite sense. You seem to
> start at the beginning . . . and in reality you have started at the
> end. . . . The end is there, transforming everything.

Incidents no longer just pile up one upon another; they are drawn together, connected, and given meaning by the ending of the story. The plots, the coherence, and the significance of narratives are always retrospective.

This recognition lies behind the contempt French social historians have for the unique, unconnected events of traditional narrative history. For a historian to emphasize one of these unique events and not another, writes François Furet, he has to assume some connecting plot in the events, that they are going somewhere; he has given them "an ideological meaning." The ending has to be present in the historian's mind, transforming everything. A historian selects one event over another because that event presumably "marks some stage in the advent of a political or philosophical ideal—republic, liberty, democracy, reason, and so forth." Such teleological narrative history cannot be truly scientific; it is simply storytelling, not essentially different from fiction.

Most historians, especially in the English-speaking world, are by no means ready to accept such Gallic logic. They still hold to a traditional epistemology, still believe that the past is real and that the truth of it can be recovered through storytelling. The rest of the intellectual world may be falling over itself with excitement in discovering the difficulty, if not the impossibility, of representing reality in any form of language or writing. But not historians. While intellectuals everywhere are promoting "structuralist" and other forms of nonlinear thought, most historians cling innocently to their Newtonian belief that one thing follows another in a coherent and causally related narrative pattern. It may be that traditional

narrative writing depends on historians' remaining mentally in the nineteenth century.

Most American historians did not have much appreciation for the intellectual fashions of the late twentieth century. Perhaps nothing is more revealing of this than the fumbling historians go through trying to deal with the work of Michel Foucault. Foucault seemed to be writing about the issues historians like to write about, such as changes through time in European methods of disciplining and punishing criminals. Thus historians try to hold Foucault up to their traditional understanding of change and their traditional standards of verification and evidence without ever appreciating that it is precisely these traditions of history writing that Foucault is out to smash.

Even more disconcerting to historians are the ways in which imaginative writers have been questioning the distinction between history and fiction, more or less in the spirit of "it's all made up anyhow." Thus E. L. Doctorow in his novel *Ragtime* claims that his fabrication of the past is no less authentic than that of the historian. "There's no fiction or nonfiction now," he has said, "there's only narrative." Facts about the past are what the writer says they are. Asked whether Emma Goldman and Evelyn Nesbit ever really met, Doctorow replied, "They have now."

In an even grander manner, the Latin American writer Gabriel García Márquez in his *One Hundred Years of Solitude* plays upon all the ways historians have traditionally organized their understanding of reality. García Márquez's story is no ordinary narrative; it levels all barriers between the real and imaginary, the past and the present. His world of magical realism has no time, no causality, no regularity, no coherent orderly succession of one thing following another, indeed no historical consciousness at all. The continued popularity of these novels and others like them testifies to the extent to which the traditional assumptions on which narrative history depends are being challenged. No wonder the distinguished literary critic Frank Kermode can casually talk about "the recognition, now

commonplace, that the writing of history involves the use of regulative fictions."

Middlekauff, like most other historians, seems to have written his story of the Revolution in all innocence of these epistemological problems. It's a good thing: the narrative form as a representation of past reality, particularly as Middlekauff has used it, may not bear much looking into.

## WRITING HISTORY: AN EXCHANGE

By Jackson Lears and John Patrick Diggins. Reply by Gordon S. Wood.

(When any of my reviews generated interesting responses from readers writing to the editor, I have included them. This review of the Middlekauff book provoked rejoinders from several prominent historians. Two are reprinted here, along with my response. All appeared in *The New York Review of Books*, December 16, 1982.)

To the Editors:

Gordon Wood's review of Robert Middlekauff, *The Glorious Cause: The American Revolution, 1763–1789*, is interesting but frustrating— interesting because he perceptively discusses the split in the American historical profession between traditional narrative and quantitative social science, frustrating because he doesn't explore alternatives to that sharply defined choice. He mentions the work of such unclassifiable thinkers as Michel Foucault, Hayden White, and Frank Kermode, but doesn't suggest that it presents a way out of the stale debate between "old" narrative historians and "new" social historians.

Both sides in that debate are hampered by the epistemology of nineteenth-century positivism. Both assume implicitly that the facts

about the past are "out there," that the historian's primary task is to collect them, and that assiduous data gathering can bring us closer to knowing the truth about the past "as it really was." The only disagreement involves whether to order those facts with an eye toward decoration and inspiration or toward precise measurement.

The debate is pointless because it never raises fundamental epistemological questions. Neither side acknowledges that historical facts are not simply "out there" but rather embedded in the questions historians frame. To keep framing intelligent questions, historians need to construct forms that give meaning to the tangle of human experience. Whether those forms are implicit or explicit and whatever labels are attached to them (theories, models, concepts, interpretations), all constitute "regulative fictions"—to use Kermode's term, which Professor Wood quotes.

The word "fiction" does not imply falsity; it does not mean that historians should play fast and loose with evidence; it does not preclude exhaustive research and rigorous accuracy. It *does* underscore the essential point that historical explanations are crafted forms—mental constructions historians use to make sense of an inchoate mass of data.

The most illuminating works of history are those governed by the most imaginative and capacious regulative fictions. (One thinks of Perry Miller on New England Puritanism, David Brion Davis on slavery, Philippe Ariès on childhood and death, E. P. Thompson on the English working class, and Wood himself on *The Creation of the American Republic*.) These works are not simply characterized either by the narration or the quantification of facts. Rather, their chief distinguishing feature is that they use regulative fictions flexibly to explain changes in human experience without flattening its variety and complexity. The current debate within the historical profession tends to overlook this analytic, synthetic tradition.

The positivist heritage is alive and well among American historians, narrowing their methodological debates and desensitizing them to some

of the most interesting developments in modern historical thought. The blurring of lines between history and fiction ought to humble historians, reminding them how fragmentary and oblique their view of the past must always be; it ought also to alert them to new possibilities. Giving up a positivist epistemology, they might explore a wider variety of regulative fictions and reveal a broader range of historical truths. They might even acknowledge the truth-telling power of literary fictions. Gabriel García Márquez's *One Hundred Years of Solitude* devastates positivist assumptions about linear causality and historical truth, as Professor Wood notes, but it also tells some profound historical truths about the "modernization" of a colonial society. That subject has inspired numerous valuable monographs but few syntheses as compelling as García Márquez's extraordinary novel. The point is not that historians should become novelists but that they might well ponder the infinite variety of paths to the past.

Historians do not need to be fashionmongers to recognize that "the intellectual fashions of the late twentieth century" could reveal a great deal about the problematic nature of their craft.

Jackson Lears
University of Missouri-Columbia
Columbia, Missouri

---

To the Editors:

In his review of Robert Middlekauff's *The Glorious Cause,* Gordon S. Wood observes that such eminent contemporary scholars as Bernard Bailyn, Eric Foner, Lawrence Stone, and Middlekauff are calling for a return to narrative history in the "storytelling" tradition of nineteenth-century historians like Henry Adams and George Bancroft. Wood believes that any return to a methodology that partakes of the "narrative form" is innocent of the problems of dealing with "causality,"

"motivation," and "human intention." These problems have been brought to our awareness, Wood states, by a whole tribe of French luminaries, including Sartre, Foucault, the "structuralists," and others who are promoting "forms of nonlinear thought." Wood seems to feel that the return to narrative history represents some kind of failure of nerve.

It might be noted that John Dos Passos, whose *U.S.A.* Sartre hailed precisely for its "structural indeterminancy," dropped that genre and went on to write narrative history, albeit pretty mawkish stuff. Perhaps the novelist realized that a "structuralist" sensibility, not to say a "deconstructionist," cannot be used to write about the Founding Fathers, since that sensibility had not entered their consciousness and hence could not have been a basis for their thoughts and actions. Jefferson assumed that the Revolution had a historical, linear explanation. "When in the course of human events it becomes necessary . . ." It is difficult to see how the eighteenth-century mentality can be reenacted with the conceptual knowledge of the twentieth-century mind. Imagine Jefferson composing the Declaration of Independence. "We hold these truths to be socially conditioned and dependent for their meaning on the 'structures,' 'paradigms,' and the 'episteme' of the epoch." If narrative history risks being antiquarian, projecting back into the past a "nonlinear" mode of explanation risks being anachronistic.

Wood's own explanation for the theoretical problems confronting the historical profession today is both geographical and chronological. "Most historians, especially in the English-speaking world, are by no means ready to accept such Gallic logic," and in particular "most American historians do not have much appreciation for the intellectual fashions of the late twentieth century." The issues that trouble Wood, and rightly so, are neither peculiar to the twentieth century nor attributable to the superior consciousness of the Parisian intellect. Actually, Henry Adams was the first great historian to grasp the impossibility of writing history. In his nine-volume study of the Jefferson and Madison administrations, Adams came to the conclusion

that he could not explain what he had set out to explain: the War of 1812. Neither his narrative form nor even his "scientific" attempt to establish sequential connections yielded causal understanding. History, like power, remained impervious to intelligence. Adams's growing sense of "chaos" and "entropy" is as "decentering" as anything found in twentieth-century "Gallic logic" (logic?). Long before Foucault, Derrida, and other contemporary movers and shakers, Adams saw that without knowledge there is only power ("authority is police") and that without narration there is no rational explanation of events and thus "silence is best." But Adams, who had the courage of his confusions, was honest enough to resign from teaching history at Harvard. What ought we to do?

John Patrick Diggins
University of California
Irvine, California

----

Gordon S. Wood replies:

Professor Lears is wrong when he suggests that historians need humbling. Historians are already very humble people. They know only too well "the problematical nature of their craft" and "how fragmentary and oblique their view of the past must always be." To be sure, most of them have not gone as far as Henry Adams and Professor Diggins to admit "the impossibility of writing history." But few historians nowadays are so naive as to believe that their task is simply to collect facts about the past. Historians realize that understanding the past requires imagination and the use of what might be called "regulative fictions" in order to make sense of the collected data. Nor are they opposed to telling what have been called "complex stories" that integrate narrative with problem solving and that rely on coherence as much as on correspondence theories of truth. Many historians have blended storytelling with analysis very nicely and, it is hoped, will continue to do so.

Yet when all is said and done, when all the concessions to subjectivity, imaginative reenactment, and the use of "regulative fictions" have been made, historians still remain necessarily tied to what Professor Lears calls "the epistemology of nineteenth-century positivism," to the view that the past "out there" really existed and that they can through the collection and ordering of evidence bring us closer to knowing the truth about that past "as it really was," even if the full and complete truth about the past will always remain beyond their grasp. It is precisely because ever-widening circles of our culture are casting doubt on this traditional epistemology that historians feel more humble about what they do. Some of the most eminent working historians, such as G. R. Elton and Oscar Handlin, know that ultimately there can be no alternative for their craft than this old-fashioned epistemology. Historians, warns Elton, "require not the new humility preached in the wake of Heisenberg, but some return to the assurance of the nineteenth century that the work they are doing deals with reality." "The historian's vocation," writes Handlin, "depends on this minimal operational article of faith: Truth is absolute; it is as absolute as the world is real." This faith may be philosophically naive, may even be philosophically absurd in this skeptical and relativist-minded age; nevertheless, it is what makes history writing possible. Historians who cut loose from this faith do so at the peril of their discipline.

## AFTERWORD

I wrote this review at a time when the problems of writing narrative history were very much on the minds of some historians, perhaps largely because of the work of Hayden White, whose *Metahistory: The Historical Imagination in Nineteenth-Century Europe* (1973) and subsequent essays had promoted the fictional character of narrative history writing. White's work had stirred up a storm of controversy among the few philosophically

minded historians who cared about such matters, examples of whom were the prominent historians who responded to my review. No doubt most working historians quite sensibly ignored the whole business of whether they were telling the truth or not. I myself had been teaching an undergraduate course on the practice of history in which I had assigned Sartre's novel *Nausea*. I subsequently dropped the novel from the course when I discovered that the undergraduates were taking it all too seriously. Reflecting on the last sentence of my review, which I came to regret, perhaps I was taking it all too seriously as well.

# 4.

# THE LESSONS OF HISTORY

*The March of Folly: From Troy to Vietnam*
by Barbara W. Tuchman (New York: Knopf, 1984)

*The New York Review of Books,* March 29, 1984

B ARBARA W. TUCHMAN is our foremost popular historian, a two-time Pulitzer Prize winner and a best-selling author. She has achieved this popular success by writing good traditional narratives on numerous subjects from the origins of World War I and Stilwell's mission to China to fourteenth-century Europe. She writes history, she once said, not "to instruct but to tell a story."

The professional historians have often given Tuchman a bad time in reviews. They have made her feel that she is something less than a professional, and she justly resents it. She does not like being called an "amateur" by all the "professionals" who have graduate training, advanced degrees, and university positions. She prefers, she said in a 1981 collection of essays covering her career, to recognize the difference between them and her "by distinguishing between academics and independents, or between scholars and writers, rather than between professionals and amateurs." She may not have a Ph.D., but she is as much of a pro as the professors are, and rather more so if making a living by your work is any criterion of being professional. She can communicate with a willing readership, which is more than the professors can do. "When you write for the public you have

to be clear and you have to be interesting." The professors have too many captive audiences—first with their dissertation supervisors, then with their students in lecture halls. They really do not know how "to capture and hold the interest of an audience."

And the reason the professors cannot capture an audience, wrote Tuchman in 1966, is that they do not know how to tell a story. They believe storytelling is "old-fashioned." They are too much caught up in "interdisciplinary techniques," in "subjects such as demography," and in "the computerized mechanics of quantification." Their efforts are directed "toward uncovering underlying patterns in history and human behavior which presumably might help in understanding the past and managing the future, or even the present." They want history, in other words, to be a science, which means that they want it "to be utilitarian and teach us lessons."

In the 1960s Tuchman had only scorn for such efforts to make history a science. "History," she said back then, "has a way of escaping attempts to imprison it in patterns." Human behavior has too many variables to be susceptible to the scientific method, and "reliable patterns, or what are otherwise called the lessons of history, remain elusive." Systems and theories therefore should not be imposed on the past. The facts of the past should be allowed to speak for themselves. Why does history have to teach lessons anyway? "Why," she asked with some exasperation, "cannot history be studied and written and read for its own sake, as the record of human behavior . . . ?" History is not a science; it is an art. History needs writers, or artists, who can communicate the past to readers, and that has been Tuchman's calling. Her "form," she said in 1966, "is narrative." She knew it was "looked down on now by the advanced academics, but I don't mind because no one could possibly persuade me that telling a story is not the most desirable thing a writer can do."

Yet all the while Tuchman was telling her stories in the 1960s and 1970s, she had a latent urge to do some teaching as well. The desire to instruct always subtly suffused her narratives, and in her occasional pieces it often

emerged full-blown. Even as she questioned the possibility of finding lessons in history, she admitted in the same breath that history might have something to teach us after all. Maybe, she said in the mid-1960s, we could learn from "past mistakes" and "manage better in similar circumstances next time." Vietnam, for example, could tell us something about mistakes "if we would only listen." Growing despair with our times, reflected in her gloomy picture of fourteenth-century Europe, *A Distant Mirror,* finally seems to have gotten the better of her. Our government's mistakes in Vietnam and elsewhere have now released all of her pent-up pedagogical urges. The result is her new book, *The March of Folly.*

This book is very different from her previous best-selling histories. To be sure, there is still some well-written historical narration here. But the tone and character of the book are different; its didactic purposes are now explicit, unmistakably clear. Her history is no longer art: it is not written for its own sake. It is now science—popular political science—which she once said she would never write. She has not taken to using computers or to calculating the prices of wheat, but she is very eager now to find patterns or lessons in the past with which to teach us.

It is all very ironic. Just as academic historians are becoming disillusioned with scientific history and are moving back toward old-fashioned narrative, Tuchman has decided to become scientific, to discover some general principles of politics that are "independent of time and recurrent in governorship" and that might tell us how to act in the present and future.

Tuchman is now nothing if she is not scientific, at least in her claims. She begins her book with a taxonomy of misgovernment. She says there are four kinds of misgovernment, often in combination: (1) "tyranny," (2) "excessive ambition," (3) "incompetence or decadence," and finally, (4) "folly or perversity." This last is the focus of her book, which she describes as "a generalized inquiry" into the ways governments have committed folly by acting against their own best interests. Political philosophers from

Plato on, she writes, have investigated the major issues of ethics, sovereignty, the social contract, freedom and order, and so on, but few of them,
"except Machiavelli," have bothered with "mere folly, although folly has
been a chronic and pervasive problem."

Tuchman aims to make up for this neglect. Examples of folly, she
believes, are "timeless and universal" and "independent of era or locality."
These constants, these scientific principles, are what she is after. All the
particulars of political events, all the peculiar and specific facts, "must be
sifted out in the hope that abiding principles may appear." By isolating
these abiding principles of politics she hopes to become a sort of
Machiavelli for the masses.

To qualify as folly for her purposes, a government's actions must meet
three criteria: (1) they must have been perceived as counterproductive in
their own time; (2) they must have been the actions of a group, not one
individual; and (3) they had to persist in the face of alternative suggestions.
In her opening chapter, Tuchman ransacks history for various examples
of such folly—everything from Louis XIV's revocation of the Edict of
Nantes to the Japanese attack on Pearl Harbor. But most of her book
concentrates on several major historical events that illustrate folly. After
a short chapter on the Trojan horse as the classic example of political
stupidity, Tuchman devotes a chapter each to the provoking of the
Protestant Reformation by the Renaissance popes, the British loss of
America, and America's betrayal of itself in Vietnam.

Like any good scientist, Tuchman is more interested in the present
and future than in the past, and she does not hide it. Each of the chapters
gets progressively longer, so that the chapter on Vietnam is nearly twice
as long as that on the Renaissance popes. And her book is sprinkled with
references to the present. "Why," she asks, "do the superpowers not begin
mutual divestment of the means of human suicide?" Why does the United
States persist in its "imbecility in El Salvador?" Political folly may have
been bearable for us in the past, but not anymore, not with the "accelerat-

ing incompetence in America." In the end, writes Tuchman, "it seems almost superfluous to say that the present study stems from the ubiquity of this problem in our time."

After describing the episode of the Trojan horse as the prototype of "policy pursued contrary to self-interest—in the face of urgent warning and a feasible alternative," Tuchman turns to the folly of the half dozen or so popes who ruled the Roman church between 1470 and 1530. "Their governance dismayed the faithful, brought the Holy See into disrepute, left unanswered the cry for reform, ignored all protests, warnings and signs of rising revolt, and ended by breaking apart the unity of Christendom and losing half the papal constituency to the Protestant secession." In vigorous and vivid prose she exposes all the examples of papal greed, corruption, and lust for power that she can find in order to indict the leadership of the Church for its folly in bringing on the Protestant Reformation.

Historians will probably wince at this explanation of the Reformation according to what the papacy did or did not do. Actually the idea that the abuses of the Church alone caused the Reformation is an old one, but it is not much supported by historians today. Well over a half century ago the great French historian Lucien Febvre made a scathing attack on the adequacy of such a view. The notion that something as complicated and profound as the Protestant Reformation—a deep-rooted upheaval in religious sentiment throughout much of Christendom—could actually spring from "nothing more than a revolt of healthy and honest minds and consciences against the nasty spectacles and wicked people around them" was to Febvre hopelessly limited and partial. And most subsequent historians have agreed with him. The abuses of the Church were neither more prevalent nor more evil in the early sixteenth century than in many earlier periods. For centuries reformers had cried out against the Church's wickedness. The papacy may even have been more degraded in the ninth and tenth centuries than it was in the fifteenth.

The Protestant reformers were moved by more than simply the abuses

of the papacy. In fact, it is doubtful how much of the profligacy of the Renaissance popes that Tuchman so colorfully describes was known to people remote from Rome. Despite all their criticism of the selling of indulgences, Luther and the Protestant reformers were far more interested in transforming the basis of faith and doctrine in the Church than in cleansing it of corruption. Any explanation of the Reformation, like Tuchman's, that ignores the emergence of powerful feelings of popular piety throughout northern Europe is bound to be one-sided.

Not only has Tuchman built her case for the folly of the papacy on this narrow base, but her chapter on the Renaissance popes is riddled with anachronism. She can never quite accept the fact that the papacy was a secular power in fifteenth-century Italy. The popes' eagerness to extend their political strength, and their obsession with "conspicuous and useless expenditure . . . for the sake of effect" are to Tuchman sheer madness. She has little appreciation of the papacy's political role and its fear of dependency in a world of aggressive emerging nation-states. To her the popes just seem so irreligious. "What kind of apostleship of Christianity" did the Renaissance popes "see themselves as filling?" she asks. It is true that the papacy's riches "nourished immortal works of art, but however much these have graced the world, the proper business of the Church was something else." Where, she might even have asked, was Pope John XXIII when the Church really needed him?

Britain's "follies" in the eighteenth century "were not so perverse as the popes'." Her ministers were not as greedy, but nevertheless they were just as arrogant and stupid, and their mishandling of America in the 1760s and 1770s cost Britain an empire. Tuchman has almost nothing good to say about Britain's ruling elite in these years. The level of British "intelligence and competence in both civil and military positions" was generally "low." George III was marked by "tragic flaws" and he "was not the most astute politician." The "upper crust of the governing class" had "few of outstanding mind." With colorful quotations from the likes of Horace Walpole, Tuchman paints a pathetic picture of British ineptitude. The government

was made up of men bred to snobbery at Eton or Westminister, close minded and woodenheaded by training and temperament, and so hung up on the punctilios of Old World etiquette that they "could not bring themselves to refer to the opposite Commander-in-Chief as General Washington but only as Mister."

George III and his ministers have never been used to gentle treatment by American historians, but certainly not in recent times have they been denounced so severely as they are here by Tuchman. It seems they could do nothing right. If they were weak, they are criticized for their lack of self-confidence; if they were strong, then they were arrogant. If George Grenville was pigheaded, then Charles Townshend was "given to reversing himself by 180 degrees if expedience beckoned."

Tuchman is aware of the possibility of anachronism: in a note she apologizes for using "on the right" in reference to the political spectrum because she realizes that it is "an unhistorical term not then in use." But at the same time, she misses all the larger and more serious anachronisms that run through her account. She seems always to be judging these British officials by some absolute rational standard of political leadership that she has in the back of her mind. Thus she caricatures Lord North, who was one of the most astute parliamentarians of eighteenth-century Britain, as a lazy, awkward slob who had no ideas or will of his own and who could scarcely stay awake in debates. She sees Townshend's "spoiling fault" to be his passion for fame—as if the desire for fame were not the ruling passion of most of the great men of the age, including Washington and Hamilton. Somehow or other, Tuchman's indictment comes down to her feeling that the "attitude" of the British leaders "toward government was less than professional." Presumably, they all could have benefited from a term at the Kennedy School of Government.

It is an incredible picture that Tuchman has drawn of Britain's political system. Her descriptions of the "unreality of 18th-century English government" and the "unsuitability for government" of its leaders refer in fact to a political system that was the marvel and envy of the age and that

despite the loss of the colonies carried Britain through an era of tumult and into the next century without serious convulsion. She has the same limited view of the American Revolution as she had of the Reformation—from the top down. She says nothing about growing American pressures and demands that would have challenged any imperial authority, no matter how talented.

When Tuchman gets to America's involvement in Vietnam, she has the real model of political folly that was in her mind all along. In vigorous polemical prose she tells the miserable story from 1945 to 1973; indeed, her chapter is probably one of the better short accounts we yet have of America's venture in Vietnam, although it does not have much to say about the war as it was viewed and conducted by America's opponents. But is it history, the kind of history that Tuchman had always wanted to write? She once said that because she was too emotionally involved in the present, "I could not write contemporary history if I tried." "A historian needs," she said, "a perspective of at least twenty-five years, and preferably fifty, to form an opinion of any value." Apparently, the present crisis has become too great for these inhibitions to apply any longer.

What can we make of Tuchman's political science? Surely we can all agree with her that there have been plenty of examples of folly in past political affairs. Folly, in fact, has been so much a "timeless and universal" constant of human behavior that it seems inherent in the process of history. Perhaps the ubiquity of folly is due to the fact that folly is not always the consequence of what Tuchman thinks it is: stupidity, woodenheadedness, and irrationality. Perhaps it is equally the result of reason and the best, most honorable and sensible of intentions. Tuchman assumes that the participants in the past knew, or should have known, they were making mistakes but perversely still kept on making these mistakes. "Persistence in error," she writes, "is the problem." But what if the historical participants, having no advantage of Tuchman's hindsight, thought they were persisting not in error but rightly and rationally?

The British leaders, for example, were not perverse in trying to pre-

serve their empire, and they did not perceive reality any more irrationally than the American Revolutionaries. Tuchman seems to expect the British officials to have realized the futility of what they were attempting. Couldn't they see all the forces against them? Certainly they were warned enough of failure. But, of course, they did not see the future and they pushed on, just as the American Revolutionaries did in the face of similar warnings. If the Americans had lost the Revolution, one could easily make a Tuchman-like case for their folly too. Imagine, the colonists attempting to fight the most powerful nation in the world, and all for a constitutional principle that probably would not have amounted to much anyway! They were a free, prosperous people who were destroying a working relationship with the greatest and most liberty-loving nation in the world.

Such were the warnings the Revolutionaries received, not just by Tories but also by frightened Whigs like John Dickinson, who refused to sign the Declaration of Independence. Yet the Revolutionary leaders were too woodenheaded, too emotional, too blind to the realities of British power, and against all the odds and all the warnings they made a revolution, even though their revolution did not cause the ruin of Great Britain as everyone had expected. Whether the historical participants' actions become examples of Churchillian determination or perverse woodenheadedness seems therefore to depend ultimately on the unpredictable outcome of events.

Folly, then, is not just a constant of history; at times it seems to be even a necessity. More often than not it is folly—false and irrational perceptions of reality—that gives people the intellectual and emotional energy to act as they do. Tuchman criticizes the British officials for believing that the Revolution was a conspiracy of designing men; it was just another example, she says, of "the self-deception that characterizes folly." But the American Revolutionaries suffered from the same sort of self-deception; they also believed in a conspiracy, a conspiracy of British officials against them. And for both sides these false and unreasonable beliefs in conspiracies were crucial in mobilizing people into action. It

was precisely the intelligent men like Dickinson, who perceived reality most accurately and doubted the existence of evil intentions on either side, who in the end hesitated to act. Reasonableness, clear thinking, and accurate perceptions of reality, in other words, are not necessarily what is needed either to make a revolution or to put one down, or even to get anything done at all.

If the political follies of history are constant and often necessary for action, can they really teach us anything? Can we in fact learn lessons from the past? Tuchman certainly hopes so, for that is the burden of her book. And most people, including many historians, will probably agree with her. Sunday supplements certainly present us often enough with George Santayana's fatuous phrase that "those who cannot remember the past are condemned to repeat it." (Actually, after all our talk during the 1950s and 1960s of the lessons of Munich and now of the lessons of Vietnam, a better case can be made for the opposite: that those who remember the past may be the ones condemned to repeat it.) Mercifully, Tuchman spares us Santayana's saying, but instead gives us Samuel Coleridge's: "If men could learn from history, what lessons it might teach us!" But Coleridge is no more right than Santayana is. History does not teach lots of little lessons. Insofar as it teaches any lessons, it teaches only one big one: that nothing ever works out quite the way its managers intended or expected. History is like experience and old age: wisdom is what one learns from it.

Unlike sociology or political science, history is a conservative discipline—conservative, of course, not in any contemporary political sense but in the larger sense of inculcating skepticism about people's ability to manipulate and control purposefully their own destinies. By showing that the best-laid plans of people usually go awry, the study of history tends to dampen youthful enthusiasm and to restrain the can-do, the conquer-the-future spirit that many people have. Historical knowledge takes people off a roller coaster of illusions and disillusions; it levels off emotions and gives people a perspective on what is possible and, more often, what

is not possible. By this definition Americans have had almost no historical sense whatsoever; indeed, such a sense seems almost un-American.

Too much of this historical sense, too much skepticism, is not, of course, very good for getting things done. Which is why Nietzsche believed that "forgetfulness is a property of all action." Too much "rumination," too much "historical sense," he wrote, "injures and finally destroys the living thing, be it a man or a people or a system of culture." Fortunately, however, there seems to be little danger of our becoming too historically minded in America today.

## AFTERWORD

I am not one of those academic historians who look down upon the popular historians who have no Ph.D.s and sell hundreds of thousands of copies of their books. I had great respect for Barbara Tuchman and have even greater respect for her successor as the premier popular historian of the country, David McCullough. As the most popular historian of her generation, Tuchman satisfied the hunger for good old-fashioned narrative history for millions of readers, just as McCullough has done for our generation. But unlike McCullough, who genuinely seems to want just to tell a good story about the past, Tuchman, as I suggest in the review, always appeared to have had a suppressed desire to demonstrate the usefulness of history, which she finally released in this misbegotten book.

# 5.

# CONTINUITY IN HISTORY

*Albion's Seed: Four British Folkways in America*
by David Hackett Fischer (New York: Oxford University Press, 1989)

*The New Republic,* October 30, 1989

D AVID HACKETT FISCHER'S book could not be much bigger or
more ambitious. It is the first in a series of volumes that he hopes
will eventually comprise a cultural history of the United States. The project has been more than twenty years in the making. It grew out of Fischer's
response to what he calls in his preface "a revolution in the writing of
history" that took place in the 1960s: the rise of "a new kind of history"
modeled on the French Annales school. Unlike traditional history, this
new history was not storytelling but problem solving. It was "not really
about the past at all, but about change—with past and present in a mutual
perspective."

It did not concentrate on great men and headline events but on the
acts and thoughts of ordinary people. Its goal was "nothing less than an
*histoire totale* of the human experience," and thus it drew upon every
conceivable kind of evidence, from statistics to iconographic materials.
And these new social historians "presented their findings in a new way."
Traditional historians had tended to offer their findings as "interpretations" discovered by intuition and supported by testimony. But the new
social historians relied on argument using "rigorous methods of logic and

empiricism." This new manner of presentation, says Fischer, represented an "epistemic revolution." It was not only "the most radical innovation of the new history" but also "the most difficult for older scholars to understand."

But, says Fischer, who is professor of history at Brandeis, the great goal of the new history was not fulfilled in the 1960s and 1970s. Instead of bringing everything together, the new history disintegrated into bits and pieces and into many special fields that became increasingly shrill and polemical. It could not accommodate the political events and individual actions of the older history, and it tended to rely too much on materialist or modernization explanations. By the 1980s the new social history had lost touch with the larger purposes that had called it into being.

Fischer hopes that his project will offer a way out of the present historiographical confusion. He is, in other words, accepting what Bernard Bailyn in his 1981 presidential address to the American Historical Association called "the great challenge of modern historical scholarship": to bring some coherence out of the incoherent mass of historical monographs and specialized studies that have been pouring from the presses in the past thirty years. Fischer expects to do this by bringing to bear on the chaos of historical scholarship "the organizing idea of cultural history"— with culture defined in an anthropological sense. He sees his series finding "a way forward by combining several elements which the old and new histories have tended to keep apart." He would like his series to synthesize the best of the old narrative history and the new scientific history.

Fischer's project, therefore, will be about both elites and ordinary people, about both individual choice and collective experience, about both society and government. His volumes will combine the "epistemic assumptions" of the old histories and the new, blending both interpretation and empiricism in a complicated "braided narrative." It will go beyond the "reductive materialist models" presently in fashion among English-speaking historians. And it will seek a new answer to the old problem about the relationship between past and present—avoiding the

extremes of antiquarianism and presentism by using a third alternative, which Fischer calls his "immediatist" solution. Finally, Fischer hopes that his work not only will teach other disciplines the indispensability of historical knowledge, but will also enlarge our ethical and moral horizons—in this first volume, for example, by discriminating historically among different kinds of liberty.

It is enough to take the breath away. Can any book or series of books do all this? There is certainly a touching earnestness, even naïveté, in the way Fischer describes his hopes and plans. And there is exaggeration and distortion. The old history was never as unempirical and as free-floating as he argues, and the new history of the 1960s was not as revolutionary and pathbreaking as he suggests. Solving problems and using logic and empirical data in historical study were not inventions of the Annales school or of the 1960s. Still, his perception that present historical scholarship is in confusion, if not in chaos, is widely shared by many in the historical profession. Thus his attempt to bring things together has to be applauded.

But breathtaking as the proposal for his series is, it is nothing compared to the particular interpretation of the origins of America set forth in this first volume. This first book starts his series with a bang—a big bang. Fischer implies that nearly every major historian writing about the origins of early America in the twentieth century has gotten it wrong. In fact, he believes that Herbert Baxter Adams and his followers in the nineteenth century were more right than not. Adams and his followers thought that American society can best be understood as an extension of Britain or Europe, that the basic determinants, the germs, of America lay in the Teutonic forests and Saxon institutions of the Old World.

It was against this nineteenth-century "germ theory," this view that the origins of American society could be found on the other side of the Atlantic, that Frederick Jackson Turner directed his writings of the 1890s and after, discovering in the western frontier of the New World the real source of democracy and free institutions in America. Although Turner's

particular "frontier thesis" has long since been modified or discredited, the general assumptions of his interpretation—that American society can best be understood as a response to the circumstances of the New World— have remained very much alive through the twentieth century. It is not too much to say that most twentieth-century American historians have been Turnerites in one form or another.

They certainly have not been followers of Herbert Baxter Adams or the "germ theory." Most historians of America have dismissed or ignored the continuities between Europe and America. Instead, like Turner, twentieth-century historians such as Daniel Boorstin, have highlighted the differences between the Old World and the New World, and have underscored the peculiarities and often the uniqueness of American development. Even historians, such as Oscar Handlin and Bernard Bailyn, who have written on immigration and have recognized connections between Europe and America, have nevertheless emphasized in their writings not the persistence of older European traditions, but the transforming impact of the American environment on those traditions.

Fischer's book directly confronts this twentieth-century Turnerite dominance of early American history. The book argues, as Fischer says, "a modified 'germ thesis' about the importance for the United States of having been British in its cultural origins." The book is thus a revisionist blockbuster; it is timely, and its implications are portentous and immense.

During the period between the early seventeenth century and the American Revolution, the British colonies were settled by at least four great waves of English-speaking immigrants. The first was an exodus of about twenty thousand Puritans, mostly from the eastern region of England, to Massachusetts in the period from 1629 to 1640. The second was the migration of a small group of royalist Cavaliers and large numbers of indentured servants from the south of England to Virginia between the early 1640s and the 1670s. The third was the migration of twenty-three thousand Quakers and Quaker sympathizers from the North Midlands of England to the Delaware Valley during the half century after 1675. The

fourth was a massive flow of English-speaking peoples from the borders of North Britain and northern Ireland to the Appalachian backcountry during the second and third quarters of the eighteenth century.

Although nearly all of these groups of migrants were alike in speaking English, in being Protestants, and in being jealous of their British liberties, they differed from one another in many ways: in their particular brands of Protestantism, in their social status, in their customs, and in the British regions from whence they came. "They carried across the Atlantic," writes Fischer, "four different sets of British folkways which became the basis of regional cultures in the New World." By the eve of the Revolution these four cultures were firmly established in America. The people of each group spoke different dialects of English, built their houses in different ways, cooked differently and ate different foods, treated the opposite sex and older people differently, raised and named their children differently, used time differently, and ordered their society and government differently.

These different British customs and practices have had decisive and long-lasting effects on American life. Although less than 20 percent of Americans today have any British ancestors, Fischer believes that "in a cultural sense most Americans are Albion's seed, no matter who their own forebears may have been." Strong echoes of these four British folkways, says Fischer, may still be heard today in the major dialects of American speech, in the regional peculiarities of American society, in the complex dynamics of American politics, and in the differing ideas of American liberty. The central thesis of his book, he writes, is the legacy of these four British folkways in early America, a legacy that "remains the most powerful determinant of a voluntary society in the United States today."

At the outset, Fischer distinguishes two dozen or so different categories of folkways, which he tediously labels speech ways, building ways, family ways, marriage ways, sex ways, religious ways, learning ways, dress ways, work ways, power ways, freedom ways, and so on through the many

other different ways cultures carry on the ordinary business of life. He has organized his book very neatly into four main parts, each dealing with one of the four waves of immigrants and the particular area in America it settled. In each part he describes in clear (if not elegant) prose the regional, social, and religious origins of the migrants, and then he goes through seriatim the various categories of folkways, depicting each in a half-dozen pages or so. In nearly every case, Fischer's conclusion is the same: the origins of the particular custom or folkway he describes can be traced directly to the English or British region from whence the migrants came.

Thus the Puritans' practices of placing single men in families and sending out children to other households were not invented in America but originated in the counties of East Anglia. So too were the food-baking practices of East Anglia carried to New England by the Puritans, just as the special tastes for frying in the south and west of England and for boiling in the north of England were brought to the New World by the migrants from those regions. Even the fabled New England town meeting was not created in America—it was transplanted from East Anglia, where it had existed for many centuries before the great migration.

In a similar manner, Virginia's culture was decisively shaped by the long-existing English customs of its immigrants. Most of the forty thousand to fifty thousand people who migrated to Virginia between 1645 and 1670 came from sixteen counties in the south and west of England. This triangle of territory between Bristol, Warwick, and Kent, whose heart was Hardy's Wessex, had its own distinctive culture that went back a millennium or more. This regional culture was dominated by a small landowning class, which had a highly developed sense of honor and a hierarchical conception of liberty.

People from this region of England, argues Fischer, were royalist in their politics and Anglican in their faith, and were used to extreme inequalities in their society, to scattered rural living, and to the production of agricultural staples. During the early Middle Ages, slavery had existed

on a huge scale throughout this area; in the eighth and ninth centuries the size of major slaveholdings had been as large as some plantations in the American South a thousand years later; and this Wessex slavery had lasted longer than elsewhere in England.

Seventeenth-century migrants to Virginia from this region brought their culture with them, and this inherited Wessex culture—not the physical environment of the Chesapeake, not the character of tobacco production, and not the demand for labor—determined most of the patterns and habits of living in Virginia. Thus American black slavery, writes Fischer, in one of the most provocative of his pronouncements, "did not create the culture of the tidewater Virginia; that culture created slavery." Fischer, however, is leaving an extensive discussion of slavery to his second volume.

In page after page Fischer details the various ways the deeply rooted traditions and customs of the south and west of England shaped the culture of Virginia and other parts of the South—its dialect, its house plans, its eating habits, its extended patriarchal families, and its open hospitality. Historians, says Fischer, often have attributed the predatory sexual habits of Southern men to the presence of race slavery. But they are mistaken. Such predatory practices appeared in Virginia before slavery became widespread; more important, they had existed in rural southern and western England.

The people from the North Midlands of England who settled the Delaware Valley, including the colonies of West New Jersey, Pennsylvania, and Delaware, likewise brought with them their peculiar customs and habits that decisively shaped the culture of the region. The Quaker architecture of the Delaware Valley, for example, was very different from the architecture in Massachusetts and Virginia, but it was very similar to the buildings in the north of England. The same was true of gender relations; marriage and inheritance patterns; customs of child naming, child rearing, and speech; and a number of other important folkways. Even the use of "thee" and "thou" as the standard second-person pronoun had been cus-

tomary in the North Midlands of England long before it was taken up by the seventeenth-century Quakers. By 1760, though the Quakers had become a minority in the colonies they had founded, their egalitarian and pluralistic values, says Fischer, were deeply embedded in the culture of the Delaware Valley.

Fischer's final group of immigrants was the largest of all—perhaps a quarter of a million people whose migrations spanned a good portion of the eighteenth century. Many of these people came from territories that bordered the Irish Sea: the north of Ireland, the lowlands of Scotland, and the northern counties of England. They introduced into America still another variety of British culture. They were a stubborn and proud border people seasoned by centuries of insecurity and disorder, suspicious of strangers, and like their famous descendant Andrew Jackson, quick to anger and fight. They brought with them to the Appalachian back settlements of America an intense xenophobia and "an indelible memory of oppression which shaped their political attitudes for generations to come."

Indeed, much of what came to characterize the culture of the southern highlands of America—from its clannishness to its instinct for personal violence—had its roots in the borderlands of northern Britain. Family feuds, distilled whiskey, leather-stocking pioneer dress, hell-fire preaching, religious camp meetings, born-again revivalism, an "elbow room" conception of liberty, and terms such as "hoosiers," "rednecks," and "crackers" were not invented by backcountry Americans. They were all transplanted from the border counties of northern Britain. All those historians who keep looking for indigenous and materialist explanations for the origins of these early American customs, says Fischer, have ignored the cultural roots of the original British migrants.

In a long one-hundred-page conclusion, Fischer summarizes his argument and traces the remarkable staying power of these regional customs, which in many cases extend even into our own time. Fischer wryly notes that the distinctive characters of these four folk cultures in early America are closer to their popular reputations than to the many academic "rein-

terpretations" of the twentieth century. (It turns out that the regional stereotypes are all essentially true and we should have known this all along, or else they would not have become stereotypes.) So the Puritans were, in fact, highly puritanical, and the Virginian leaders were cavaliers after all. If you want to know about Puritan and Yankee New England, Fischer implies, you cannot do better than to read Harriet Beecher Stowe's *Oldtown Folks.* The historical truth about the distinctiveness of these regional cultures, says Fischer, is finally emerging from "beneath the many layers of revisionist scholarship."

If this conclusion were not controversial enough, Fischer goes on to hop, skip, and jump through the rest of American history right up to the presidential election of 1988 in order to demonstrate the persistent influence of these four regional cultures in America. Thus the seventeenth-century Puritan system of nucleated central villages with small satellite hamlets has held on in New England for three centuries. So too have peculiar voting patterns, low rates of homicide, and high rates of public spending for government compared to other regions of the United States.

Southern violence is not the product of racial diversity or frontier conditions, and the lower levels of education in the southern highlands cannot be attributed to the legacy of slavery or poverty. These customs are rooted in regional practices that go back to the borderland culture that British immigrants in the eighteenth century brought with them. There is not much in America that cannot be traced back to Albion's seed. The black soul food of the twentieth century resembles the diet of seventeenth-century Virginians. Even the dour color of the ceremonial gown of the president of Brown University, "which," says Fischer, "is approximately the color of used coffee grounds," can be attributed to the Puritans' preference for "sadd colors."

In his zeal to demonstrate persistence and continuity, however, Fischer ultimately misses the point of history, which is to show not how things have remained the same through time but how they have changed. Of course it

is necessary to know, for example, that the vernacular architecture of the New England Puritans remained basically similar to that of East Anglia, but gross similarities and continuities are not what historians are really after. It's the differences, the discrepancies through time, however slight, however marginal, that intrigue and interest them, for cumulatively they tell us how that different, distant past world evolved into our own.

In the architecture of seventeenth-century Massachusetts, as in all aspects of the regional cultures the British migrants brought with them to America, innovation and adaptation to new circumstances began at once and gradually modified what the migrants had known. Sometimes, as Fischer admits, the transplanted regional folkways changed quite dramatically and, like the Anglican parish in the Delaware Valley, were abolished overnight. Why people radically transformed some parts of their inherited culture and clung tenaciously to other parts is precisely what historians want to discover. Still, they cannot understand the nuances of adaptation and change until they know what came before. And to that knowledge Fischer has made an invaluable contribution.

It is not just the predilections of historians that Fischer is implicitly challenging in this book. He also takes on the immigrant myth of America, the basic belief that American culture is a blending and melting of many different immigrant cultures. According to Fischer, the nineteenth-century and twentieth-century immigrants to America "did not assimilate American culture in general." Instead, "they tended to adopt the folkways of the regions in which they settled." But Fischer never satisfactorily explains why they should have done so, never adequately explains why these original British regional folkways should have had such powerful effects on subsequent non-British immigrants, especially since the argument of his book rests on his belief in the staying power of people's particular cultures. Apparently, he thinks that the British regional cultures were so deeply seated and so effectively institutionalized in the colonial period that non-British immigrants over the past two hundred years have felt compelled to adapt to them. So becoming an American for most immi-

grants has usually meant becoming a regional variant of an Anglo-American. Indeed, Fischer at one point refers to the nineteenth- and twentieth-century United States as "Anglo-America."

Since we have long since learned that history books are as much a product of the present as the past, does the appearance of Fischer's remarkable book suggest anything about ourselves at this moment in American history—when the promotion of pluralism and the resistance to assimilation are being publicly voiced more vehemently than ever before, and when the idea of the United States being "Anglo-America" seems increasingly absurd? As Fischer points out, as late as 1900 nearly 60 percent of Americans were still of British stock. By 1980 that proportion had fallen below 20 percent.

In subsequent decades, as that proportion becomes more and more insignificant, will there be any great cultural consequences? Will the British seed that Fischer has so elaborately described lose its potency? If people hold on to their cultures as tenaciously as Fischer says they do, and if the future Americans of the twenty-first century, the majority of whom will likely be of Hispanic, Asian, and African heritage, continue to believe and behave much as their ancestors believed and behaved, then is it not possible that the continuities Fischer has seen in American history from its seventeenth-century beginnings from Albion's seed may at last come to an end? Fischer never raises such a possibility. But why Albion's seed should continue to remain so strong in competition with the cultural seeds of other more numerous peoples is a question that his very provocative book leaves hanging in the air.

## AFTERWORD

In graduate school I was taught that the task of a historian is to describe how people in the past moved chronologically from A to B, with B always closer to us in time. It seems self-evident, but for me it is the

most important lesson I received in my training to be a historian. Since people rarely stay the same between A and B, describing and explaining change through time always seems to me to lie at the heart of historical reconstruction.

Although Fischer has not yet published a second volume in his projected cultural history of America, he has written a number of books since the publication of *Albion's Seed* and has established himself as one of America's most eminent historians. He is a historian of many talents. He is quite capable of writing about radical change, as demonstrated by his superb and pathbreaking *Growing Old in America* (1977); and he can also write very exciting narrative history, as demonstrated by his Pulitzer Prize–winning *Washington's Crossing* (2004). Perhaps the heated controversy stirred up by *Albion's Seed* has made Fischer hesitate to continue his multivolume cultural history, but given Fischer's combative temperament, that seems unlikely. Those interested in the kinds of criticism the book aroused among various experts in early American history might consult the "Forum: *Albion's Seed: Four British Folkways in America:* A symposium," *William and Mary Quarterly*, 3d Ser., 48 (1991), 223–308.

# 6.

# HISTORY AND THE NEW HISTORICISM

*The Letters of the Republic: Publication and the Public Sphere in Eighteenth-Century America* by Michael Warner

(Cambridge, MA: Harvard University Press, 1990)

*The New Republic,* November 12, 1990

H ISTORIANS OUGHT TO BE very happy these days. Everywhere we look, historical thinking (of a sort, at least) is exerting "hege-monic power" over a wide variety of academic fields. What is called "new historicism" is now infecting everything from scientific thinking and law to philosophy and women's studies. We are being told to abandon all uni-versal values and standards and to recognize that everything is relative—or that everything is, in other words, a product of specific historical circumstances. Scholars in a number of disciplines are urging us to un-derstand the peculiar historicity of every person, event, value, or ideal, to acknowledge once and for all that there are no truths outside of that his-toricity.

So blatant, so prevalent have these calls for a "new historicism" be-come that even historians have become aware of them—historians being usually the last to know about avant-garde theories, which is, of course, their saving grace. No group of scholars is wielding this "new historicism" with more confidence and excitement than postmodern literary critics. To

these avant-garde literary scholars, "historicism" seems to have become the latest theoretical weapon in their continual battle to destroy what they commonly refer to as the hegemonic forms of the existing culture.

Michael Warner's book is a good example of this new literary historicism, though he never explicitly invokes the term. His subject is the transformation of printing and reading that took place in eighteenth-century America. Warner, an associate professor of English at Rutgers University, is especially eager to contest, and to subject to historicist criticism, the work of scholars such as Elizabeth Eisenstein and Walter Ong, who have written about the importance of printing in a McLuhanite manner in which the medium becomes the message. These scholars assume printing to be an unhistorical constant; they take the historically developed characteristics of printing as inherent to the technology and project them backward in time, believing that the technology of printing has "a logic internal to itself, a logic which then exerts causative force in human affairs," and which encourages, all by itself, "rationalization and democratization." This, says Warner with undisguised contempt, is a "kind of technological determinism."

The McLuhanite scholars are not historical enough for Warner, but even Jürgen Habermas, whose book *The Structural Transformation of the Public Sphere* (1962) forms Warner's starting point, is insufficiently historical. Habermas argued that the invention of printing led, by the late seventeenth century, to a fundamental change in the political life of the West. It created a new bourgeois public sphere in which political discourse was separated both from the state and from private life (including the economy), and thus became capable of regulating and criticizing both. Warner aims to extend this argument to eighteenth-century America, but to refine and further to historicize it.

Habermas, says Warner, saw printing simply as creating new opportunities for individuals to make public use of their reason; he simply assumed as a constant a modern consciousness that developed, he should

have realized, only historically. In his book Warner wants "to analyze the historical transformation in print discourse as fully historical—to analyze it without attributing its significance to a historical point of reference, such as the intrinsic nature of individuals, reason, or technology." Such an analysis, Warner realizes, will treat "the textuality of printed works . . . as a feature of specific historical contexts rather than as what makes them 'literature.' " Consequently, he says, in his book the works of the period will "remain alien to us in fundamental ways."

Although this distancing of literary works from the present may bother literary scholars, it is something that historians will applaud. Historians have long winced at the crude ways that literary scholars and others have wrenched past writings out of their historical contexts for aesthetic and other present-minded purposes. Warner's approach, therefore, resembles what historians have always celebrated as the central thrust of all historical reconstruction: the attempt to shed our present-mindedness in order to recapture the integrity of the past in all its different and alien pastness.

Despite this resemblance, however, few historians or ordinary readers will be able to make much sense of Warner's book. This is not because, as Warner thinks, the book avoids the kinds of simple one-way causal explanations that historians and others expect (for example, "printing caused the growth of democracy"). It is because the book is cast in the postmodern, post-Marxist, deconstructionist theories and terms currently fashionable among literary scholars. The book is full of the special language that literary critics now use to separate themselves from the power structure as well as the common herd of us ordinary readers: "interpellation," "exfoliation," "ambiguation," "valorized," "intellection," "narrativized," and "meta" this and "meta" that. Everything is "mediated" (the literary substitute for "caused") and "overdetermined," "redetermined," and "retrodetermined," and, of course, "discourse" becomes the ubiquitous term describing every oral and written exchange of opinion.

Warner invents principles—"the principle of supervision," "the principle of negativity"—that confuse rather than clarify his argument. And he writes sentences that defy understanding for all but the initiated: "This personal tactic of depersonalization both requires and enables a specialized subsystem of public discourse"; "The very idea of the diffusion of literature presupposes a recalcitrant social difference. Its implicit center-periphery metaphorics registers the centralization of literacy that the thematic content of the discourse disavows"; "It must be emphasized also that the mutual recognition promised in print discourse was not an interaction between particularized persons, but among persons constituted by the negating abstraction of themselves"; "Public discourse and the market were mutually clarifying, then, in both their positive and negative characters: positive, because both public and market were metonymically realized in printed, mass-produced artifacts; negative, because the private subject finds his relation to both the public and the market only by negating the given reality of himself, thereby considering himself the abstract subject of the universal (political or economic) discourse." So it goes: sentence after sentence of this sort of "ambiguation," written in this "specialized discursive subsystem."

This is lamentable because such esoteric language will severely cut down the number of readers of the book, and Warner, beneath his opaque lit-crit post-Marxist jargon, has some very interesting things to say. It is ironic, to say the least, that scholars eager to deconstruct "texts" in order to expose the ways they wield power in our society should themselves create texts that mask and obscure much of what they want to say. And that bright younger scholars like Warner should be induced by the fashions of their discipline to use this jargon is an especially poignant form of "hegemonic coercion."

Warner and other literary critics believe, no doubt, that to look at the world in new ways requires new words and new conceptions. But in the case of Warner's book, at least, this is not true. Most of his "new histori-

cist" ideas about the socially constructed nature of reality and the textuality of print are the stock-in-trade assumptions of good historians, and demand only a good historical imagination to be made effective. All the intricacy and the subtlety of his argument, all his many insights into the nature of literature and public life in eighteenth-century America, are not dependent on post-Marxist and "deconstruction" theories and the new postmodern jargon; they easily and more clearly could have been expressed in ordinary language.

Warner is centrally concerned with the relationship between the development of printing and the rise of the republican ideology that accompanied the American Revolution. Of course, historians a generation ago, most notably Arthur Schlesinger, Sr., long tried to find some causal connection between the growth of newsprint in the eighteenth century and the coming of the Revolution. But Warner is not interested in crude explanations of historical causality; he is interested, rather, in the reciprocal relationship between printing and eighteenth-century culture and in the ways each interacted upon and changed the other, in particular in the ways the culture "refashioned the textuality of print." Beneath Warner's heavy theory and clumsy jargon is an important argument trying to get out. Warner contends that the emergence of print and publication as we know it reconceptualized "the public sphere," articulated "a new representation of the political order," and "restructured relations of power." A traditional premodern society had no clear understanding of our separation between public and private or state and society. Governmental office was generally regarded as a burden to be shouldered by those who had wealth, talent, and social preeminence. The political leaders were the social leaders, and the authority to govern flowed from the social position and the personal power of these men. Hence such officials were understandably sensitive to public criticism of their private character, and were quick to invoke the common law of seditious libel to protect the personal reputations that underlay their capacity to govern.

Modernity changed all this. It separated the public world from the private world, and state from society; and it made the criterion for holding governmental office something other than personal or social power. As Warner argues, these changes were very much involved in what happened to print and publication. The traditional society had no conception of a press that ought to be "free" to criticize the government; consequently, the print that existed rarely defied or criticized governmental authority.

As the society became larger and more impersonal, however, writers lost immediate touch with their readers and found themselves writing for a more anonymous public. The result was the creation of a public sphere of publication in which the participants were unknown and unknowable. This public sphere of print, Warner argues, formed the real basis for the rise of republican government. The spoken word of traditional society had been too closely tied to men's personal authority to allow for criticism and defiance, but the growth of print created "the abstraction of the public" and allowed for debate and controversy without endangering the unity of society. People came to realize that they could, in their publications, argue and differ over means while still wishing the good of their country. In other words, print made it possible for Americans to imagine themselves as a republican people who could act "in distinction from the state."

This argument is set forth in the first two chapters of the book. The remaining four chapters, though they deal in general with literature and eighteenth-century republican culture, are essentially separate essays on particular themes. The third chapter focuses on Benjamin Franklin as "the first American to fashion a career entirely of letters." This is Warner's weakest chapter, and the only one that does violence to his historicist aim. It is based on a questionable, indeed, anachronistic reading of Franklin, who scarcely thought of his writing as "a career."

In his fourth chapter Warner delves into the interesting problem of the "textuality and legitimacy" of written or printed constitutions in the revolutionary era, but his theoretical apparatus of "textuality" and "signi-

fication" unnecessarily complicates his investigation. He does, however, appreciate some of the widespread popular mistrust of discretionary judicial authority that lay behind all the codification movements of the period. Many revolutionaries actually thought that written texts, getting things down in black and white, would eliminate judicial and magisterial interpretation and restrict the power of "official hermeneutics": they needed some postmodern literary critics to tell them how naive they were in believing that texts could be determinate and stable.

In perhaps the best chapter in his book, Warner argues convincingly that modern literary scholars have misunderstood the literature of late eighteenth-century America. Critics have been disappointed with the writings of the 1780s and 1790s because they have judged them in accord with modern and hence anachronistic "literary" expectations that the eighteenth century had no intention of realizing. Eighteenth-century Americans defined literature broadly and nearly equaled it with knowledge itself. Thus, in simply expanding the number of readers and in diffusing knowledge through print, they could believe they were successfully achieving their literary goals—even if subsequent generations of romantic and modern critics thought otherwise. A final chapter attempts to clinch this point through a detailed reading of one of Charles Brockden Brown's "novels," *Arthur Mervyn*, which, of course, was not meant to be a novel at all in any modern sense. Thus Warner is "struck by the final incommensurability between our own standards of appreciation and those of Brown's republican literature."

If this is the sort of judgment that the new literary historicism will lead to, historians can only wish it well. But much of the new historicism will not be satisfied with merely demonstrating the differentness and the remoteness of the past, as Warner's book seems to. Ultimately much of the new literary scholarship has radical Foucault-like agendas and New Left goals that are antithetical to real historical understanding. (Indeed, at one point Warner says that "the argument of my book presupposes the arguments" of the post-Marxist work *Hegemony and Socialist Strategy*, 1985,

by Ernesto Laclau and Chantal Mouffe.) The new historicism wants to deconstruct the past in order to show us that all the values, all the institutions, all the canons, all the truths, and all the texts by which we live our lives are simply imprisoning fictions that were created by some people in the past (usually white males) for self-serving purposes. These fictions are, therefore, readily susceptible to being destroyed by us in the present, in preparation for the emergence of a new, more just, more democratic order.

Such a Rousseauian view, which assumes that knowledge of the fictional character of custom will itself free us, severely underestimates the power of the past and the power of culture. All the beliefs, values, and institutions of the culture may indeed be artificial fictions; but the historical fact of the matter is that they are fictions created by a process so complicated, involving so many participants with so many conflicting purposes over such long periods of time, that no amount of deconstruction, no degree of unmasking, can ever undo them. The culture, of course, can be—indeed, it will be—changed, but in ways that no one, including the radical post-Marxists and the deconstructionist literary critics, ever intended or wanted. Understanding this fact about the process of historical change is true historicism.

## AFTERWORD

It is sometimes difficult for people to appreciate that history is a separate and peculiar discipline. So many other disciplines—sociology, anthropology, economics, political science, political theory, and literature—so commonly deal with the past that it is not easy to see the distinctiveness of history's relationship with the past. Warner, the literary scholar, is someone who is very much interested in the past, but he is not the kind of historian who simply wants to reconstruct the past as accurately as possible. Many literary scholars have other agendas these days,

legitimate agendas no doubt, but agendas that are not those of ordinary historians. Warner is one of the best of the literary scholars interested in the past, and *The Letters of the Republic* has become extraordinarily influential among literary and cultural scholars of the eighteenth century. That speaks volumes about what has been going on in scholarship over the past several decades.

# 7.

# HISTORY AS FICTION

*Dead Certainties (Unwarranted Speculations)*
by Simon Schama (New York: Knopf, 1991)

The New York Review of Books, June 27, 1991

IT WAS BOUND to happen. Sooner or later a distinguished historian had to cross over, had to mingle the writing of fiction with the writing of history. The circumstances were ripe; the pressures were enormous. Everyone else was doing it. Novelists like E. L. Doctorow have long been blurring fact with fiction without apology. They not only set their invented characters among real historical figures, but they have these authentic historical figures do and say things they had never done. Journalists and TV writers have been doing it too, creating hybrids called "faction" and "docudrama." Television has even begun simulating the news, adding made-up pictures to otherwise apparently lifeless words.

These examples, however important, are merely the manifestations of a larger, more significant force at work. The blurring of fact and fiction is part of the intellectual climate of our postmodern time, dominated as it is by winds of epistemological skepticism and Nietzschean denials of the possibility of objectivity that are sweeping through every humanistic discipline, sometimes with cyclonic ferocity. Historians are usually the last to know about current fashions, but so powerful have the postmodern,

deconstruction theories become that even historians can no longer remain ignorant of them.

Most historians are not yet ready to admit that they simply make up the past as a fiction writer does or to deny outright the possibility of representing a past reality, but the signs of doubt and anxiety are in the air. Hayden White and the journal *History and Theory* have, of course, long been writing about the fictional character of historical narrative and urging historians to recognize the complex nature of what they do. Peter Novick, in an important and widely acclaimed book, *That Noble Dream: The "Objectivity Question" and the American Historical Profession* (1988), offered his fellow historians an elegiac and anguished account of the demise of the founding ideals of the discipline of history with little or no hope for their rebirth. Literary scholars have been very busy bringing their postmodern, deconstructionist theories onto the historian's turf and calling themselves "new historicists" while further undermining the old-time faith in an objective past reality. Although historians have scarcely experienced the kinds of epistemological quarrels that have torn apart the literary disciplines over the past several decades, some signs of change have become ominous, and Simon Schama's book, *Dead Certainties (Unwarranted Speculations)*, is the most portentous of them.

*Dead Certainties*, which loosely combines two separate stories about the past—one about the death of General James Wolfe at the battle of Quebec in 1759 and the other about the murder of George Parkman by Professor John Webster of Harvard Medical College in 1849—is a self-proclaimed experiment in narration. In his storytelling Schama has avoided neat chronological sequences and has, in fact, "deliberately dislocated the conventions by which histories establish coherence and persuasiveness." Both stories "begin with abrupt interventions . . . and end with accounts at odds with each other as to what has happened." He has given us what literary scholars would call interior monologues, shifting voices, and multiple points of view; and if these were not enough, he has even invented whole

passages, including a fictional account by one of Wolfe's soldiers of the battle of Quebec and a made-up dialogue between two of the figures in the Webster trial. It is an extraordinary book, with important implications for the discipline of history, especially because of who Schama is.

Schama is no small-time renegade in the historical profession. He is not a philosophically inclined critic of history like Hayden White, who carps at the margins of the discipline and preaches skepticism and subversion to the halfway converted but writes no history. Schama is a prominent practicing historian. Indeed, at the outset of his career he was marked by his mentor J. H. Plumb as "the outstanding historian of his generation." Whether or not he is that, he has certainly risen rapidly to the top of the historical profession.

He was born in London in 1945 ("the night we bombed Dresden," he says), educated at Cambridge University, and taught at Cambridge and Oxford until moving a decade or so ago across the Atlantic to Harvard. Though only in his midforties, Schama has already published four highly acclaimed history books, the last two of which have sold widely in several nations and languages. Not only have these books brought him professional acclaim, they have also made him something of an international celebrity. Shortly before *Dead Certainties* was published, the London *Sunday Times Magazine* devoted its weekly feature "A Life in the Day of" to this university professor—a bit of fame usually reserved for politicians and film stars. Even in Boston, local television stations occasionally invite Schama to comment on current events, including the upheavals in Eastern Europe, about which he presumably knows not much more than the rest of us.

So when a professional historian of Schama's status and significance deliberately decides to mingle fact with fiction and try an experiment in narration, the result can be no trivial matter. In writing this book, however, Schama seems to have no hidden political purpose or dark schemes in mind. Indeed, there is a certain guilelessness about him. Upon publication of the book, he explained to the *Guardian* that he was being "held cur-

rently guilty of committing a fiction," saying this, according to the interviewer, "with a big pleased grin . . . , the bad boy of the class enjoying the trouble he didn't quite mean to cause." He didn't want to change the world. He wanted to tell stories. He has said that "all history tends toward autobiographical confession," which his experiment in fictional history confirms. It is no momentary aberration for him; it is the natural development of his work.

Schama is a born storyteller. From the beginning of his career he has had a powerful desire to write something more aesthetically pleasing and imaginatively exciting than the prescribed rules of history writing currently allow. To be sure, his two earliest books were more or less traditional historical studies, heavily footnoted and based on intensive archival research, but they were certainly more narrative than they were analytical, and big narratives at that. His first work, *Patriots and Liberators: Revolution in the Netherlands, 1780–1813,* published in 1977, began, he admits, "as a trim monograph" but "came to assume proportions of . . . indecent corpulence"—745 pages worth—a problem of volubility Schama has continued to struggle with. Telling the story of the complicated process that destroyed the Dutch Republic and established the Kingdom of the United Netherlands under William I required Schama's mastering the Dutch language and the Dutch archives, and that alone was an awe-inspiring achievement. Most reviewers believed that there was nothing to rival Schama's study of this important period of Dutch history—in any language. Still, even in this very scholarly work dealing with a relatively recondite subject for an English-speaking historian, Schama nevertheless expressed an aspiration to break out of the "pedantic specialisations" of the historical profession. "It is time, perhaps," he wrote in his preface to the book, "to poke our heads above our several molehills and to take in a view, however nervous and blinking, of the broader historical landscape." He knew too from his teacher J. H. Plumb that "history must at least strive to be art before it can pretend to be a science." Already this early book revealed the richness and garrulousness of his narrative style, where words

and sentences seem to spill out as fast as the storyteller can speak. One reviewer said that Schama's writing sometimes "approaches the ripeness of late eighteenth-century prose, but it never goes beyond the bounds of decency."

His second book, *Two Rothschilds and the Land of Israel* (1978), dealing with the contribution of Edmund and James de Rothschild to the creation of a Jewish community in Palestine, was an even more traditional history than his first book, based as it essentially was on the single archive of the Palestine Jewish Colonization Association. The book grew out of an informal seminar on Jewish social and intellectual history that Schama had been teaching to undergraduates at Cambridge University in the 1960s and 1970s. It was a very personal story, which at one point in his life he felt he had to tell, but one he says he would never have finished except for the "goading of those two kindly but purposeful bullies, my mother and father," especially his father, who was "a passionate enthusiast of Jewish history."

His move from England to Harvard in the late 1970s allowed fuller scope for Schama's deep desire and remarkable ability to tell stories, an activity that in origin is, after all, an oral process. At Harvard, unlike Oxford or Cambridge, he became, as he says, the examiner of his own curriculum and thus became free to develop his lecture courses at will. "I do anything I want to," he says. By his own count his courses now number twenty or so, ranging in subject from baroque art and architecture and eighteenth-century French politics and painting to Dutch art and Pieter Brueghel, and most recently to the reading and writing of narrative history, which, he says, has become "a major concern" of his. This concern *Dead Certainties* bears out. Nearly all of Schama's courses combine art with history and so rely heavily on the showing of slides. He says he never has a prepared text for his lectures, only his slides, "just a series of shuffled images." His very popular lectures at Harvard thus become awesome feats of extemporaneous speaking, extraordinary displays of the ancient art of oral storytelling with the modern addition of pictures.

His third book, *The Embarrassment of Riches: An Interpretation of Dutch Culture in the Golden Age* (1987), revealed fully Schama's remarkable talent for telling stories and shuffling images, and it brought him to the attention of a wider public. Like his first book, *Embarrassment of Riches* was huge—698 pages—but it was not old-fashioned linear narrative history; as Schama admitted, it "strayed a good deal from the straight and narrow of the historical method." The book was essentially a cornucopia of stories, dozens if not hundreds of them, with over three hundred interspersed illustrations. Schama roamed all over seventeenth-century Dutch society, gathering what he called "bits and pieces of culture"—incidents and anecdotes, curiosities and delights, paintings and engravings on a wide variety of subjects from criminal punishments to dike building, from Calvinist patriotism to beached whales, from Dutch eating, drinking, and smoking habits to tulip sales, from cleanliness to child rearing—all designed to reveal a collective self-portrait of the Dutch people. The "shameless eclecticism" of the study was very controversial, one critic calling the book the "triumph of ingenuity over evidence." Some experts in Dutch history or art history were reluctant to praise this eccentric and imaginative book, but many others did. Still, Schama himself expressed concern that the collective image of the seventeenth-century Dutch people that he had tried to recover "might at best be fugitive and ghostly."

His next book, *Citizens: A Chronicle of the French Revolution* (1989), carried Schama even closer to pure storytelling. "*Citizens* came tumbling out of me—it poured out," he says; "I was even writing it in the shower!" The book, which is 948 pages long, has no pretensions to being scientific or dispassionate. Unlike *Embarrassment of Riches,* which retained conventional documentation, *Citizens* has no reference notes. Although the book was "in no sense fiction (for there is no deliberate invention)," Schama realized that "it may well strike the reader as story rather than history." It represented "a deliberate turning away from analytical history" and an un-

abashed revival of an old-fashioned nineteenth-century narrative "with a beginning, middle, and end that tries to resonate with its protagonists' own overdeveloped sense of past, present and posterity."

Schama rejected the objectivity that historical distance presumably confers and opted for the proximity of the historical participants. Like a novelist, he concentrated not on society and impersonal historical forces but on the contingent thoughts and actions of particular individuals, allowing what they said and did "to shape the flow of the story . . . year after year, month after month." Consequently, he comes close to viewing the past reality of at least the period of the French Revolution as simply a story waiting to be told. "It is not in the least fortuitous," he says, "that the creation of the modern political world coincided precisely with the birth of the modern novel." His rejection of the "conventional barriers" of history writing is clear; he had learned that "to write history without the play of imagination is to dig in an intellectual graveyard, so that in *Citizens* I have tried to bring a world to life rather than entomb it in erudite discourse."

Thus Schama's rendezvous with fictional history in *Dead Certainties* was ordained almost from the beginning. He begins his first story, entitled "The Many Deaths of General Wolfe," with a six-page monologue by an imaginary soldier involved in Wolfe's scaling of the cliffs of Quebec, 1759, which resulted in Wolfe's death and the British victory over the French in Canada. With this device Schama certainly captures the tone and language of an eighteenth-century character. But his invented soldier's account, though it contains nothing that is untrue, ultimately lacks verisimilitude: no ordinary soldier in the ranks could have heard about or experienced all that he describes about the battle of Quebec. Which is why Stendhal's description in the opening chapters of *The Charterhouse of Parma* of Fabrizio's bewildering experience in the battle of Waterloo is so wonderfully effective: it undercuts the view, which is the basic premise of Schama's book, that participants have a privileged access to knowledge of the events they are involved in. The opposite is in fact true: it is the his-

torian removed from the events who is in a better position to put together the confused, disparate, and sometimes contradictory accounts by the participants into a plausible whole. This problem runs through Schama's entire experiment in fictionalized history.

Schama next shifts to a brilliantly concise twelve-page "Life of General Wolfe" written from Wolfe's point of view; sometimes, in fact, the account enters directly into Wolfe's mind. Then in the second chapter Schama jumps to the opening of the exhibition of Benjamin West's great painting *The Death of General Wolfe* at the Royal Academy on April 29, 1771. This is followed by an incisive essay on West and the significance of his decision to paint Wolfe in contemporary dress. West's deliberate deviation from the conventions of history painting was not done, however, for the sake of realism but, as Schama is at pains to point out, for the sake of rhetorical effect. Indeed, the effect was so great that for future generations of British children "drilled in the pieties of imperial history, it was West's scene they imagined rather than any more literal account. . . . After West, nothing could dispel the odour of sanctity that lay over Wolfe's memory. . . . What more could possibly be said?"

With this question hanging in the air, Schama then dramatically takes the reader to the Massachusetts Historical Society on November 21, 1893, on the occasion of a memorial tribute to the great historian Francis Parkman, who had recently died. Next, Schama moves back in time into Parkman's house and mind in 1880, concluding the chapter with a brief summary of Parkman's life, which concentrates on his pain in both body and soul as he struggled to write his multivolume masterpiece, *France and England in North America*, whose climax is the battle of Quebec. In the end, says Schama, Parkman wrote of the neurotic and disease-ridden Wolfe on the eve of the battle as if he were Wolfe himself. "Past and present dissolved at this moment. He became Wolfe and Wolfe lived again through him."

Schama then resumes the imagined first-person account of the battle of Quebec by the anonymous soldier, which had begun the story. The

soldier recounts the rather sordid and inconspicuous gurgling and groaning death of Wolfe, whose "face had gone stiff and greenish" with blood from his wounded belly "oozing through his shirt and coat." Schama's story ends with a poignant letter (presumably authentic) written a month after the battle by Wolfe's betrothed, Katherine Lowther, to Wolfe's mother, who had disapproved of the match, begging to have any messages or marks of endearment Wolfe might have left sent to her.

This story, "The Many Deaths of General Wolfe," takes up less than a quarter of Schama's book; the remainder is devoted to the "Death of a Harvard Man," which has no relation to the first story, except that the murdered man, George Parkman, was Francis Parkman's uncle. For Schama this is enough: "the Parkman inheritance . . . ," he says, "deeply colours both stories."

This story opens cinematically in 1850 with Governor George Briggs of Massachusetts pondering the possibility of commuting the execution of John Webster, a Harvard professor of chemistry, who had been found guilty of murdering George Parkman after Parkman had demanded that he pay back a loan of $483. Schama has the governor shuffling through the piles of letters arriving at his desk from all over the country, letters that both affirmed and denied Webster's guilt. "Yes, yes, folly and lies, fairy tales and fables," he has the governor think to himself.

> But where lay the truth, the real history of George Parkman
> and John White Webster? Much as he respected the stern
> proceedings of the trial, he was too much of a lawyer himself
> (or perhaps too much of a smithy's son) to imagine that it told
> the whole story. [Webster's] defence, after all, had opened with
> one account and closed with another—a fatal strategy; even
> the prisoner's own confession could not wholly be credited.
> Indeed, confessions were two a penny. . . .

From this beginning, characteristic of Schama's novelistic technique throughout, he proceeds to tell the whole fascinating and macabre story. George Parkman disappears one afternoon just before Thanksgiving in 1849. A week later pieces of a body are discovered at Harvard Medical College. The corpse is identified from barely recognizable false teeth by the dentist who swears he made them. Professor John Webster of Harvard is arrested and tried for the brutal murder. It is a story so sensational that a century and a half later it still makes present-day Boston murder cases seem tame by comparison.

Using the same novelistic devices he used in the first story—interior monologues, shifts from one mind and point of view to another, and straight third-person narratives interspersed with the printing of presumably authentic documents—Schama develops his exciting tale with great skill. He introduces us to the principal characters and develops them fully and imaginatively as a sensitive novelist would: the victim, George Parkman, eccentric real estate speculator and landlord whose early desire to establish a modern and humane insane asylum in Boston had been thwarted; the accused, John Webster, whose income was insufficient to support the style of life of a Harvard professor and who had therefore been compelled to borrow money from Parkman; Ephraim Littlefield, janitor at the Medical College, who was suspicious of Webster and discovered the cut-up remains of Parkman in the basement of Webster's laboratory; the prosecuting attorneys, specially George Bemis, who kept a diary; the defense attorneys, who could never quite agree on a consistent defense for Webster; the marshal who arrested Webster; the chief justice of the Massachusetts Supreme Court, Lemuel Shaw, whose mountainous presence overawed all courtrooms; and a host of lesser figures who fade in and out of the narrative. It is a tour de force of storytelling, but is it history?

Schama concedes in the end that it is not. "Though these stories may at times appear to observe the discursive conventions of history," he writes, "they are in fact historical novellas." Nevertheless, despite this

disavowal, Schama seems to believe that he is doing something more than writing historical fiction like Sir Walter Scott or Kenneth Roberts. It is not clear, however, just what his experiment in narration is designed to accomplish.

No doubt Schama believes that his new novelistic techniques and his deliberate violation of the conventions of history writing allow him to tell a better, more convincing story. But is it a better and more convincing story than a novelist could write? And if not, then why the experiment? Schama cannot have it both ways. He cannot write fiction and still assume that it will have the authenticity and credibility of history. His problem in mingling fiction with fact in history writing is similar to that of mixing simulations with authentic documentary material in television news. The readers or viewers are never sure which is which, and therefore come to doubt the truthfulness of the whole. One reads *Dead Certainties* with admiration and credulity until suddenly something in the narrative provokes the question of whether or not there is documentary evidence for it. Maybe Schama actually has a diary or a letter he could point to that would clinch his point, but in his fictionalized account there are no references, no conventional proof, and the purely invented parts taint the credibility of the whole. In retrospect, even Schama himself seems to have some doubts. "I have a slight pang that I did invent anything at all," he told an interviewer. "I could see a genuine nonfiction book that would have a lot of immediacy without narrative invention."

The loss of credibility far outweighs any aesthetic gains that Schama might have gotten from his narrative experiment. Indeed, his violation of the conventions of history writing actually puts the integrity of the discipline of history at risk. Those conventions of history writing, like any conventions, are fragile and always vulnerable to challenge; they are scarcely more than a century old. Of course, there is no inherent reason why these conventions of objectivity and documentary proof should continue to guide and control the writing of history; they certainly did not

control much of the history writing in the distant past and still do not control what passes for history in other cultures. But they have been painstakingly developed in the Western world and have respectable justifications for their existence; they ought not to be abandoned without a fight either to postmodern skepticism or to Schama's playful experiments in narration.

In an eight-page "Afterword," Schama attempts to explain why he tried his experiment in narration. Although he is far from a postmodern deconstructionist and does not "scorn the boundary between fact and fiction," he does seem to share some of the epistemological angst that is so prevalent these days. Events did actually happen, he has admitted on another occasion, but they "can't be very clearly determined even with the resources we have available." Since historians can never truly enter into a past world, they "are left forever chasing shadows, painfully aware of their inability ever to reconstruct a dead world in its completeness, however thorough or revealing their documentation." We are unavoidably remote from our subjects, he says, and therefore "we are doomed to be forever hailing someone who has just gone around the corner and out of earshot."

In both of the cases he has dealt with in his book, "alternative accounts of the event compete for credibility, both for contemporaries and for posterity." Thus both of his imaginative stories, he explains,

> end with accounts at odds with each other as to what has
> happened, as to the significance of the deaths and the character
> of the protagonists. . . . Both dissolve the certainties of events
> into the multiple possibilities of alternative narrations. . . .
> Thus, General Wolfe dies many deaths, and though a verdict is
> rendered and a confession delivered in the case of John
> Webster, the ultimate truth about how George Parkman met
> his end remains obscure. . . . These are stories, then, of broken

bodies, uncertain ends, indeterminate consequences . . .

flickering glimpses of dead worlds.

All this seems a bit overdrawn and overwrought—as does much of the epistemological doubt currently being expressed by scholars. We know a good deal more about these events than Schama implies; he is certainly not the first historian to write about them. We know about the difference between Wolfe's actual death and West's rhetorical portrayal, and we know too where Parkman's histories have been superseded by new research. And we have more than a shadowy sense that John Webster killed George Parkman. We know, in fact, more about these events than any of the participants could or did, which may suggest that Schama has got it backward: that it is the participants in the events who chase shadows and the historians who have a more comprehensive grasp of past reality. Of course, as Schama says, there are multiple points of view and alternative ways of recounting these events. But it is no good for the historian to wring his hands and simply lay out, as Schama says he has done in this book, "all the accidents and contingencies that go into the making of an historical narrative." It is the historian's responsibility to analyze and evaluate all these different views and narrations and then arrive at as full and as objective an explanation and narration of the events as possible.

Still, the question remains: What did Schama hope to accomplish with this experiment in narration? Did he want seriously to affect the writing of narrative history, or simply fulfill a personal aesthetic desire to tell stories in a richer and fuller manner? Maybe he has become too enamored of the visual arts he spends so much time teaching and writing about. Paintings, after all, are no longer judged on the basis of the accuracy with which they represent reality but on other bases. Some postmodern philosophers of history, like F. R. Ankersmit, would like historical narratives to be judged in the same way: on the basis of their style or other aesthetic features and not on their capacity to represent past reality accurately.

Whether he intends to or not, Schama is certainly playing into their hands. Or perhaps Schama is too much affected by his recent reading of imaginative fiction. He tells us in the *Sunday Times* feature that he is a "voracious" reader, much of it apparently in modern experimental fiction. "Jeanette Winterson's views on time are so like mine—it's quite spooky," he says. He also admires "Julian Barnes's mixture of fiction and nonfiction," and he finds Penelope Lively's *Moon Tiger* (1987), which moves back and forth between the past and present of its historian/heroine's experience, "wonderful." What he really likes about these modern novelists is "the attention they pay to ghostly echoes and the historical perspective." "All derivative, all in the mind—the confection of fact and fantasy that is how we know the world," says Lively's heroine. If historians ever really do take seriously as models for their work the fiction of new experimental novelists like Patrick McGrath who say that they "don't want to be constrained by the actual—there's more freedom to invent when the fiction is not accountable to a reality," then they surely will put themselves out of business.

Schama apparently believes that because naive nineteenth-century positivism—"the certainty of an ultimately observable, empirically verifiable truth"—is dead, all we have left are ghosts and shadows and indeterminacy. If we cannot recover the truth about the past with finality and completeness, then must we resort to the techniques of fiction in order to fill in the shadows and embody the ghosts? Are those the alternatives? If we cannot have old-fashioned positivist history, then must we write historical novellas?

Although, says Schama, both his stories "follow the documentary record with some closeness, they are works of imagination, not scholarship." These are not contraries. Historical scholarship should not be set in opposition to imagination. History writing is creative, and it surely requires imagination, but it is an imagination of a particular sort, sensitive to the differentness of the past and constrained and constricted by the documentary record. Schama in his better moments knows this, knows that "even

in the most austere scholarly report from the archives, the inventive faculty—selecting, pruning, editing, commenting, interpreting, delivering judgements—is in full play." He does not deny the existence of a past reality. But he "does accept the rather banal axiom that claims for historical knowledge must always be fatally circumscribed by the character and prejudices of its narrator."

That "fatally" is mistaken; and it has led Schama into his experiment in fictional history. One can accept the view that the historical record is fragmentary and incomplete, that recovery of the past is partial and difficult, and that historians will never finally agree in their interpretations, and yet can still believe intelligibly and not naively in an objective truth about the past that can be observed and empirically verified. Historians may never see and represent that truth wholly and finally, but some of them will come closer than others, be more nearly complete, more objective, more honest, in their written history, and we will know it, and have known it, when we see it. That knowledge is the best antidote to the destructive skepticism that is troubling us today.

## AFTERWORD

My review of his book angered Schama. An interviewer in an article published in the *Harvard Magazine* (November–December 1991) stated that Schama in *Dead Certainties* was not attempting to challenge the conventions of historical scholarship but only trying to allow his powerful imagination greater scope. According to the author of the article, Schama seemed to want to play down his little venture into historical fiction. What harm could there be, Schama suggested, in his emulating the great historical novelists? Besides, Schama said, "so far from the intellectual integrity of history being policed by the protocols of objectivity, distance, and scientific dispassion, its best prospects lie in the forthright admission of subjectivity, immediacy, and literary imagination." Imaginative works

like his, he declared, are more likely to yield truths "closer to the truths of the great novels and the great poets" than the so-called scientific monographs.

All this may be true enough, but what does this kind of truth have to do with writing fictitious history? As the historian Richard D. Brown has pointed out, the claim that we historians are telling the truth is what distinguishes us from fiction writers. "This is the claim that supplies the distinctive appeal and power of historical writing." In his reaction to criticism, Schama seems to have forgotten that he was not Walter Scott or E. L. Doctorow, but instead an important and influential academic historian who was supposed to be writing history.

In his "Afterword," Schama implies that he initially regarded his book not as fiction but only as a legitimate display of his robust historical imagination. But with his experimental stretching of the boundaries of historical imagination, he ignored both the epistemological climate of the early 1990s and the devastating effects such a work by such a distinguished historian could have on the conventions of the discipline. It turns out that the Library of Congress, followed by many university libraries, has cataloged the book not as fiction but as history.

# 8.

# HISTORY AS HIGH POLITICS

*The Age of Federalism* by Stanley Elkins and Eric McKitrick
(New York: Oxford University Press, 1993)

*The Atlantic Monthly,* December 1993

W HEN I ENTERED graduate school in history, thirty-five years
ago, many of us beginning graduate students thought that some
of the most exciting work in history was being written by a pair of young
historians named Stanley Elkins and Eric McKitrick. This dynamic duo,
whom we somehow thought of as a single entity, had not yet published a
book, but they had written three or four imaginative and provocative articles: on slavery and capitalism, on a new meaning for Frederick Jackson
Turner's frontier thesis, and on the youth of the Founding Fathers. We
could scarcely wait for what they would do next. Because we thought them
to be inseparable—like Ben and Jerry or Sears and Roebuck—we were
surprised when they eventually published separate books, Elkins on slavery and McKitrick on Andrew Johnson and Reconstruction. But we solved
our puzzlement by accepting the rumor that they needed to split up and
publish individually in order to get tenure at their respective colleges,
Elkins at Smith and McKitrick at Columbia. After their highly acclaimed
books appeared, these two historians published virtually nothing else, either separately or together, for three decades.

Now, at last, we know what they have been up to all this time: *The Age*

*of Federalism*, a mammoth study that covers the period from the beginning of the United States government under the Constitution in 1789 until Thomas Jefferson's election as president in 1800. They have read everything having to do with high politics and diplomacy in this turbulent decade: unpublished manuscripts, British foreign office documents, dissertations from both sides of the Atlantic, newspapers, statesmen's papers, and hundreds of books and articles. Suddenly they have revived the once noble but now presumably dying dream that history can be an accumulative science, gradually gathering truth through the steady and plodding efforts of countless practitioners turning out countless monographs. In this book they have brought together and made meaningful hundreds of these unused and unread monographs written over the past century or more on obscure and seemingly insignificant topics of history dealing with this single decade of the 1790s—from an 1878 biography of George Cabot to the most recent analysis of the XYZ affair. No historian, or pair of historians, is likely to do again what they have done.

In their rich and detailed study the authors aimed at recovering something of "what it was like—the difference it made—becoming a 'nation' after having been something else, especially in the experience of those persons most directly implicated in bringing this entity into being and setting it afoot." Something called Federalism is what defined America's purposes and guided its affairs during this decade. This Federalism did not have, the authors admit, a very long life, and therefore they want in their book "to account, to whatever extent is possible, for Federalism's ascendancy, decline, and eclipse, and to discern something of what displaced it."

The result is a truly remarkable book—a blockbuster of over 750 pages of text and nearly 200 more pages of notes. It is not its length that makes it remarkable but its character and scope. The book seems to be a throwback to an earlier time of large narratives of great men and grand events. It is reminiscent of Henry Adams's multivolume account of the administrations of Jefferson and Madison; indeed, it appears to do for the decade

of the 1790s what Adams did for the succeeding two decades. It is certainly history from the top down, not from the bottom up. It is all high-politics history, without the slightest concession to the social history of the past generation of history writing, or even to the kind of social history that Adams attempted in his famous first six chapters. Elkins and McKitrick concentrate almost exclusively on the headline political and diplomatic events of the period.

All the great characters of the period are insightfully portrayed in beautifully crafted vignettes: George Washington, the heroic first president, who brought legitimacy to the new government; Alexander Hamilton, the brilliant secretary of the treasury who fashioned its financial program; Thomas Jefferson, the learned secretary of state who together with James Madison in the House of Representatives eventually created a Republican opposition that ultimately brought down the Federalist government. Sometimes in just a few pages or a few lines Elkins and McKitrick capture more about these characters than biographers have in whole volumes, and with more humor. Jefferson, for example,

> had an agreeable enough exterior presence, though he was not very ardent in personal relationships. He was entirely accessible but always fastidious and a bit distant; he could occasionally even exhibit—though shirking from open hostility—a touch of the cold fish. But for the most part he was quite amiable, especially in small groups, where his shyness left him: knowing a great deal about a great many subjects made him endlessly interesting. . . . One imagines that he would have been all but ideal as a professor.

But it is not just the great men who stride through these pages. The authors have provided sketches of a dozen or more lesser figures involved in the story of this passionate decade in the nation's history—from the

irascible Philip Freneau, the sometime poet and journalist who became a principal voice of Republican invective, and the sardonic Gouverneur Morris, who was the only foreign minister to remain in Revolutionary France through the period of the Terror, to the worldly Talleyrand, the French foreign minister who survived multiple changes of regime in France by simply never adhering to any principle.

All the great and many of the not-so-great political and diplomatic events are also described: there are two chapters on Hamilton's financial program, one chapter on locating the capital and building the federal city, another on the French Revolution in America, a large section of a chapter on the 1790 Nootka Sound controversy between Britain and Spain, another section on the Convention of 1800 with France, and so on. They are not just described, but analyzed, examined, turned over and over, explained, and expounded in astonishing and often loving detail. Sometimes the authors set forth fully the existing historical literature on a problem—for example, Washington's Farewell Address or the Whiskey Rebellion—and then wind their way through that literature and the circumstances of the time in order to find a balanced and satisfactory explanation or conclusion. Other times the authors describe all the contemporary elements pointing toward a particular solution of a problem—for example, evidence of the French proclivity in 1797 to negotiate with the Americans—and then state that the particular solution that seemed so obvious never resulted, and ask why.

So the volume becomes much more a series of problem-solving essays than a simple linear narrative of the period. This approach means that small things are sometimes left unexplained. We are never told, for example, why Jefferson and Hamilton resigned from Washington's cabinet, or why Washington had to go to his seventh choice to fill the position of secretary of state after Edmund Randolph's resignation and to his fourth choice to fill the office of secretary of war. But it is not just little things that the authors ignore. Despite the book's extraordinary length and its

detailed analyses of almost every major political and diplomatic event in the period, much of importance is simply not dealt with. There is virtually nothing, for example, on slavery, the development of law and the judiciary, the Yazoo land frauds, or religion.

Actually, the authors did not intend to write an ordinary narrative that moves directly from one event to another in chronological order. Instead, they want the historical process to "be shown happening, to whatever extent our capacities can control it, and not in one way but many." Thus they wander to and fro, stop, backtrack, and cover old ground from new directions. They do not simply tell what happened; they ruminate on what happened, often slowly and accumulatively, considering over and over an individual or an event from different perspectives, building layer after layer of analysis until the reader has a subtle, rich, deep, and multidimensional picture of a world very different from ours. They aim to bring a literary sensibility to their history, one similar to that of Lionel Trilling or of their mentor, Richard Hofstadter, to whose memory they dedicate the book. When the authors discuss the election of George Washington to the presidency, they pause to ponder the meaning of character. When they consider the location of the national capital, they meditate at length on the antiurban bias of Americans and the thinness of their cultural life. And in writing their chapter on the reaction of Americans to the French Revolution, they start with a short essay on the way Americans and the French have viewed each other throughout their histories.

Such a meditative technique inevitably slows down the prose and results in a good deal of repetition, interruption, and diversion. In the authors' continual backing and filling and their multilayered analyses of problems, such things as Alexander Hamilton's West Indian experience, Lord Sheffield's report on British trade policy, Citizen Genet's plans as French minister to the United States, and America's vision of an Atlantic free-trade community necessarily get mentioned and described more than once. This makes for an ever-deepening understanding of particular is-

sues (and, incidentally, it allows the reader to dip in and read sections here and there without having to read everything that went before), but it does tend to break up the narrative—as do the authors' many vignettes and digressions. Their sketch of James Madison, for example, quickly slides off into a description of Madison's college in Princeton, which turns into a discussion of the college's Scottish president, John Witherspoon, which leads to a consideration of Scotland and its vibrant intellectual life in the eighteenth century.

Given so much reading and research and such multilayered presentation, the authors' judgment inevitably takes on a magisterial and authoritative quality that few if any historians of the period have possessed. Sifting through the contradictory evidence and the conflicting and sometimes polemical historical monographs, as they frequently and conscientiously do right in their text, they strain for objectivity and impartiality, and most of the time they achieve it. It may be the most balanced account of the politics of this contentious decade ever written.

Many readers, especially those with a bias toward Jefferson and the Republicans, will probably disagree. The book will seem to be too pro-Hamilton and too much a defense of the Federalists. And to some extent such readers will have a point. In the contest over Hamilton's financial program of funding the national debt and creating the Bank of the United States, which began the rift among the Founding Fathers that led to the emergence of the Republican Party, the sympathies of Elkins and McKitrick clearly lie with Hamilton. The authors can scarcely stop shaking their heads at how little understanding Jefferson and Madison, the agrarian Virginia leaders of the Republican opposition, had of banking or money, and they therefore imply that the Republicans' criticism of Hamilton's financial program could have had little substance. Indeed, the authors' account of the debate over the debt and the bank reads at times like a present-day editorial from the *Wall Street Journal* lecturing all those simple-minded liberal Democrats on their inability to comprehend the

most elementary workings of money and stock markets. Nonetheless, Elkins and McKitrick are absolutely right about the Virginians' ignorance of banks, finance, and public credit.

When the authors couple this innocence in money matters with Jefferson's and Madison's extreme and apparently irrational hatred of all things British, it is not surprising that they have a hard time understanding the grounds for the formation of the Republican Party and its bitter accusations that the Federalists were trying to establish a monarchy. Since Elkins and McKitrick believe that "there was small likelihood of anyone's setting up a monarchy in the American republic, and no critical observer should have had much difficulty perceiving this at the time," they can only conclude that Madison and Jefferson were deluded in some sense ("the coolest minds may be unsettled, as is shown by the case of James Madison") and that the entire Republican effort at opposition was based on a misperception of reality. All the Republican invective, all the charges of the Federalists being "monarchists" and "aristocrats," the authors can therefore dismiss as mere "tag-words, . . . formulas that seemed to tie all these suspected men and their principles together in a system of ready reference." The Republicans, the authors suggest, became prisoners of their own farfetched ideology.

Yet there was truth in that Republican invective, for Hamilton and other Federalist leaders were interested in more than stock markets and banks and commercial prosperity. They in fact wanted to turn the United States into a fiscal-military power that would rival the great European states and achieve the honor and glory that all such great states aspired to. This meant establishing for the United States a strong national government with an elaborate administrative bureaucracy, a standing army and navy, and the financial wherewithal to accomplish great and noble deeds. The whole structure would be held together not by republican virtue, which Hamilton thought was chimerical, but by patronage, interest, ceremony, and force—the kind of ligaments monarchies used. So although the Federalists technically did not want to set a king upon an American

throne, they were indeed seeking to infuse enough monarchical elements into American life to lend weight to the Republican fears of Federalist monarchism. Elkins and McKitrick never quite bring themselves to admitting that those Republican fears might have been justified.

Their praise of the Federalists' political economy and their criticism of the Republicans' irrationality notwithstanding, the authors ultimately have not written a brief for Federalism. Over and over they emphasize that the Federalists brought about their own demise: that Hamilton in his impatience and pride misunderstood the speculative nature of those who would execute his financial program; that the Federalists invested nearly all of their moral authority in the figure of Washington, and therefore had nothing to hold them together when he left office; that their Alien and Sedition Acts and their plans for a huge standing army in 1798 were as stupid and clumsy as they were unpopular; and that they ultimately turned against the very principle—the sovereignty of the people—that they themselves had created.

Nevertheless, in the end the authors' account of Federalism's decline and fall has an elegiac tone. With the demise of the Federalists, they imply, something important in American life was lost, and it was doomed to be lost from the very beginning. The Federalists, they conclude, attempted to stand against what the authors call "the American idea," a worldview, born of the Revolution, that was suspicious of far-removed and energetic government, of manipulators of money, of taxes, of English entanglements, of great military and naval establishments, of the use of force at home or abroad. This American idea, the authors say, was preempted by the Republicans; it "was a popular temper, in the long run better matched in season and out to the ordinary pursuits of the spreading Republic than were the more demanding and exclusive standards of Federalism even at its best."

In the long run of the nineteenth century perhaps, but surely not for our own time. When we look at the United States during the last two-thirds of the twentieth century, is it not possible that the Federalists may

have the last laugh after all? For is it not true that the great bureaucratic and fiscal-military state that they wanted for America in the 1790s has at last been achieved, and that that achievement has been brought about largely through the efforts of the very party that Thomas Jefferson founded?

## AFTERWORD

Academic history writing over the past four decades or so has virtually eliminated high politics and old-fashioned diplomatic history as subjects for serious study. This made Stanley Elkins and Eric McKitrick's mammoth study of the 1790s all the more remarkable. The work even garnered a Bancroft Prize. The book was originally designed to be the fourth volume in the Oxford History of the United States, covering the period 1789 to 1815, but when the two authors came in with such a huge book on only half the period, Oxford decided to publish it separately and not include it as part of the original series. In the aftermath Oxford University Press commissioned me to write the volume that Elkins and McKitrick were supposed to write; so I have benefited in several ways from their marvelous passion for detail.

# 9.

# MICROHISTORY

*The Kingdom of Matthias: A Story of Sex and Salvation in Nineteenth-Century America* by Paul E. Johnson and Sean Wilentz

(New York: Oxford University Press, 1994)

*The New York Review of Books,* October 20, 1994

E ARLY NINETEENTH-CENTURY America witnessed the greatest outpouring of religious feeling in Christendom since the religious turbulence of seventeenth-century England or perhaps the Reformation. Amid all the momentous events of what came to be called the Second Great Awakening, one year, 1830, seems to stand out. (Is it just coincidental that 1830 was also the year that Americans reached a level of consumption of alcoholic spirits—four gallons per person—that was the highest for any year in all of American history and one of the highest in the world?) In that spirit-soaked year the great evangelical preacher Charles Grandison Finney came to Rochester, New York, the fastest-growing community in the United States, and launched a religious revival that eventually shook the nation. In that same year the celibate communitarian sect called the Shakers attained the greatest number of members than at any other time in its history.

At the same time, Alexander Campbell, a seeker of primitive Christianity, broke from the Baptists and began publication of the *Millennial Harbinger* in preparation for the momentous alliance of his Campbellites with

Barton Stone and the creation of the Disciples of Christ, which within decades became the fifth-largest denomination in America. In 1830 a twenty-five-year-old failed farmer from Palmyra, New York, Joseph Smith, Jr., having translated some golden plates given to him by the angel Moroni, published a six-hundred-page American bible, the Book of Mormon, which began the Church of Jesus Christ of Latter-day Saints. And in that same crucial year, 1830, a down-and-out carpenter in Albany, New York, named Robert Matthews experienced a revelation that turned him into the wandering Jewish prophet Matthias.

Of all these religious events of 1830, it is the last and least familiar— the story of Robert Matthews, or Matthias—that historians Paul E. Johnson and Sean Wilentz have chosen to tell. Perhaps because it is the least familiar event, the story of it is especially enthralling.

Matthews was born in 1788 to a Scottish immigrant family in the farming village of Cambridge in Washington County, New York, located midway between the Hudson River and the Green Mountains of Vermont. He was raised in a world of strict Calvinism that, as the authors say, nursed "ancient ecclesiastical grievances unknown to the rest of the world." Unsuited for farming, Matthews apprenticed as a carpenter and by 1808 turned up in New York City as a skilled journeyman in his craft. Taunts from his fellow workers over his religiosity and a conviction for assaulting a woman in 1811 eventually led to his return to his hometown of Cambridge, where he became a country storekeeper and married and began a family. But he went bankrupt in 1816, when credit became tight, and he was forced to return to New York with his family and once again take up carpentry. The deaths of two of his children and the difficulty of finding work drove him into despair and fits of rage.

At the same time, Matthews began experiencing ever-stranger religious sensations. Following his excitement over hearing a service in an African Methodist church, he began professing that he was no Christian at all but a prophesying Hebrew, just as Jesus the carpenter had once been.

He became involved in the plans of a New York newspaper editor, Mordecai Manuel Noah, who hoped to build a Jewish homeland on Grand Island on the Niagara River. When these plans fell through, Matthews moved his family back to Washington County.

After moving about, he ended up in Albany sometime in the mid-1820s. His black moods were more frequent now, and he took to whipping his wife when angry. She in turn became increasingly convinced that he was insane. After trying out the Dutch church in Albany, he moved to a schismatic Presbyterian church under the evangelical ministry of a follower of the great evangelist Charles Grandison Finney. By the late 1820s Matthews was working only occasionally, spending the rest of the time furiously reading the Bible and religious tracts and stopping people on the street to tell them of his visions.

In 1830 he suddenly ceased shaving and announced to his wife that Albany was to be engulfed by a flood. When his wife refused to leave Albany with him, Matthews fled alone with his children. He was picked up several days later and confined for two weeks as an insane pauper in the Albany almshouse. After several arrests for beating his wife, he left home alone once again, wandering to the western part of New York State, then to Rochester, and back to his wife and family in Albany. When his wife told him to get work or leave, he traveled west again, then south and east to Washington, D.C., before ending up in 1832 in New York City.

In the meantime, the Prophet, as he was called, had decided to assume the name Matthias, which was the name of the disciple chosen by God to replace Judas after he had betrayed Christ. Although Matthias was only the latest in a series of deluded religious fanatics preaching to crowds in the streets of New York, he was more conspicuous than most. He was tall, stately in his bearing, with fury in his eyes, and at a time when most men were clean-shaven, in possession of a huge, luxuriant ash-colored beard.

Soon after arriving in New York, Matthias met Elijah Pierson, a once well-to-do businessman who himself had become a religious seeker and

prophet. The meeting was a turning point for both men. Johnson and Wilentz devote one of the four sections of their book to describing Elijah's career, which was almost as strange as that of Matthews.

Elijah Pierson was born in 1786 in rural New Jersey near Morristown and was reared as a strict Calvinist Presbyterian. As a young man he left for New York City to take a job as an apprentice clerk. By 1820, at the age of thirty-four and unmarried, he had succeeded to the point where he and a partner could set up their own mercantile firm on Pearl Street.

The new business world of the city was very different from the farming community of Morristown. As the authors make clear, "Elijah's fortunes were now tied not to an inherited farm set within a network of kin but to individual ambition, risk-taking, and the accumulation of money." In place of a wife and family, Elijah sought solace in religion, and soon he became caught up in the missionary work of some evangelical Presbyterians. Involvement with the Female Missionary Society for the Poor led Elijah not only to the evangelical woman who would become his wife but to the very un-Calvinist conclusion that even the lowliest of persons could be cleansed of sin. Elijah and his wife were attracted to ultraevangelical reformist movements that attacked male authority and domestic luxury. Before long they became involved in a sect of perfectionist Methodists who believed among other things in the direct inspiration of the Holy Ghost. After three years of praying with this sect Elijah began talking with the Holy Ghost and recording what He said.

In 1829 the Piersons moved to Bowery Hill and under the direction of a woman named Frances Folger set up a perfectionist community called the Retrenchment Society. They were joined by Frances Folger's cousins by marriage, Benjamin and Ann Folger, and their children. Benjamin was a wealthy hardware merchant, but his riches had no place in this ascetic community. The members shed all their fashionable clothing and furnishings, radically simplified their diets, fasted regularly, and threw themselves into religious frenzies, once meeting continually for three weeks,

pausing only for naps and light refreshments with Elijah doing much of the preaching.

What is astonishing is that the larger evangelical community did not denounce this fanaticism, "for," as the authors say, "in the religious excitements of the late 1820s, who was to say what was excessive and what was not?" Instead Elijah and his friends built alliances with more mainstream evangelicals, including leading reformers like Lewis and Arthur Tappan. They began rescuing prostitutes from the slums, which only further convinced the group of the evils of male authority. Gradually the community, which moved from Bowery Hill to Fourth Street, picked up new members: a carpenter, an elderly Jewish widow from Newark, a wealthy merchant and widower named Sylvester Mills, and a tall, deep-voiced black servant named Isabella Van Wagenen, who had once been a slave.

The lingering sickness and death of his wife in 1830 further unsettled Elijah's mind, and he announced that God had called him to become the Prophet Elijah the Tishbite, with his first task being to raise his wife from the dead. Although that proved impossible, Elijah now quit his business entirely and devoted himself to full-time praying, preaching, and talking with Jesus. One by one his old evangelical friends abandoned what the authors say was "an obviously deranged Elijah Pierson." Soon his only social contacts were with Jesus and the members of his little community.

In 1832 the Prophet Matthias joined the Prophet Elijah and his group on Fourth Street in New York City. Matthias soon convinced Elijah that it was not Jesus' Kingdom that was imminent but that of the Father, and that Matthias as God's instrument for bringing about the reign of Truth and for redeeming the world from devils, disobedient women, and humiliated men. Jesus had once been the Spirit of Truth, but after his Crucifixion that Spirit had entered Matthias and had remained latent until the Christians were nearly finished ruling the world. Now after eighteen hundred years of degenerating Christianity, which had been weak-

ened and taken over by women, the time was at hand for Truth to return. (As scholars have noted, American Christianity was indeed becoming increasingly feminized in these years.)

Matthias declared that as the Spirit of Truth (and male authority) he would preach until 1836; all who had not entered the Kingdom by then would be damned. Christian confusion would continue for another fifteen years until Matthias, in 1851, brought the gentile world to an end by fire. In the new pure green world that Matthias foresaw for those who had joined the Kingdom there would be peace and prosperity without money and a marketplace. Matthias would rule this world and at his right and left hands would be the former wealthy merchants Pierson and Mills. After hearing this message, Elijah stopped preaching forever and turned his ministry over to Matthias; at the same time, Mills turned his large house over to Matthias's cult.

With all the wealth of Pierson and Mills available for use, Matthias could see no sense in the asceticism of the old perfectionist community. The Spirit of Truth demanded clothing, food, and furnishings befitting his status. His wardrobe was one of the most extravagant the city had ever seen: a cone-shaped black leather cap, a military frock coat of the best green cloth lined with silk and decorated with gold braids, a fine silk vest and a crimson sash, green or black pantaloons, and (depending on the weather) sandals or highly polished Wellington boots. (One reporter said he looked like a cross between a drawing-room dandy and a Spanish or Italian brigand.) Although Matthias arrived at Elijah Pierson's door in poverty and in secondhand clothes, within weeks he was living as a wealthy man.

Matthias's community soon attracted attention. Relatives of Sylvester Mills eventually had Matthias arrested and thrown into the ward for the insane poor at Bellevue. But the police could not prove that the Spirit of Truth was not who he said he was, and Matthias was released. When the community was ousted from Mills's house, Pierson rented another. When it looked as if the tiny group might wither away, it was rescued by Benjamin

and Ann Folger, the young, attractive well-to-do couple who had once been part of Elijah's old congregation.

What remained of the cult moved to the Folgers' country mansion near Sing Sing, a thriving village on the Hudson some thirty miles north of New York City. Matthias named his new house Mount Zion. He attracted some new members, called himself Father, and as the authors put it, "used prophecy and terror—not to mention his disciples' money—to make Mount Zion the first perfectly reformed rural household in the coming Kingdom." Central to that reformation, Johnson and Wilentz suggest, were the Prophet's attempts to return to his half-remembered, half-idealized Presbyterian youth in a patriarchal authoritarian world. "From his seat at the head of the table, Matthias disciplined his house and delivered the meandering, often angry sermons that became the one source of Truth at Mount Zion."

Everything in the Kingdom began to change with Ann Folger's seduction of the woman-hating Matthias. For months Ann charmed the Father and sought to anticipate his every need and every thought. Finally, Ann and Matthias announced that they were "match spirits," and that they should marry and have a son who would be the Messiah. Benjamin, Ann's husband, was not happy with this announcement but eventually consented to having his wife become Mother of the Kingdom. The Mother soon became pregnant (with a girl, as it turned out). Matthias next brought his twenty-year-old married daughter and eleven-year-old son to Mount Zion. Benjamin promptly seduced the daughter; Matthias reacted by whipping his daughter and then marrying her to Benjamin. Through it all the shrewd black ex-slave, Isabella Van Wagenen, carried on the bulk of the household work and observed everything.

When the husband of Matthias's daughter brought charges against the Kingdom, the Father had to give up his daughter; but he promptly married Benjamin to another member of the community. Benjamin, however, began having suspicions that Matthias was a fraud, but he was placated by his former wife, Ann, who continued to sleep with him off and

on. Finally, Elijah Pierson, who was only forty-eight but with no teeth and outlandishly long hair and fingernails and suffering from periodic fits, looked much older, decided that he, too, wanted a match spirit. He seems to have had his eye on the Mother, but one day in July 1834 he had another fit and died.

Outside the Kingdom, rumors spread that Pierson had been murdered. Inside the Kingdom, members began turning on one another. Matthias accused Ann Folger of disloyalty, and Benjamin Folger offered to pay Matthias to leave his house. When the Prophet left, Folger brought charges of fraud and had Matthias arrested. Although Folger dropped the charges of fraud in the midst of the trial, Westchester County officials were already preparing a case against the Prophet for the murder of Elijah Pierson. By this time, the New York penny press had picked up the scandal and made it a topic of national news. All of the newspapers were hostile to Matthias—calling him Matthews the Imposter—but they differed greatly in their analyses. Some thought Matthias a fool, some a charlatan, others a lunatic. Many thought that he represented a species of disorder that Jacksonian Americans had begun to label "fanaticism."

During the trial, the murder charges came to nothing, but the charges made by the husband of Matthias's daughter that the Prophet had beaten his daughter and thus violated the rights of the husband were made to stick, and Matthias was sentenced to four months in jail. After his release, the now shaven Prophet showed up briefly at his wife's home; from there he journeyed to the pioneer Mormon settlement in Kirtland, Ohio, to meet another prophet, Joseph Smith, and was last heard of preaching to the Indians in Iowa Territory. Sylvester Mills was released from a lunatic asylum and once again became a stylish and respectable merchant. The Folgers got back together, with Benjamin continuing to make real estate deals through the 1840s. Most marked by the whole affair was the ex-slave Isabella Van Wagenen. Like her mentor the Spirit of Truth, Isabella had her own visions, became a traveler, and eventually an abolitionist and

women's rights advocate. God renamed her too: the world would come to know her as Sojourner Truth.

It is a fascinating story, and Johnson and Wilentz have written it with all the skill and verve of novelists. (Perhaps because the book reads like a novel, the authors and publisher decided, unfortunately, that it needed no index.) Fascinating or not, this sensational scandal quickly lost the public's attention, overwhelmed by a profusion of New York crime stories that became a staple of American reading in the late 1830s and 1840s. And after the initial excitement of reading the story passes, some important questions linger: what is the historical significance of this event, why should two distinguished historians take the time to write about it, and why should readers bother to read it?

The book very much represents a new genre of history writing that has become increasingly popular over the past couple of decades. Called at various times microhistory or ethnographic history, this kind of history writing takes small events in the past involving inconspicuous people and a limited number of sources and teases out of them stories and meanings that presumably throw light on the larger society. Italian scholars in the 1970s, eager to find some alternative to the dominant influence of the French Annales school, with its stress on deep-lying structures and the long term of quantitative and serial data, coined the term "microhistory" and with works like Carlo Ginsburg's *The Cheese and the Worms* (1976, English edition, 1980) have done the most to develop its potentialities.

At the same time, anthropologists and ethnographers, led by Clifford Geertz, began promoting "thick descriptions" of ordinary events, not to formulate social laws but to uncover cultural meanings that required literary-like interpretation rather than scientific investigation. So Geertz's cultural analysis of the symbolic action of a cock fight became a means of gaining insight into the culture of a Balinese community. As the practice of reading cultural behavior as texts became more and more popular, ethnography was transformed. Ethnographers like James Clifford and George E.

Marcus became increasingly self-conscious about the literary and inventive character of this kind of anthropological storytelling, and they began exploring its various implications.

Ethnography, some said, has become "the discourse of the postmodern world." It has abandoned the scientific search for origins and has become fragmented—all pieces, all flashes of experience, no wholes. There is not a single story of a culture anymore, only "a story among other stories," with almost no thought given to the questions of why the stories should be about this group or this subject rather than another. Ethnographers are not interested in how their little episodes of experience are "embedded in larger, more impersonal systems" or "in the sort of events and processes that make history, so to speak." They "cannot see the forest for the trees" in their microstudies because many of them have come to believe that "there are no forests."*

Without accepting or perhaps even being aware of the implications of such fragmentation, American historians have recently begun exploiting this microhistorical, ethnographic technique, some quite brilliantly. One thinks of Natalie Zemon Davis's *The Return of Martin Guerre* (1983), which was first a film and then a small book; Robert Darnton's *The Great Cat Massacre* (1984), whose thickly described episodes interpret the way some ordinary people of early modern France made sense of the world; Laurel Thatcher Ulrich's marvelous story, *A Midwife's Tale* (1990), based on the diary kept between 1785 and 1812 by a midwife and healer living in a small town on the Kennebec River in Maine; and John Demos's recent book, *The Unredeemed Captive* (1994), which tells the story of a seven-year-old daughter of the minister of Deerfield, Massachusetts, who was captured by the Indians in 1704 and refused to return to her home. Although all these microhistories hope to say something important about the societies in

---

* James Clifford and George E. Marcus, eds., *Writing Culture: The Poetics and Politics of Ethnography* (Berkeley: University of California Press, 1986), 123, 109, 172, 166, 131.

which they are set, sometimes the sheer intensity and interest of the particular stories overwhelm their larger significance, turning them into little trees in search of a forest. This seems to be true of Johnson and Wilentz's book as well.

At times Johnson and Wilentz appear to take the same line some postmodern ethnographers do by implying that their small story has no larger significance. They seek to evade the problem of significance by making fun of all those contemporaries (presumably including subsequent historians as well) who picked over the evidence about Matthias and his cult, "looking for clues to some grander meaning, hoping to support their conflicting views respecting humankind, God, and the United States of America." All such cults in our history, like those of James Jones and David Koresh, the authors write, "burst into public notice, usually because of some confrontation with the law; immediately, they win notoriety, which in turn leads Americans to wonder about themselves and about what has become of their country to foster such lunacy. Just as suddenly, however, the prophets fail and then fade from public memory, until the next strange prophet comes along, and the questioning begins all over again." The authors insinuate that they are not such fools as to be caught finding any grand meanings about America in the story of Matthias.

Yet beneath all this subtle mocking of the search for significance, Johnson and Wilentz do have some ideas about what was happening in the larger society that can explain Matthias's cult and, indeed, can explain how America in the early nineteenth century experienced "one of the most extraordinary spells of sectarian invention that the nation, and world, has ever seen." The most important underlying force, they suggest, was what they and other historians have called "the market revolution," that transformation peaking in the years between the 1820s and the 1840s "that took the country from the fringe of the world economy to the brink of commercial greatness."

There are problems with this market revolution as a device for explaining the outbreak of religious enthusiasm. No one doubts that England experienced an even more impressive and extensive market revolution in these years, yet early nineteenth-century English religious developments, though certainly enthusiastically wild and evangelical, were never as confused, explosive, and fragmented as those in America. Johnson and Wilentz also suggest that much of the religiosity and revivalism of these years "emerged primarily not from the new middle class but from Americans whom the market revolution had either bypassed or hurt." Yet their own evidence indicates that the most dominant members of Matthias's cult— Elijah Pierson, Benjamin Folger, and Sylvester Mills—were successful middle-class businessmen. The relation between religion and the development of a market society seems so complicated as to defy almost all generalizations.

Similar problems emerge with another of the authors' explanatory suggestions: the transformation of gender relationships and the family. At one point the authors maintain that all the extremist prophets throughout American history have spoken not to some quirks of the moment "but to persistent American hurts and rages wrapped in longings for a supposedly bygone holy patriarchy." It is undoubtedly true that changes in the roles of men and women in the late eighteenth and early nineteenth centuries lay behind the many utopian and often eccentric proposals for a new sexual harmony, but many of these proposals, like the radical celibacy of the Shakers, were hardly for a return to patriarchy; indeed, the Shakers, founded by Mother Ann Lee in 1776, became the first American religious group to recognize formally the equality of the sexes at all levels of authority.

What does seem fundamental to this explosion of religiosity in the late eighteenth and early nineteenth centuries are the great numbers of radical changes that took place in people's personal and social relationships, relationships that compared to other early modern societies

were often weak and tenuous to begin with. Whatever transformed these relationships—whether it was the so-called market revolution, or the disestablishment of the Old World churches, or rapid population growth and movement, or the cries of equality coming out of the American Revolution—created needs and anxieties that often found resolution in religion. The sudden emergence in the early nineteenth century of new sects like the Mormons and weird cults like that of Matthias was certainly expressive of changes in social relationships and in American religious thinking that historians have only begun to explore.

Whatever the ultimate significance of Matthias and his cult may be for American history, however, there is no doubt that these two imaginative historians have written a splendidly readable and fascinating piece of history. That is no small achievement.

## AFTERWORD

According to many in the historical profession today, any sort of grand narrative of the past is frowned upon. Even as hard-nosed a historian as Richard D. Brown, who has written several substantial synthetic studies of early America, has succumbed to the postmodern skepticism of the present climate to the point where he doubts the possibility any longer of historians' writing large-scale synthetic accounts of the past. In his presidential address to the Society of the Early Republic, published in 2003, Brown stated that historians' claims to be telling the truth now stand on shaky ground. "Syntheses cannot make the strongest truth claims because they are based on such selectively chosen facts." He suggested that historians should escape from this dilemma by writing microhistories, small studies of particular localities, persons, or events. "By exploring a finite subject exhaustively (though not definitively), the microhistorian commands the evidence on that subject beyond challenge; so within that topic

readers learn to accept his or her authority." Certainly microhistory has flourished since the mid-1990s, when Johnson and Wilentz published their book. But, interestingly, Wilentz has recently gone on to publish the kind of grand narrative of political history (*The Rise of American Democracy: Jefferson to Lincoln* [2005]) that Brown thought could no longer be written. Wilentz's book even won a Bancroft Prize—a welcome sign of change.

# 10.

# TRUTH IN HISTORY

*Telling the Truth About History* by Joyce Appleby, Lynn Hunt,
and Margaret Jacob (New York: W. W. Norton, 1994)

*The New Republic,* November 7, 1994

I T  I S  O N L Y  within the context of our ongoing cultural war that this
book can be understood. For essentially it is an attempt by its authors
to mediate this cultural struggle, to use their good offices and their influence to find some solution, some middle way between the extremes, and
thus end the fighting. One can only hope that their efforts at mediation
will be successful.

Confused and complicated as this war is, it can be described basically
as a struggle between the traditionalists or modernists and the postmodernists, or as these three authors see it, between the defenders of the
status quo and the relativists. This basic dichotomy can be extended out-
ward to encompass and to explain the struggles now going on between the
universalists and the ethnicists, between the pluralists and the multiculturalists, between those who stress America's essential unity and those
who stress its essential diversity. So what might seem to be a petty academic debate about the nature of historical writing has, in fact, momentous implications for the kind of nation we Americans want to be.

Although the three authors are well aware of the pervasive influence
of postmodern thinking on everything from architecture to the

movies, their concern in this book is with the discipline of history—understandably so, since they are all historians. Although they write their book with one voice, each author is a distinguished historian in her own right. Joyce Appleby is an expert in early American history. Lynn Hunt writes on the French Revolution and on women's history. Margaret Jacob specializes in the history of science. It is hard to think of three historians better equipped to deal with threats to the discipline of history, particularly threats that come from the left of the political spectrum. For it is the peculiar burden of their book to try to rescue history from attacks from the left without at the same time repudiating much of what the left believes.

History is one of the last of the humanistic disciplines to be affected by deconstruction and postmodernist theories. These theories are not the same as ordinary historical relativism, which, as historian Gertrude Himmelfarb describes it, "locates the meaning of ideas and events so firmly in their historical context that history, rather than philosophy and nature, becomes the arbiter of truth." Most historians these days, including Himmelfarb, have become comfortable with this kind of contextual relativism, which accepts the reality of the past and our ability to say something true, however partial, about that past. But as Himmelfarb and these three historians agree, the radical relativism of postmodernism threatens all that. Postmodernism challenges all the fundamental assumptions of Western social science and calls into question everything that makes historical reconstruction possible.

Postmodernists are attacking the entire Enlightenment project on which the natural and social sciences are based. They hold that there is no truth outside of ideology and, indeed, they suggest that the search for truth is itself the prime Western illusion. Truth, they believe, is invented, not discovered. Strip away the political and cultural coverings that pass as "truth" in each society and the will to power by hegemonic interests will be revealed. The idea that the historian masters facts and recovers past reality is, in the words of the authors, describing the postmodernist point

of view, "simply a figment of the Western, capitalist imagination." History is seen as "a useful fiction for modern industrial society, nothing more." As one postmodernist has put it, "History is the Western myth."

Insofar as postmodernists recognize a "new historicism" at all, it is one practiced mainly by literary critics and involves essentially the unmasking and revealing of "hegemonic" relations of power. Postmodernism, in fact, subverts all conventional history writing. It denies that there is a reality in the past beyond that described by language, and this barrier of language forever prevents historians from telling any truth about the past. Because of the impossibility of historical reconstruction and the postmodern subversion of our conventional sense of time, some postmodern literary critics, such as Elizabeth Deeds Ermarth, have gone so far as to predict "the disappearance of history," which in turn may mean the end of all the things bound up in "historical time," including our ideas of human rights, the structure of the human sciences, and the informational functions of language. In fact, in place of the plot and character of traditional history writing, Ermarth offers an "interminable pattern without meaning," a form of writing that resembles modern music or some modern novels.

Not all the postmodern theorists are as wild as Ermarth, but Appleby, Hunt, and Jacob are keenly aware of the threat postmodern theories pose for history. So far it is mainly a threat. Although postmodernism has profoundly transformed the studies of literature, art, and anthropology, it has only begun to scratch the surface of the discipline of history.

Yet there are straws in the wind, of which this book is one, that suggest a destructive storm may be closer than we think. Multicultural studies that use the postmodern theories seem new and exciting and are attracting some the best young minds in the discipline. Fashionable postmodern jargon—"decentering" this, "deconstructing" that, "inventing" this, and "constructing" that—is cluttering up more and more historical writings. Some respected historians, such as Simon Schama and John Demos, have become frustrated by the constraints that documentary evidence places

on their imaginations and their writing and consequently have chosen to invent thoughts and words for their historical characters, thus contributing, however inadvertently, to the postmodernist blurring of fact and fiction. Other historians, like Peter Novick in his widely read book, *That Noble Dream*, have become increasingly skeptical of the possibility of writing detached and objective history and have concluded that each historian has "agendas" and does only what is right in his or her own eyes. This skepticism is reaching the point where all defenses of objectivity and impartiality, even as ideals, are ridiculed as naive and self-serving. It seems evident that the discipline of history is being fundamentally challenged in new ways.

The authors realize that not all of these challenges have been bad. Some feminist historians like Joan Wallach Scott have found the postmodern theories very useful in showing the social constructiveness of gender distinctions and in formulating a new women's history. As women and "outsiders" in academia, the authors have been "especially sensitive to the ways in which claims to objectivity have been used to exclude us from full participation in the nation's public life." Claims of objectivity also have been used to exclude other groups from America's past; thus in destroying canons and deconstructing authorities, postmodernism has no doubt been helpful in the creation of a multicultural perspective on the past.

Consequently, in drawing out the implications of postmodernism these three historians do not see themselves "looking into the abyss," as Himmelfarb has described her recent confrontation with postmodernist history. They have no desire to reject "out of hand everything put forward by the postmodernists." They, in fact, accept relativism as a necessary part of historical thinking and celebrate the changes that have taken place in history writing over the past generation. They "embrace a healthy skepticism" and "applaud the research that has laid the foundations for a multicultural approach to human history." Still, they do believe that "truths about the past are possible, even if they are not absolute, and hence are worth struggling for." Thus they are willing to "take on both the relativists

on the left and the defenders of the *status quo ante* on the right." They want to save the new history from its friends as well as its enemies.

They are historians, and so they have organized their book historically. The eighteenth century, they write, made natural science the measure of all human truth. Natural science was neutral, value-free, and objective, and as such it became the guarantor of progress and power in the West. The success of science in understanding nature inevitably led people to aspire to apply the scientific method to an understanding of society. Thus arose the human sciences—first history, then psychology, sociology, and anthropology—and with the emergence of these human sciences came the belief in linear progress. If historians behaved like scientists, then history, it was thought, could contribute to this progress, particularly by applying its findings of how the West became modern to the whole world.

Following this opening, the authors quickly run through what they call "the three main schools of Western historical interpretation of the twentieth century": Marxism, the French Annales school, and American modernization theory. All three schools sought to create "a modern, scientific history [that] could incorporate every place on earth into one secular universal story with the aim of understanding the patterns of development." All three were heirs of the Enlightenment; all three promised progress and an emancipation from the darkness of the past. Yet now all this hope, all this vision, has come under increasing attack, to the point, the authors say, where the future of history itself has been brought into question.

The second part of the book is titled "Absolutisms Dethroned." In it the authors describe the various ways American historians, beginning with Charles Beard and the Progressives, have unmasked and demystified the myths, institutions, and ideologies of the United States in order to reveal the underlying gritty and exploitative reality. Although radical critics of America during the first half of the twentieth century tended to see that gritty and exploitative reality as an economic one, in their political out-

look and in their desire to penetrate beneath the surface of things they were, in fact, the progenitors of the deconstructionists, postmodernists, and the new historicists of our own time. According to the authors, however, the immediate source of the present crisis in history was the remarkable outburst of social history writing that began in the 1960s.

The effects of the upheavals of the 1960s were felt everywhere in American culture, but especially in the colleges and universities. The 1960s democratized higher education in America. Never before did so many men and women from so many different social backgrounds go to college and earn higher degrees. Among the people from diverse backgrounds entering the historical profession were increasing numbers of women. The number of new female Ph.D.s in history steadily grew through the decade and the decades following. In 1970 only 13 percent (137) of new Ph.D.s were awarded to women; by 1989 that had increased to 37 percent. As the character of the history profession changed and became more diverse, so did the subjects the historians wrote about. Between 1958 and 1978 the proportion of doctoral dissertations written on social history quadrupled, and social history surpassed political history as the primary area of historical research.

More important than the change in subjects, however, was the radical shift in perspectives. Instead of focusing on statesmen, generals, diplomats, and elite institutions, the new social historians over the past thirty years have concentrated on "America's outsiders—the poor, the persecuted, and the foreign," and thus they have "put their research on a collision course with the conventional accounts of the American past." For the most part, the stories of these outsiders have not been celebrations of heroic achievement and patriotic glory; rather, they have been "tales of frustration and disappointment which cannot be easily assimilated to the monolithic story of American success."

The authors contend that our present pessimism and skepticism and preoccupation with multiculturalism are in large part a consequence of these three decades of work in social history. By attacking the older nar-

rative history as "always partial, always political, always propagandistic, indeed, mythical . . . the social historians fostered the argument that history could never be objective." At the same time, the new social history worked to weaken the ties that bound Americans to the nation. Since much of this social history "is unassimilable into any account written to celebrate the nation's accomplishments," it "raises very fully the disturbing possibility that the study of history does not strengthen an attachment to one's country. Indeed, the reverse might be true, i.e., that open-ended investigation of the nation's past could weaken the ties of citizenship by raising critical issues about the distribution of power and respect." The new social history challenged the possibility of absolute truth and patriotism and thus it helped to pave the way for the introduction of postmodern theories into history.

But this introduction took time. The authors contend that controversy over the methods and goals of social history worked to delay the use of postmodern theories in history writing in comparison with their use by the other humanistic disciplines. For a long while social history by itself seemed to satisfy the political urges and utopian aims of its practitioners. When it no longer sufficed, many historians turned more and more to cultural history, which became another way station on the road to postmodernism. Even the Marxists, under the influence of theorists like Antonio Gramsci and Raymond Williams, abandoned old-fashioned economic materialism in favor of the new cultural history. Borrowing heavily from anthropology and literary theory, cultural historians broke up the past into unconnected ethnographic moments and turned all cultures into texts that had no relationship to anything outside of themselves. As the authors point out, this kind of cultural history "could be used to further the attack on reason and universal values" and could therefore contribute to making history over in a postmodernist fashion.

What the authors call "discovering of the clay feet of science" reinforced this growing skepticism, relativism, and multicultural criticism that helped propel historians toward postmodernism. In the years following

World War II, the heroic model of science came undone. Revealing of this intellectual unraveling and a sign of the times, say the authors, was Thomas Kuhn's *The Structure of Scientific Revolutions*, which appeared in 1962. By showing how scientists operated within theories and conventions that changed through time, Kuhn's book unintentionally reinforced the rising skepticism about science. If even the scientific process was historically conditioned, then it seemed that nothing was immune from relativism.

Probably because of Jacob's expertise and influence, the three authors tend to see the intellectual struggle of the 1960s taking place centrally in the history of science. Although the authors describe the historians of science as one of the major forces undermining the absolutism of science in the postwar world, in the end they also make them the redeemers of what they had wrought. Beginning in the 1960s historians of science used richly contextual studies of the heroic figures of science like Newton and Darwin to reveal just how prejudiced, irrational, and ideological these great men of science had been. Yet these historians of science also showed that it was precisely the scientists' involvement in the major currents of opinion of their day that enabled them to make their great discoveries. Newton's deep religious conviction made possible his conceptualization of universal gravitation. Darwin's Malthusian perspective on the struggle of the poor in nineteenth-century Britain made possible his formulation of the mechanism of natural selection. Thus these recent historicist studies of great scientists, the authors conclude, "suggest new understandings of how objective truth can be produced by deeply subjective people." No lesson is more important to Appleby, Hunt, and Jacob: the fact that "science can be historically and socially framed and still be true" is the basis of all their hopes of mediating and ending our cultural war.

All may be contingent; all may be relative. But, the authors claim, this prevalence of contingency and relativism does not mean the end of objectivity and the possibility of arriving at practical workable truths in history writing. It is true that historians, like all humans, are subjective: they have passions, desires, political and personal agendas. But so did

Newton and Darwin, and they were still capable of discovering objective scientific truths. We can never return to the absolutist world of nineteenth-century positivism, but the alternative to that world is not the postmodernist world of total subjectivity. There is another way of seeking truth, another way of demonstrating objectivity, and the authors are determined to show it. The instability of language, the subjectivity of human thought, the social construction of reality, the deconstruction of texts—none of these postmodern arguments can ultimately "undercut the ability to say meaningfully true things about the world."

By the time the authors get to the third and final part of their book, entitled "A New Republic of Learning," they are prepared to offer a new theory of objectivity based on the "practical realism" developed by philosopher Hilary Putnam. This practical realism, which owes a great deal to twentieth-century American pragmatism, recognizes that there cannot be an exact correspondence between words and what is out there; still, it continues to aim for as much accuracy and completeness as possible in the historical reconstruction of the past. Our interpretations of the past may be imperfect, but practical realism knows that "some words and conventions, however socially constructed, reach out to the world and give a reasonably true description of its contents."

The consequences of not being able to make such distinctions between truth and falsehood can be terrifying. Nothing has been more jarring to the postmodern relativists, for example, than all those bogus scholars who assert that there was no Holocaust and back up their assertion with the postmodernist view that one person's view of the past is as good as another's, since there is no reality out there that can be verified. Examples like this one of denying the Holocaust have been far more effective in discrediting postmodernist theories than dozens of books.

In a final chapter, entitled "The Future of History," the authors offer a glowing vision of a new post–Cold War world in which history will be able to be "imagined in markedly different ways." Here all the authors' neutrality and sagacity displayed earlier in the book seem to give way to

partisanship and sentimental hopefulness. It is almost as if the authors, having so severely criticized the postmodernist history identified with the left, now felt the need to reestablish their credentials as liberals, lest anyone confuse them with Gertrude Himmelfarb. They admit that "muscular ideologues" exist on both the right and the left, but they now want to emphasize that most of the absolutism and rigidity in our cultural war can be blamed on the right, on the defenders of the status quo, whom they call traditionalists. "Even though they have identified some real weaknesses in postmodernism," these traditionalists have actually had the nerve to attack an array of educational initiatives that the authors very much favor, including multiculturalism. Himmelfarb, for example, has charged that multiculturalism not only politicizes and trivializes history but by pluralizing and particularizing history to the point where people have no history in common, it demeans and dehumanizes people and denies their common humanity. Himmelfarb sees no merit in multiculturalism and dismisses it as a natural consequence of the destructive and disintegrative tendencies of postmodernism.

Since the authors themselves link multiculturalism to postmodernism, they have a tricky problem: trying to get rid of the evils of postmodernism without losing the benefits of multiculturalism in the process. There is no doubt that our understanding of American history has been profoundly enriched by what might be called a soft multicultural approach to history. In hundreds of books and articles written over the past several decades, the histories of hitherto neglected persons and groups, including women, Indians, and African Americans, have been brought to life and made integral parts of our national history. Much of this soft multiculturalism is not new; we used to call it pluralism, which assumed a process of assimilation. Celebrating the distinctiveness of one's group or ethnicity has always been part of the process of becoming American. Nineteenth- and twentieth-century immigrants, as historian John Higham has pointed out, often "constructed an ethnic identity and a new American identity concurrently."

What is new and alarming at the present time is the use of "identity politics" and what might be called hard multiculturalism to break up the nation into antagonistic and irreconcilable fragments. Such hard multiculturalism denies the possibility of assimilation and erodes our national sense of ourselves as Americans. The authors are certainly aware of the disintegrative dangers of this hard tendency of multiculturalism, but offer little to thwart it. They make a feeble attempt to defend the oneness of the nation, but actually spend most of their time praising diversity and the recent expressions of ethnic identity. Indeed, they go so far as to compare the demands for an Afrocentrist education for African Americans with what American colonists in 1776 did in providing a collective identity for themselves as detached Europeans—as if the Declaration of Independence were once just a piece of identity politics and no longer has any relevance for those Americans of non-European origin. And the authors wonder why so-called traditionalists, like Himmelfarb or Arthur Schlesinger, Jr., are opposed to this sort of multiculturalism!

In the end, the authors can only blame the Cold War for everything. All that has gone wrong in contemporary American intellectual life—all the extreme relativism and skepticism, all the cynicism and bitter criticism, all the postmodernistic nihilism—the authors attribute to the Cold War. "The Cold War," they assert, "politicized all social thought. . . . For almost a half century, it determined identities, magnified anxieties, and permeated every intellectual enterprise." Even the traditionalists' opposition to multiculturalism is laid at the feet of the Cold War, for such opposition "bears striking resemblances to the ideological marching orders of the Cold War." Poor Dinesh D'Souza, who is too young to have experienced very much of the Cold War, gets the brunt of the authors' attack because it is in his book *Illiberal Education* where "the workings of Cold War logic can be seen most clearly."

But now the Cold War has suddenly ended. And with the ending of the Cold War the cultural struggle that has been tearing up America's intellectual life can presumably come to an end too. Removing the re-

straints imposed by the Cold War, the authors believe, has lowered "the stakes for ideologues on both the right and left" and has increased the opportunity for examining the enterprise of truth seeking in history in a dispassionate manner. A new era, "a new republic of learning," is now possible.

Appleby, Hunt, and Jacob's attempt to connect our present cultural war to the Cold War seems seriously misguided, but it is understandable. They have a vested interest in this linkage because of their ultimate faith and confidence in science. Science, they say, was tainted and corrupted by the Cold War in which it was enlisted to fight. Now, with the end of the Cold War, science will be able to regain its rightful place as the model of objective truth seeking. And with the revitalization of science and the opening of a truly democratic arena of discourse, "relativism and the intellectual postures that feed into it will recede, departing in the company of the alienation engendered by the rigidities of the Cold War." The authors have very high hopes for what will come out of the disappearance of the Cold War. "In time of war," they write, "one attacks; in time of peace, one tries to find a common ground." The lions will lie down with the lambs and all will be well across the land.

## AFTERWORD

That a book such as this one by Appleby, Hunt, and Jacob was published in the 1990s tells us a lot about the scholarly climate of that decade. Indeed, *Telling the Truth About History* offered support to Richard D. Brown's pessimistic claim that postmodernism would inevitably lead to the writing of microhistories. The three authors believed that the social historians who experienced the changes of the 1960s had come to wonder "whether their work could ever be other than fragmentary and partial, with little relevance to the grander narratives of the past." Consequently, these social historians, "despairing of the validity of what they describe as

macrohistories . . . embrace irony and claim only to be writing microhistories." But irony hardly seems to be the preserve of microhistory. Grand narratives, like that of Henry Adams, can employ irony as well.

And as we have seen, microhistory has not commanded the field after all. Consequently, *Telling the Truth About History* now seems overanxious and somewhat dated. The Cold War is over, but we now have another war, the "war on terror." It is not at all clear yet how this new "war" will affect history writing.

# 11.

# HISTORY VERSUS
# POLITICAL THEORY

*If Men Were Angels: James Madison and the Heartless
Empire of Reason* by Richard K. Matthews

(Lawrence: University Press of Kansas, 1995)

*The New York Review of Books*, October 19, 1995

P OOR JAMES MADISON! Think of who he was and what he achieved.
The major architect of the Constitution; the father of the Bill of
Rights and one of the strongest proponents of the rights of conscience
and religious liberty in American history; coauthor of *The Federalist*, surely
the most significant work of political theory in American history; the
leader and most important member of the first House of Representatives,
in 1789; cofounder of the Democratic-Republican Party in the 1790s; secretary of state in Jefferson's administration; and the fourth president of
the United States—all this, and still he does not have the popular standing
of the other Founding Fathers, especially that of his closest friend, Thomas
Jefferson.

Madison seems unable to escape from the shadow of Jefferson and
seems smaller than his Virginia colleague in every way. He was, after all,
only about five feet six inches tall compared to Jefferson's six three or four,
and somehow that difference in height has carried over into the different
degrees of popular esteem that the country has paid to these two founders.

Jefferson has a huge temple erected in his honor in the nation's capital; but until 1980, with the naming of a new Library of Congress building after him, James Madison had no such memorial. Jefferson's ringing statements on behalf of freedom and democracy are inscribed everywhere, but very few of Madison's are. Jefferson's home, Monticello, has been restored to Jeffersonian perfection and has become a shrine visited by thousands of people every year. Madison's home, Montpelier, has only recently been opened to visitors, and it remains dominated by the twentieth-century horsey tastes of the Duponts, who once owned it.

Although the two men collaborated on many things throughout their careers, especially in passing Virginia's bill for religious freedom and in organizing the Democratic-Republican Party, Jefferson has received all the glory while Madison did much of the work. Indeed, Jefferson has come to symbolize America and America's ideals to an extent that no other single figure in our history has matched. Certainly, Madison has not even come close. Until now, that is.

It is the burden of this book, *If Men Were Angels,* by Richard K. Matthews, professor of government at Lehigh University, to show us that Madison, not Jefferson, is the more accurate symbol of America. Madison, not Jefferson, says Matthews, stands for the America of the past two hundred years; he, not Jefferson, articulated the beliefs and values that have made us what we are. Matthews contends that Madison is the most influential and most representative thinker among the founders of the United States. Madison is the "quintessential liberal" whose "passionless notion of reasonable liberal politics" has shaped our culture as no one else has.

As the term "passionless" and the word "heartless" in the subtitle jarringly suggest, however, Matthews's book is not meant to enhance Madison's reputation. For Matthews does not much like the reasonable liberal values and beliefs that Madison articulated; indeed, the picture that Matthews paints of the kind of American people that Madison's thinking presumably represents is anything but attractive. In fact, it is downright ugly: a picture of a coldhearted, fragmented, and undemocratic people

marked by fear and loneliness, a people engaged in a "war of all against all . . . with no hope of fraternity, equality, or community." Madison, it seems, is the symbol of a selfish individualistic people who have no sense of benevolence and care only for their material wealth and property. For Matthews that is what being "liberal" means.

Few American academics writing today have as despairing a view as Matthews does of what he calls "the political and cultural wasteland" that constitutes present American reality. Despite this despairing view, however, *If Men Were Angels* is not primarily a work of social criticism. It is not, in other words, a long hand-wringing jeremiad or lamentation about the sorry state of contemporary American culture. Far from it. For the most part, this clearly written and vigorously argued book is a straightforward work of historically grounded political theory; it stays pretty much in the eighteenth and early nineteenth centuries.

The book tries to do three things: "to construct the complete political theory of James Madison," to provide "a critical analysis of Madisonian politics," and to understand Madison's politics "in comparison with what America has failed to become" by setting his vision of politics alongside Jefferson's very different vision.

*If Men Were Angels* is the second volume in a revisionist trilogy of books that Matthews hopes will open "a public debate on the meaning of America's pasts and thereby initiate a dialogue on the possibilities for alternative, democratic futures." His first volume, *The Radical Politics of Thomas Jefferson,* published in 1984, described "a Jefferson who not only presents a radical critique of American market society but also provides an image for—if not a road map to—a consciously made, legitimately democratic future." The trilogy will eventually conclude with *Alexander Hamilton and the Creation of the Heroic State.* With Jefferson as the radical democratic hero in the trilogy, we can expect an unflattering portrait of Hamilton in the volume to come. What is surprising about this second volume is the harshness of Matthews's indictment of Madison, who, after

all, has usually been thought to have been the most intimate and loyal of Jeffersonians. Matthews shows us otherwise.

Harsh as the indictment of Madison may be, however, the book is in no way a crude debunking of Madison; in fact, much of the time Matthews seems to admire the energy, design, and intellect that went into Madison's conception of politics even as he strongly disagrees with its assumptions and values. Given the current scholarly opinion of Madison's political thinking, Matthews perhaps had little choice.

The general public may now have only begun to glimpse the importance of Madison among the Founding Fathers, but that is no longer the case with scholars. During the past several decades historians like Ralph Ketcham, Jack Rakove, and Robert Rutland have written excellent biographies of Madison, and Irving Brant's six-volume work has been completed. The definitive edition of Madison's papers is now well under way, modeled, however, as all the great publication projects of the founders' papers are, on Julian Boyd's edition of Jefferson's works and correspondence. And perhaps most important, several scholars, including Drew McCoy and Neal Riemer, have written excellent studies of various aspects of Madison's political thought, all more or less contributing to the now widely accepted view that Madison was the most astute, profound, and original political theorist among the Founding Fathers.

So widely accepted is this view of Madison that Matthews makes no effort to dispute it head on. In fact, he spends an extraordinary amount of time detailing the various ways Madison, with his "brilliant liberal mind," contributed to the making of the liberal American republic. In the process he draws out starkly the pessimistic implications of Madison's liberal thinking. Madison, he tells us, was no democrat; democracy for Madison was "a fool's illusion." And since Madison's ideas stand for American culture, America is no real democracy either. Madison's dream, like any "liberal's dream," was "life without others," which, says Matthews more than once, was really a "nightmare." His politics, which are American

politics, was "the politics of sin, cynicism, and suspicion." A liberal like Madison has an accountant's mentality with no place for compassion and caring. All that matters in Madison's liberalism is the individual and his property, especially his property. And so it goes. Despite his acceptance of Madison's brilliance, Matthews has written a devastating critique of Madison's political thought.

James Madison was born in 1751 into that class of Virginia slaveholding planters who dominated their society as few aristocracies have. Although his father was the wealthiest landowner in Orange County, Virginia, he was not far removed from the raw frontier; and young Madison, like most of the Founding Fathers, became the first of his family to attend college. In Madison's case it was the College of New Jersey (later Princeton), where he was introduced, through the president John Witherspoon, to the enlightened ideas of eighteenth-century Scottish thinkers, such as Francis Hutcheson, Adam Smith, and David Hume. In college he revealed an intellectual intensity and earnestness that he never lost. His father's plantation wealth enabled Madison, who complained endlessly of his poor health, to return home to study and contemplate participating in the provincial politics of colonial Virginia. The Revolution, of course, changed everything.

In 1776 Madison, at age twenty-five, was elected to Virginia's provincial convention and became caught up in the Revolutionary movement. His first great liberal passion was religious freedom, and through that concern he became friendly with Jefferson, who, eight years his senior, was already a major force in Virginia's Revolutionary politics. It was the beginning of a lifelong friendship.

Madison moved up fast in politics, and by age twenty-eight he was elected to the Continental Congress, where he was confronted with national problems. The glaring weaknesses of the Articles of Confederation convinced him, along with many others, that some sort of reform of this first national constitution was needed, and throughout the middle 1780s he wrestled with various schemes for overhauling the Confederation. In the

meantime, service once again in the Virginia Assembly, where many of his and Jefferson's plans for reform were mangled by factional fighting, convinced him that popular politics at the state level and majoritarian legislative tyranny were as dangerous to republicanism as executive despotism. Not only Virginia but other states as well were passing various inflationary paper-money laws and other debtor relief legislation that were victimizing creditor minorities. All this experience during the 1780s sparked new thoughts, and Madison began working out for himself a new understanding of American politics, a new understanding that involved questioning conventional wisdom concerning majority rule, the proper size for a republic, and the role of factions in society. No American in the 1780s thought so seriously or so originally about the problems of constituting republican governments—it was probably the most creative moment in the history of American politics.

Matthews concedes much of Madison's creativity; he simply does not like the uses to which Madison put that creativity, nor does he share Madison's realistic assumptions about human nature and society. Madison, he says, had a Calvinist and almost Hobbesian conception of human beings. People had little virtue. They were selfish and passionate and had to be watched constantly. It was true that they were rational as individuals; but when collected together in a group, they became dangerous. As Madison wrote in *The Federalist,* and Matthews quotes more than once: "Had every Athenian citizen been a Socrates, every Athenian assembly would still have been a mob."

In such circumstances the best that could be done was to create a strong, balanced government to maintain stability and protect individual rights, especially the rights of property, from encroachments by others. The executive branch of government, of course, could abuse its power and threaten people's rights and liberties, and this possibility of abuse had to be checked. But for Madison, the people themselves, either in the mass or in representative legislative majorities, were even more threatening to the rights of minorities than were governors and other executive administra-

tors. What Matthews refers to as "the liberal Prince" had to shift back and forth depending on where the threat to individual rights was greater and throw his weight onto one or the other side of the seesaw in order to achieve social stability, which, says Matthews, always remained Madison's "primary political concern."

By the 1780s Madison had worked out a Malthusian view of the future before Malthus. Because population increased faster than the resources available to sustain the increases, the lot of people in time would become ever more vicious, ever more miserable, and ever more poor. This was already happening in Europe, and it would eventually happen even in America, despite its being blessed with so much land. The great populous cities of Europe and the growth of urban manufacturing were to Madison the results of social decay and the desperateness of people without agricultural land. No one in his right mind would ever move to the city and become a manufacturer if he had land to till.

Although the end of America's frontier might not come for a century or more, Madison had a more immediate fear. The growing numbers of American farmers needed outlets for their produce; if they did not find them, they would stop working and slip into idleness, barbarism, and savagery. To Madison, as to many other thinkers in this premodern world, men were naturally lazy and would not work unless they were driven by necessity. Madison had nothing but contempt for those utopians like Robert Owen and William Godwin who believed that people would work for the love of it and would use positively any increased leisure they got from machinery and technology by cultivating their minds. People were simply not like that, said Madison. Even civilized individuals were only one step removed from savages, he said, and in groups or factions and under the influence of passion they could sometimes behave like savages.

Following his description of Madison's pessimistic view of human nature and the future, Matthews turns to what he considers to be "the heart and soul of Madisonian politics": Madison's obsessive concern for private property. In this discussion Matthews clearly reveals his deep

aversion to a capitalist market society, a present-minded aversion that leads him into an anachronistic misreading of Madison. Although Matthews senses at times that Madison's view of property was different from our own, he eventually concludes that Madison was just another advocate for a "bourgeois notion of property."

No doubt he wishes Madison had not been so property loving. In 1790 Secretary of the Treasury Hamilton proposed to pay off in full the present holders of the Revolutionary War debt, even though many of them were speculators who had bought up the debt at a fraction of its face value. Madison rejected Hamilton's proposal as unjust because it did nothing for the people who had originally lent the money to the government, an action that Matthews applauds as one of Madison's "finest public moments." At long last Madison "specifically attacked the cold calculus of the market." But alas, this sort of rejection of "the norms of modern market economics" was all too rare for Madison. Most of the time, says Matthews, Madison lived in dread of any popular assault on private property.

There is no question that Madison was centrally concerned with protecting minority property interests from the encroachments of government, particularly from what he called the "majoritarian tyranny" of rampaging state legislatures. But Madison's conception of property was not quite the kind of modern bourgeois property that Matthews has in mind. Madison was still thinking of property in premodern, almost classical terms: rentier property, proprietary property, property as a source of authority and independence, not as the source of productivity and capitalistic investment. The most traditional kind of proprietary property was, of course, land; but it could take other rentier forms, such as government bonds or money on loan. Both Madison and Jefferson wanted as many American white males to have as much of this kind of proprietary property as possible, for such property, particularly in land, would help guarantee the independence of these citizens and help secure republican government.

This kind of fixed property was very vulnerable to inflation, which is why Madison and other gentry were so frightened of the paper-money emissions and other debtor relief legislation passed by the state assemblies in the 1780s. Inflation threatened not simply their livelihood but their authority and independence as citizens. Although gentry like Madison could at times regard the advocates of paper-money and debtor relief schemes as little better than levelers, those advocates were neither the propertyless masses nor radicals opposed to the private ownership of property. Such debtors believed in the sacredness of property as much as Madison, only it was a different kind of property they were promoting: modern, risk-taking property; dynamic, entrepreneurial property; venture capital; not money out on loan, but money borrowed—in fact, all the paper money that enterprising farmers and protobusinessmen clamored for in these years. Matthews has placed Madison in the wrong Marxian class. Madison is the aristocrat; the paper-money advocates that he feared are the bourgeoisie.

To conclude his argument Matthews offers an extensive comparison of Madison's politics with that of Jefferson, drawing freely on his earlier book on Jefferson. Although historians have generally lumped the two men together as great collaborators, Matthews contends with some cogency that as political theorists they were actually "worlds apart." Jefferson, says Matthews, was an authentic American democratic radical, who believed in permanent revolution, a kind of communitarian anarchism, and widespread political participation by the people. His political theory was based on the moral sense of each individual and on faith in the future and the people. Madison, by contrast, says Matthews, was neither a democrat nor a civic humanist. He was simply a liberal defender of bourgeois property whose political theory was constructed on instrumental reason and fear and the atomization of society. Matthews is not wrong in pointing out these differences between the two men, but his contrast seems greatly overdrawn.

It is true the two men had different temperaments: Jefferson, high-minded, optimistic, visionary, and quick to grab hold of new ideas;

Madison, cold-eyed if not pessimistic, analytical, and skeptical of utopian schemes. But Jefferson's often fanciful and exaggerated opinions were usually curbed or brought down to earth by his very practical and cautious behavior, which is why he was so frequently charged with hypocrisy and inconsistency. So the two men in day-to-day political affairs appeared to be very similar. Certainly, they seemed to each other and to contemporaries to be closer and more alike in their thinking than Matthews allows. (Jefferson, for example, despite Matthews's categorical denial, did sometimes seem to suggest that property was an individual natural right.) Indeed, if the two men differed as much as Matthews says they did, then their entire life together was a long and extraordinary act of bad faith.

Matthews tends not only to exaggerate differences between the two men but to attribute too much originality to Jefferson. Jefferson's conception of the moral or social sense that presumably adheres in each individual was very important for the development of democracy, but it was scarcely unique to Jefferson. It was a commonplace of enlightened thinking in the eighteenth-century English-speaking world, and Madison certainly shared it, though it is true that he did not emphasize it to the extent that Jefferson did.

Matthews is apt to take much of what Jefferson said too seriously and to put more weight on Jefferson's overcharged language than it will bear. He does not, in other words, heed Madison's warning of allowing "for a habit in Mr. Jefferson as in others of great genius of expressing in strong and round terms, impressions of the moment." So Jefferson's many impetuous opinions expressed in various private letters throughout his career—that the earth belongs to the living and that therefore all laws and constitutions should come to an end every nineteen years; that a little rebellion now and then was a good thing; that the Terror and other French Revolutionary excesses on behalf of liberty, even having half the earth desolated, could not be too extreme; that the only politics was local politics in which people participate in tiny ward republics—cannot be taken as seriously as one would take them if they had been worked out and pub-

lished in a treatise. His "earth belongs to the living" letter to Madison, for example, written in the heady atmosphere of Paris in 1789, was never published in his lifetime, and the ideas it contained were known only to a handful of his intimates. Although the ideas set forth in this letter certainly embodied assumptions Jefferson had about the world, he never followed up his specific proposals, most of which were tactfully shot down by Madison. The fact is Jefferson never developed or acted upon half of the opinions he so freely and impulsively expressed in his correspondence.

Nevertheless, there were differences between Jefferson's and Madison's political thinking besides Jefferson's hastiness of expression; but some of those differences do not seem to be quite what Matthews believes them to be. Jefferson could at times be very conventional in his thinking—idealistic and enlightened no doubt, but nonetheless conventionally idealistic and enlightened, always acutely sensitive to what the best people in the cosmopolitan centers of culture believed. In this respect the inquisitive, original, and skeptical Madison was very different.

Take, for example, their different views of the Constitution's omission of a bill of rights. Matthews, like many other scholars attuned to our exclusively twentieth-century preoccupation with the Bill of Rights, simply assumes that Jefferson had it right when, writing from Paris in 1787–88, he complained to Madison that the Constitutional Convention had made a mistake in not adding a bill of rights to the Constitution. But Jefferson supported a bill of rights not because he had thought through the issue and related it to a developed understanding of an entirely new political system the way Madison had, but mainly because a bill of rights was what good governments were supposed to have. All his liberal aristocratic French friends said so; indeed, as he told his American correspondents, "The enlightened part of Europe have given us the greatest credit for inventing this instrument of security for the rights of the people, and have been not a little surprised to see us so soon give it up." One almost has the feeling that Jefferson advocated a bill of rights out of embarrassment over what his liberal French associates like Lafayette might think.

Yet the two friends and founders did differ from each other in some important ways, and Matthews is right to bring home to us those differences. Both men were suspicious of governmental power, including the power of elected representative legislatures. But Jefferson's suspicion was based on his fear of the unrepresentative character of the elected officials, that they were too apt to drift away from the virtuous people who had elected them. Madison's suspicion, in contrast, was based on his fear that the elected officials were only too representative, only too expressive of the passions of the people who had elected them. It is true, as Matthews says, that Jefferson always invested much more of himself in the future of popular democracy than Madison did. He was inspired by a vision of how things could and should be; Madison tended much more to accept things as they were.

Yet despite these real differences between the politics of Jefferson and Madison, do we have to choose between them? Surely a country as democratic and as diverse as ours needs the outlooks of both founders, needs both utopian visions of the future as well as realistic assessments of what is possible, needs both the Jeffersonian faith in the popular will of the majority as well as the Madisonian concern for minority rights. Perhaps American history has been a great collaboration between these two founders and their politics after all.

## AN EXCHANGE ON JAMES MADISON

By Richard K. Matthews. Reply by Gordon S. Wood.

*The New York Review of Books,* May 23, 1996

To the Editors:

Like Newt Gingrich, I always read Gordon Wood. His writings are insightful, elegant, balanced, and fair. So too his review of my *If Men*

*Were Angels: James Madison and the Heartless Empire of Reason.* Nevertheless, there are a few points in his essay that need additional comment.

As Wood explains, my book tries to construct and critique Madison's political ideas and compare them to, among others, Jefferson's. He notes as well that this effort is part of a larger project designed to open a public dialogue on the character of America's pasts and the possibilities for alternative, democratic futures. A dialogue, however, requires all those involved to understand the arguments and ideas being presented. I suspect that Wood does not appreciate fully my perspective, since he predicts an "unflattering portrait of Hamilton" as the final volume in the trilogy. While still in the gestation stage, I anticipate a different Hamilton book than does Wood. Why the differences in perception?

Wood is a historian, arguably one of America's finest. I am a political theorist. As such, our training, our interests, our concerns are somewhat different. My focus centers on the differences among the founders' political beliefs—their ideologies—the ideas and ideals they believed in even if they never were manifested in action in the public arena. What they actually wrote and thought, rather than what they did while in office, comprises the primary research material of this endeavor. As a historian, Wood focuses more on the behavior of political actors and on the material record, while I concentrate more on their philosophic ideas.

The differences, in part, may also stem from the style of the Madison book. It is at moments, as one earlier reader observed, an "in-your-face" analysis of Madison. As a reviewer inevitably must, Wood collapses some of the book's more extended discussions down to the nittiest grit. Consequently, some of the book's meaning becomes obscured if not lost. Perhaps two examples will suffice: first, his description of what "being 'liberal' " means "for Matthews"; and second, my "deep aversion to a capitalist market society," which, if Wood is correct, leads "into an anachronistic misreading of Madison." To be sure, Madison is a liberal of the Calvin-to-Locke variety. But liberalism has a history, spanning centuries and including many different voices. I

do not collapse liberalism down to the size of Madison, or Hobbes, or Locke, but rather conceive of liberalism spanning a historical and ideological spectrum of thinkers such as Jeremy Bentham, both Mills, and T. H. Green as well as contemporary figures such as C. B. Macpherson and Isaiah Berlin. To comprehend Madison's ideas and import, I situate him inside this larger liberal (cum liberal-democratic) tradition and thereby implicitly draw the reader into beginning the dialogue about alternative futures.

Capitalism also has a history. That I am not particularly fond of the present-day manifestations of a cultural system designed to produce ever more efficiently ever greater amounts of capital remains beside the point. Madison never lived to see even the beginning traces of the consequences of monopoly capitalism. Moreover, it remains impossible for me to conceive of his embracing today's Wall Street ethos. Still, he did accept the cold and inescapable logic of a Malthusian nature trapped inside a Calvinist universe run on market principles and Madisonian politics. Furthermore, rather than presenting Madison as "just another advocate for a 'bourgeois notion of property' "—a position Wood declares "wrong"—my fifth chapter, "Property: Rights and Possessions, Democracy and Despair," presents a lengthy account of a much more complex Madison, who, not unlike other liberals, appeared torn between concerns of economic justice and the logic of the emerging market society. Madison cannot be understood simply as an (eighteenth-century) aristocrat. While there certainly is an aristocratic flavor to Madison's notion of property (hence his nostalgic concerns with economic justice), portions of his 1792 essay "Property" and his 1818 "Agricultural Address" could have come straight from John Locke's chapter "Of Property" in his *Second Treatise of Government.* If this Locke does not contain the seeds of market society, who does?

Lastly, Wood finds a "greatly overdrawn" contrast between Madison and Jefferson. To be sure, I strove to bring as much analytic clarity as possible to the philosophic differences between Madison and Jefferson.

After all, the myth of the "great collaboration" between the two of them has been gospel for some time. To soften the differences between these two political giants, Wood reminds readers of Madison's observation of "a habit in Mr. Jefferson as in others of great genius of expressing in strong and round terms, impressions of the moment." The exact context of those words of Madison that Wood quotes may be at least as supportive of my position as it is of Wood's. Madison wrote them to N. P. Trist in 1832 when he found himself having considerable difficulty trying to rationalize the significant differences between himself and Jefferson on the political issues of states' rights and nullification that had been generated by the Virginia and Kentucky resolutions. Since Jefferson was dead, and the reality of the historic record surrounding the resolutions clearly documented their philosophic differences in this collaborative effort, Madison had little choice but to attempt to gloss over them. As political thinkers, Madison and Jefferson held vastly different pictures of the past and the future. And Jefferson's radically democratic notion that "the earth belongs in usufruct to the living" was not the "impression of the moment" but rather an ideal he maintained throughout his life.

Richard K. Matthews
Lehigh University
Bethlehem, Pennsylvania

————————

Gordon S. Wood replies:

In his letter Professor Matthews tries to soften some of the harsh, "in-your-face" arguments of his book, and suggests that I did not fully understand those arguments because I am a historian and he is a political theorist. Although it's certainly true that we come from two different disciplines, and that explains much of our disagreement, I don't believe he appreciates clearly the difference between the two. He

says that the difference is largely one of focus: that political theorists concentrate on the ideas and beliefs of persons in the past, while historians concentrate on their behavior and the material record. This is not where the difference lies. Historians are as interested in the ideas and ideologies of the founders as political theorists like Matthews. What is different about the two disciplines is their purpose. Historians attempt to recover a past world as accurately as possible and try to show how that different world developed into our own. Political theorists who work with the ideas of the past have a different agenda. They are primarily interested in the present or future conditions of political life and see past ideas as merely the sources or seeds for present or future political thinking. They are, as historians like to say, very "whiggish"; they usually see the past simply as an anticipation of our present, and thus they tend to hold people in the past responsible for a future that was, in fact, inconceivable to them. So if you think modern liberalism is heartless, then go back and blame John Locke or James Madison or any of the other presumed contributors to a modern "bourgeois notion of property." Or if you want an alternative future for America, then go back and find in Jefferson's thought some idiosyncratic notions about ward democracy and the earth's belonging to the living.

There is nothing wrong with this sort of ransacking of the past by political theorists; lawyers and jurists do it all the time. But we should never confuse these manipulations of the past for present purposes with doing history. In his book, for example, Matthews wants to show that Madison was "committed implicitly to the market principle of possessive individualism." So he is compelled to argue that he understands Madison's "actual position" on property better than Madison himself, even "in spite of his words." His book is full of these kinds of distortions and manipulations of Madison's thought. Whatever Matthews is up to, it is not history, and his book is not a historically accurate account of Madison's political thinking.

It's true that I did jump the gun in presuming that Matthews's

portrayal of Hamilton in his final work of his trilogy would be unflattering. Since Jefferson is Matthews's hero and since Jefferson and Hamilton were so deeply at odds with each other in their lifetimes, I naively assumed that Matthews's account of Hamilton would inevitably be disparaging. But from the imaginative ways Matthews has misrepresented Madison and grossly separated him from his good friend and collaborator Jefferson, I should have realized that anything might be possible in his forthcoming interpretation of Hamilton.

## AFTERWORD

Matthews has not yet published his volume on Hamilton's political thought. But when it appears, it will be a study in political theory, not history. Our exchange over the review nicely explains some of the differences between political theorists and historians. Political theorists, especially those influenced by the ideas of Leo Strauss, tend to believe that the history of political thought can be studied as a search for enduring answers to perennial questions that can enhance contemporary political thought. Historians, on the other hand, tend to hold that ideas are the products of particular circumstances and particular moments in time and that using them for present purposes is a distortion of their original historical meaning. It doesn't follow from this distinction that past ideas cannot be legitimately used in the very different circumstances of the present; of course, they can be used and are used all the time. Jefferson's idea of equality, for example, has been used time and again throughout our history, by Lincoln as well as Martin Luther King, Jr. Historians contend that such usages violate the original historical meaning of the ideas and cannot be regarded as historically accurate, but they don't deny the rationality and legitimacy of such violations.

Such distortions and violations are indeed necessary for contemporary discussions of political thought and are no great sin, as long as the

theorists are aware that they are not being historically accurate. It's the theorists' claim that their present-day use of past ideas is true to the original way they were used in the past that historians quarrel with. Ideas, of course, do not remain rooted in the particular circumstances of time and place. Ideas can, and often do, become political philosophy, do transcend the particular intentions of their creators, and become part of the public culture, become something larger and grander than their sources. Political theory, studying these transcendent ideas, is a quite legitimate endeavor; it is, however, not history.

# 12.

# HISTORY WITHOUT IDEAS

*A Struggle for Power: The American Revolution*
by Theodore Draper (New York: Times Books, 1996)

*The New Republic,* February 19, 1996

WITHOUT DOUBT Theodore Draper is one of America's most acute observers of contemporary events. Indeed, at age eighty-three he is the grand old man of contemporary history writing. But he still wonders whether he is a historian. Although he has written over a dozen books on a variety of subjects over his long and distinguished career, he is not quite sure how to categorize himself. He says he is "surely not an academic, because he does not hold an academic post." Besides, he writes much better than most academics. Yet he is certainly much more than a journalist. Although he has engaged present-day events while they were "still hot, even boiling," he has always sought to analyze them "coolly with convincing documentation and reasoned judgment." He wants to write not merely for academics but for the general educated reader, for the reader who is "no longer merely interested in the daily or even weekly ration of news," and who wants to understand present events "in some organized form and in some historical perspective."

Draper likes to think of himself "as a historian of a special kind," a writer of what he calls "present history." Although he studies his subjects "as seriously as a professional historian might," he generally has worked

on "subjects closer to the present than most historians deal with." He likes to investigate "subjects of the greatest urgency and controversy while they were still urgent and controversial," yet he wants to treat them "from a larger historical perspective" than journalists do while using "traditionally historical methods." So over the past fifty years Draper has written histories of a wide range of events while the events were, so to speak, still on the front page—from the collapse of France in World War II, written in 1944; Castro's Revolution, written in 1962; Viet Nam, written in 1967; to the Iran-Contra affair, written in 1991. No one has taken on so many contemporary events over such a long period of time and written so objectively and impartially about them as has Draper. Always, he says of his fifty-year career, his aim has been "to analyze present-day events historically."

Until now, that is. This remarkable study of the origins of the American Revolution is Draper's first attempt to account for an event that took place a long time ago. It is no small event that Draper has taken on. The Revolution is the most important event in American history, not only because it legally created the nation but also because it infused into our culture all of our noblest beliefs and ideals, in truth, all of what actually makes us a nation. Consequently, its origins have been studied by more people over a longer period of time than any other subject in American history. It takes courage, therefore, to write another book on the American Revolution. It is as if Draper at the age of eighty-three wants to show himself and the world that he has always been a real professional historian at heart, and a superb one at that.

Draper has brought to his account of this two-centuries-old event the same approaches and techniques that he brought to his histories of present-day events. In referring to his use of traditional historical methods, Draper has always meant laying out the evidence "clearly, accurately, and as fully as possible" so anyone could check on it. Those methods have also meant using mostly primary rather than secondary sources and not hesitating "to quote at whatever length necessary from those sources." Yet

these are not the only characteristics of his writing of present history. Some historians, he wrote in 1982, believe in reinterpreting the past in terms of the present; even when they write about the distant past, they believe that it has to be shaped by some concern in the present. In his writings, he said, he has always taken an opposite course. Although his subject was the present, he has always tried to understand it in terms of the past or whatever parts of the past seem to have shaped it. He takes a present event, say the Iran-Contra affair, and goes back in time in order to understand it, indeed, "as far back as necessary if I thought some useful perspective could be gained."

Draper also tells us that he has paid special attention to the thoughts and words of the participants—especially those of the statesmen and politicians of the time—who did not know the future and whose statements often revealed far more than they intended. He usually quotes at great length from these participants, letting, as he says, "the facts speak as much as possible for themselves." Such a method requires dogged patience and a great capacity to go thorough mountains of material. So in his prize-winning study of the Iran-Contra affairs, *A Very Thin Line* (1991), he waded through well over fifty thousand pages of documents and then, as he said in the preface of that book, "used a good deal of the documentary material to carry the story forward, so that the reader may get a more intimate sense of what the material is before I say anything about it."

Without explicitly saying so, Draper has applied the same approaches and techniques to this history of the American Revolution. In effect, he has treated the Revolution as if it were a contemporary event, as if it had just occurred and needs explanation, just as the Cuban revolution needed explanation. He has pored through masses of primary sources from both Great Britain and the colonies, going all the way back to the seventeenth century and has quoted extensively from these original sources, aiming, as he says in his preface, "to let many of the actors speak for themselves" in the hope "that the reader will gain a more immediate impression of ideas and events than might be possible if I merely summed up what they

had to say." The result is an extraordinarily readable but peculiarly old-fashioned history of the Revolution. Not since Lawrence Henry Gipson's fifteen-volume history of the *British Empire Before the American Revolution* (1936–70) has anyone written such a full account of the breakup of the first British Empire.

The book opens with a discussion of the debate in 1759–61 over whether Britain ought to claim either the rich sugar island of Guadeloupe in the Caribbean or the vast continental territory of Canada captured from France in the Seven Years' War. Britain could not claim both, and the possession of one or the other of these territories would determine the future nature of the British Empire. Some said the sugar island was already commercially valuable, while others pointed to the promise of a populous Canada buying British manufactures. Others argued that Britain's primary interests lay in Europe, not in North America, and therefore it was wise to leave the French in Canada. Besides, it was claimed over and over, the French presence on the North American continent was the best means for ensuring that the British colonies there would continue to submit to the direction of the mother country. Without the restraining presence of the French in Canada, many warned, the rapidly multiplying colonists would begin to claim freedom from their dependence on Britain.

Despite these forebodings, however, Britain chose Canada in the Peace of Paris in 1763, and thereby set in motion a chain of events that led in little more than a decade's time to the breakup of the greatest empire the world had seen since the fall of Rome. Draper uses these British warnings, in 1759–61, of eventual American independence as the hook on which to hang his lengthy narrative investigation of the history of the British-colonial relationship. Convinced that one has to go far back "for a full understanding of the formative period of the Revolution," Draper uses several chapters to survey the colonies' history from their beginnings in the seventeenth century to the onset of the Seven Years' War in the 1750s. The colonies were founded by private entrepreneurs and religious zealots in the seventeenth century, during the decades that England itself was

torn apart by religious passion, the execution of its king, and a civil war. By the time the newly restored English Crown in 1660 got around to organizing its hodgepodge of colonies in North America, it was already too late. A whole generation in the early colonies had enjoyed a feeling of independence, and this would prove impossible to reverse.

Although the English government repeatedly tried over the next century to extend its control over the colonists' lives—taking over several of the private colonies, appointing royal governors and provincial councils, and establishing networks of bureaucrats—the empire remained essentially a trading empire, not an empire in depth, but one that touched only the surface of colonial society. The colonists were left remarkably free to pursue their own economic and social interests. Even the trading restrictions of the empire were blatantly evaded when they conflicted with the colonists' interests. Smuggling, bribery, and corruption became everyday facts of life for colonial merchants dealing with the British navigation system.

Draper is remarkably accurate in his history of the colonies, and his judgments are often shrewder than those of many specialists. Yet his newness to the material sometimes shows, especially in his discussion of eighteenth-century British politics, for which he has little real feel. He rightly notes that the empire was the Crown's empire, yet assumes that Parliament was some sort of independent entity that might or might not intervene in colonial matters if it so desired. Draper thus has no way of explaining the long period of what Edmund Burke later called the "salutary neglect" of the colonies by the Whig governments of Sir Robert Walpole and his successors up to the 1760s, except to say that "Parliament was usually too busy, too divided, or too uninterested to assert itself."

This misunderstands the peculiar position of the Whig administrations in the early eighteenth century. Walpole and his successors sought to keep colonial matters out of Parliament not, as Draper would have it, because they had "weightier things to preoccupy them," but because colonial issues were the issues most likely to unite the opposition elements

in the House of Commons against the government. The ministers were usually able to use the traditional Whig fear of royal power to keep reform-minded bureaucrats from stirring up opposition groups in the Commons and strengthening the Crown's empire.

After describing the creation of the empire up to 1750, Draper begins a detailed narrative of the momentous events during the next twenty-five years that culminated in the battle of Lexington and Concord. Always his aim is to explain what he sees as the inherent conflict between Britain and the colonists in a system of "dual power." It was a system, he believes, in which the colonists' future strength as a nation was not far from the consciousness of people on both sides of the Atlantic.

Draper recognizes, of course, that these North American provinces were not colonies in the modern meaning of the term. The white Anglo-Americans were not alien peoples conquered and oppressed by a foreign power; they were Britons who happened to live on the periphery of a huge empire, three thousand miles from the metropolitan center. And they were not exactly oppressed. Almost from the beginning, these colonists grew and prospered. Indeed, they had the highest standard of living and were probably the fastest-growing people in the Western world in the eighteenth century. (Their population doubled in size about every twenty-five years.) They grew so fast, says Draper, that many British officials and intellectuals worried about them and their prospects for independence, even a century before the Revolution. What was most striking about these predictions and forebodings of independence, Draper observes, was that they "most frequently rested on a calculus of power rather than of rights, grievances, or ideologies. When the colonies came of age and made themselves rich and strong, they were bound to become dangerous and rebellious." Or so many on both sides of the Atlantic prophesied. The colonies were steadily increasing in population and power; they had less and less need for British protection; and sooner or later they would become independent.

From beginning to end, the history of the British North American

colonies was a struggle for power between what Draper often refers to as the "two sides"—the mother country and her dependencies. Often this struggle was hidden from view, masked by a common sense of Englishness, but latently it was always present. This is Draper's argument in a nutshell. He repeats it over and over again, drawing on a multitude of sources designed to show that many people throughout the colonial period had premonitions of the colonists' eventual liberty. Draper realizes that he is someone who needs "a good many words to get to the end," though he usually starts out his projects "by intending to write something shorter." "I would like to think," he once wrote, "that it takes all those words to tell the reader why and how I have come to a position on a pending issue. The verdict may be disputed, but the evidence should stand."

There are certainly a lot of words here, with many long quotations from various contemporaries. In fact, the book is a throwback to the kind of history that used to be written a long time ago. Yet despite all the words and quotations, the book reads surprisingly well. Draper's prose is so vigorous, his choice of quotations so apt, that the reader is carried along with unexpected ease. It is a measure of Draper's skill as a writer that he is even able to build up a certain amount of suspense about an outcome that we already know: the breakup of the empire.

Great Britain came out of the Seven Years' War the dominant power in the world. France was humbled and was driven from the continent of North America; and Britain stood astride an empire that extended from India to the Mississippi. Yet the future was ominous. The war had altered power relations between Britain and the colonies, and left in its wake a host of problems and costs that could not be evaded. The newly acquired territory in America required policing and the maintaining of an army in scattered western posts—a very expensive matter, costing between three hundred thousand and four hundred thousand pounds a year. Yet the British debt from the war itself was already monstrous, demanding five million pounds a year in interest payments alone compared to a total

peacetime government budget of only eight million pounds. The English gentry already thought themselves taxed to exhaustion. They expected a peace dividend—but, instead, they got, in 1763, a new cider tax, which provoked uprisings in the apple-growing counties that had to be put down with troops. Thus it seemed only natural that the colonies should bear some of the costs of the recent war—a war that, after all, had been fought in their interest—especially since returning British military officials brought back reports from America of the colonists' prosperity.

From these circumstances flowed the new British policies of the 1760s: the tightening up of the navigation system in the effort to cut down smuggling and raise revenue, the closing off of the western territories in order to protect the Indian trade and avoid costly Indian wars, and the Stamp Act, which was the first direct tax levied on the colonists. "To the British," writes Draper, "each of the measures made good sense. No one decision stood by itself; each created the necessity for the next. All seemed to follow reasonably and inexorably from the legacy of the Seven Years' War." The decisions were not made haphazardly, and no one British minister was responsible. Most of the measures were deliberately submitted to Parliament and approved by it without substantial opposition.

Here, in an uncharacteristically crude touch, Draper says that "Parliament had awakened to the importance of colonial issues and had decided to use its long dormant power." He shows little awareness of the new political situation in Britain that emerged with the end of the Stuart pretension to the throne, the breakup of the old Whig oligarchy, and the accession of George III in 1760. Suddenly, for the first time in a half century, the governments of the 1760s discovered that colonial issues were the one thing they could count on to divide the opposition in Parliament rather than to unite it. So Parliament was now brought into the formation of colonial policy, with momentous implications for the empire. Defying the Crown was one thing—all good Whigs might condone that sort of defiance, which is why the British put up with a remarkable degree of

rioting and disorder both in the home island and in the colonies—but defying the sovereignty of Parliament was quite another thing: that was challenging the nation itself.

The colonists never quite understood the emotional significance Parliament had for eighteenth-century British Whigs. (Draper suffers from the same lack of understanding.) Parliament was the bastion of all English liberty. From time immemorial, it seemed, it had stood between the ever-encroaching power of the Crown and the English people's rights and liberties. Charters and bills of rights were important, no doubt, but most Englishmen never lost sight of the fact that these documents were acts of Parliament and protected by Parliament. For most metropolitan Englishmen, tyranny came only from the Crown, and Parliament was the only real defense against it. Thus it was quite understandable, and not some "common British illusion," as Draper would have it, that most British officials would instinctively expect the colonists to defer to Parliament's authority even while they were defying the Crown.

The experience of the colonists, of course, was different. For them too the source of tyranny had always been Crown power, usually embodied in their royal governors, but their defense against this power had not been Parliament. Their defense had been their several colonial assemblies. When confronted in the 1760s with Parliament's authority, therefore, they shared little of the traditional awe and respect that most Englishmen had for Parliament. Eventually they were even willing to promote a relationship with Great Britain that avoided Parliament altogether. In the end, this different experience was crucial to the breakup of the empire. The British could not accept the colonists' challenge to Parliament's sovereignty, and the war came.

True to his reputation as a clear-eyed and impartial analyst of politics, Draper is remarkably evenhanded in his assessment of the imperial relationship. There is no British bashing here, no suggestions of the tyranny or even the stupidity of George III. At the same time, however, Draper has no brief for the British government against the colonists. He is as

sympathetic to the Americans as he is to the British. From their point of view, he writes, the Americans' response to the new British measures in the 1760s was reasonable. Neither side was more right than the other. "Seen this way, the incipient revolution could only be decided by the capitulation of one side or the other, by some sort of compromise between them, or by a final conflict that would separate them forever." Was an armed struggle inevitable? To Draper that is "the most demanding question of the American Revolution."

The answer he gives to this question of the inevitability of the conflict is, essentially, yes. The Stamp Act represented much more than a mere tax. It released the pent-up desire for American autonomy, which, says Draper, was "the secret of the American Revolution." The colonists, he says more than once, became "an irresistible force" moving toward the "immovable object" of the British government, and there was little anyone could have done to stop the clash. The Americans' move toward independence in the 1760s and 1770s "seemed to spring out of nowhere," but "it had been foreshadowed in the seventeenth century." By 1765 the colonists already had the framework of an ideology worked out. "It ruled out all British—in practice, parliamentary—interference in American internal affairs and recognized a connection only with the king. It implied independence—or at least self-rule—in American domestic affairs. It took its stand on a platform of equality between Americans and British, within a still unified empire." The next ten years were only variations on these themes.

Draper's description of the maneuverings of these years between 1765 and 1775 takes up nearly half the book. But however many twists the story of these years took, there was no escaping the inevitable ending of the long struggle for power.

> Both sides tried to avoid responsibility by making demands
> that neither had the intention of meeting. The British said that
> they were prepared to relent, if the colonies showed proper

deference to the authority of Parliament. The colonies said
that they were ready to go back to the status quo ante of 1763 if
the British retracted everything they had done afterwards. Yet
neither wanted to show weakness in the face of the other's
perseverance. As usual in such circumstances, they spoke of
peace and prepared for war.

The conflict might have come sooner, Draper maintains, if the British had
sufficient force in the colonies to compel the colonists' obedience or if
they had fewer illusions about the colonists' deference. For their part, the
"Americans were long loath to admit even to themselves" their ultimate
purpose. They "needed time and goading to develop an ideology and a
leadership that brought them the full realization that they were aiming at
independence." Under the circumstances, war between the two sides was
just a matter of time. By 1774 the Americans were ready to fight for what
they believed, while the British thought it was high time they took a stand:
they had surrendered so often to colonial pressure—repealing the Stamp
Act, withdrawing most of the Townshend duties—that one more time
would mean the end of the empire. But "the government decided on a
policy of coercion without having sufficient powers of coercion to back
it up—until it was too late." The decision by the British commander in
chief in America, General Thomas Gage, to seize an arms depot in
Concord, Massachusetts, on April 19, 1775, touched off the long-expected
conflict.

Draper ends his story with this initial outbreak of hostilities. His history of the American Revolution, he says, does not include the war, but
only "why and how it came about." What are we to make of this lengthy
account of the coming of the Revolution as a struggle for power? Draper
is not the first historian to stress the underlying anticipation of eventual
American independence, but he is the first to build an entire book around
this anticipation. It is a very tricky theme. His desire to find premonitions
of the colonists' drive for independence even as far back as the seven-

teenth century runs the risk of committing what English-speaking historians commonly call Whiggism: the anachronistic foreshortening that makes the past a mere anticipation of what would later occur. One may get a very distorted view of the colonial period simply by garnering all the statements people made about the possibilities of the colonies' eventual independence, for there exist even more statements about the colonists' pride in being English and in belonging to the greatest empire in the world.

Draper's repeated reference to the "two sides" throughout the colonial period seems to exaggerate anachronistically the colonists' sense of having a distinctive identity. Draper assumes what has to be explained. No doubt Draper's evidence about the colonies' extraordinary growth and prosperity is important; and he is surely right in contending that sooner or later some adjustment in the imperial relationship was unavoidable. But was that need for adjustment the cause of the American Revolution?

Draper obviously has gone through an enormous amount of material, both primary sources and secondary accounts. He cites a good many of these secondary works, but, interestingly, most of those he cites were written during the first half of the twentieth century: works by Charles M. Andrews; Arthur M. Schlesinger, Sr.; George Louis Beer; Sir Lewis Namier; and Lawrence Henry Gipson. His attraction for these early twentieth-century historians is important. It suggests an affinity of thinking between him and them, between his conception of human behavior and theirs; in fact, Draper's book could have been written by any of them, though perhaps not as vigorously or engagingly.

Most of the scholarship on the American Revolution written since 1950 has focused on the importance of ideas in bringing on the Revolution. In his account Draper either dismisses or ignores this more recent scholarship. He apparently does not believe that ideas or the meanings that people give to their behavior are of great significance in explaining events. For Draper, as for many early twentieth-century historians influenced by Marx, Freud, and behaviorist psychology, ideas are epiphenomena. They

are symptoms, not causes; and they do not count for much in the determination of human events. For Draper, ideas and power are separate elements: ideas, self-consciousness, exist on the surface of life; the struggle for power, on the other hand, is one of those "large" and "deep" "forces" that make things happen.

Owing to his separation of ideas from power, Draper can make plausible the colonists' talk about themselves as Englishmen while carrying on an underlying struggle for power with the mother country. For Draper, the Revolution was the consequence not of "intellectual exercises between rival groups of ideologues" but of "something of longer range and deeper significance." He often goes out of his way to stress that "no ideological factors entered into" the controversies that the colonists had with their governors or with the home government. Even at those moments when ideas may have been important, moreover, they were only conjured up to meet the particular needs of an "elite [that] managed to hold on to its leadership and directed the Revolution where it wanted it to go." In fact, no ideas at all were really required until the very eve of the Revolution. "If power, not ideology, was driving the colonies on to their appointed breakaway," Draper writes, "self-awareness was not needed until the very last stage of the process."

Draper thus has little patience with seeing the Revolution either as the result of a consistent struggle over constitutional principles, in the way Edmund S. Morgan did in the 1950s, or as the consequence of a long-existing and explosive radical ideology, in the way Bernard Bailyn did in the 1960s. He has little sympathy with the Americans' fumbling efforts in the 1760s to clarify their previous experience in the empire and define their relationship with Great Britain. All he can see are what he calls the "extraordinary intellectual gymnastics" of the Americans as they "repeatedly" shifted from position to position in their debate with the British, "looking," as he puts it, "for a convenient scapegoat" to blame for the difficulties.

That the Americans "went from objecting to taxation only, to rejecting

the legislation of Parliament in all cases, to accepting the weak link with the king, to declaring absolute independence" is not, however, a sign of flightiness or inconsistency, as Draper implies. It was an indication of the seriousness with which the Americans attempted to respond to the British arguments and to explain their previous experience in the empire while clinging consistently to their basic position staked out clearly by the Stamp Act Congress in 1765: that they could be taxed only by their several provincial legislatures.

Similarly, Draper's view of the Revolution as a struggle for power without ideological meaning cannot fully account for the extraordinary nature of the popular ideas and passions that possessed the colonists by the early 1770s. He knows that many ordinary colonists were "trigger-ready" by 1775, but the mindless drive for power cannot really explain why. Nor can his argument account for the soaring aspirations and the ameliorative idealism expressed up and down the continent in 1776—aspirations and idealism that became permanently embedded in American culture.

One would never understand from Draper's account why the English radical Richard Price, in 1784, called the American Revolution, next to the birth of Christ, "the most important step in the progressive course of human improvement." Draper's dismissal of the Americans' struggle with black slavery suggests some of the pinched nature of his approach. As far as he is concerned, the white Americans, despite all their talk of being enslaved by the British, "paid little attention to the real slavery of blacks that was all around them." This misses the significance of the American Revolution in putting slavery, for the first time in American history, on the defensive. Until the Revolution, most colonists had taken slavery for granted as the most base and degraded status in a hierarchy of many un-free statuses. With the Revolution, most of the American leaders, contrary to what Draper says, suddenly devoted a great deal of attention to slavery, and concluded that it was an aberration that had to be eliminated. It is no coincidence that the first antislavery society in the world was formed in Philadelphia in 1775. Of course, by modern standards, the Revolutionaries

failed to do all that they should have done; but to stress that point exclusively ignores their substantial achievement in abolishing slavery at least in the North.

Theodore Draper's argument can account, at best, only for the American war of independence. What it cannot explain is the American Revolution.

## AFTERWORD

Draper, who has died since he wrote this book on the American Revolution, was not alone in disparaging the role of ideas in human behavior. Many historians likewise play down the influence of ideas in history. Those tough-minded historians of the first half of the twentieth century who especially influenced Draper always believed that ideas never counted for much in the movement of events. "What matters most," declared Lewis Namier, the hard-nosed historian who dominated British history writing in the 1930s and 1940s, "is the underlying emotions, the music, to which ideas are a mere libretto, often of a very inferior kind." These early twentieth-century historians knew that ideas existed, but they tended to dismiss them as propaganda, as manipulated rationalizations covering more deep-lying motives, which were usually economic. Ideas, they said, could not realistically be considered as motives for action, as causes of events.

Even if this realist or materialist position is true, however, ideas are still important for explaining human behavior. Although ideas may not be motives for our actions, they are nevertheless the constant accompaniment of our actions. There is no human behavior without ideas. Ideas give meaning to our actions, and there is almost nothing that we humans do that we do not attribute meaning to. We give meaning to even our simplest actions, a wink, for example, and these meanings—our ideas—are part and parcel of our actions. These meanings or ideas are the means by

which we perceive, understand, judge, or manipulate our experiences and our lives. They make our behavior not just comprehensible but possible. We have a human need to make our actions meaningful.

Although we have to give meaning to nearly everything we do, we are not free at any moment to give whatever meaning we wish to our behavior. The meanings we give to our behavior are necessarily public ones, and they are defined and delimited by the conventions and language of the culture at that time. It is in this sense that the culture creates behavior. It does so by forcing us to describe our behavior in its terms. The definitions and meanings that we seek to give to our behavior cannot be random or unconstrained, which is why the concept of "propaganda" as freely manipulated meanings is flawed. Our actions thus tend to be circumscribed by the ways we can make them meaningful, and they are meaningful only publicly, only with respect to an inherited system of conventions and values.

What is "liberal" or "tyrannical," "democratic" or "aristocratic" is determined by this cultural structure of meanings. Our intellectual life, like that of participants in the past, is made up of struggles over getting people to accept different meanings of experience. The stakes are always high because what we cannot make meaningful—cannot conceive, or legitimate, or persuade other people to accept—in some basic sense we cannot do. What is permissible culturally affects what is permissible socially or politically, so that even if ideas may not be motives for behavior, as the realists and materialists like Draper tell us, they do affect and control behavior.

That is why Draper's account of a struggle for power without ideas is so limited.

# 13.

# HISTORY AND HERITAGE

*American Scripture: Making the Declaration of Independence*
by Pauline Maier (New York: Knopf, 1997)

*The New York Review of Books*, August 14, 1997

S CHOLARS WHO TALK about America's "civic religion" often don't appreciate the half of it. Not only have we Americans turned profane political beliefs into a hallowed religious-like creed, but we have transformed very secular and temporal documents into sublime sacred scriptures. We have even built a temple to preserve and display the great documents consecrating the founding of the American creed: the Declaration of Independence, the Constitution, and the Bill of Rights. At the National Archives in Washington, D.C., these holy texts are enshrined in massive, bronze-framed, bulletproof, moisture-controlled glass containers that have been drained of all harmful oxygen. During the day these "Charters of Freedom" are on display in the rotunda of the National Archives for the faithful to pay homage to, but at night the documents and their containers are lowered into a vault, of reinforced concrete and steel that is twenty-two feet deep and weighs fifty-five tons. Once inside the vault with the massive doors on top swung shut, the sacred texts, the National Archives assures us, are safe.

Pauline Maier opens her history of the making of the Declaration of Independence, the most sacred of these documents, with this vivid de-

scription of the rotunda of the National Archives. In Maier's eyes the shrine where the documents are displayed resembles nothing so much as the awesome, gilded, pre-Vatican II altars of her Catholic girlhood, raised three steps above where the worshippers assembled. The whole shrine seems to belong in a baroque church somewhere in Rome. On the altar's surface are spread out the Constitution and the Bill of Rights, but at the center of the shrine, held above the altar in what looks like a tabernacle or monstrance, is the most holy document of all: the Declaration of Independence. Every day hundreds of believers file by the altar looking up reverentially at this document, "as if it were handed down by God or were the work of superhuman men whose talents far exceeded those of any who followed them."

Maier, as an experienced student of the American Revolution, has no patience with the religious-like adoration paid to a document whose actual historical origins she has come to know so well. She is "uncomfortable," she says, "with the use of religious words and images for what are, after all, things of this world." The whole business of erecting a shrine for the worship of the Declaration of Independence strikes her as "idolatrous, and also curiously at odds with the values of the Revolution," which was suspicious of Catholic iconographic practices. More important, the Declaration of Independence seems to her to be "peculiarly unsuited" for the role that it eventually came to play in America—"as a statement of basic principles for the guidance of an established society." At the beginning, in 1776, it was not meant to be that at all.

In her book Maier wants the American people to know that the Declaration of Independence was created by human beings just like them and that they are its master, not its supplicants. She wants to liberate the Declaration from its tomb by recovering the actual historical circumstances of its creation, circumstances whose mundane nature puts the origins of the Declaration greatly at odds with the quasi-religious character it later acquired. In confronting this contradiction, Maier found herself with two different but related stories to tell: "that of the original

making of the Declaration of Independence and that of its remaking into the document most Americans know, remember, and revere." Her book is thus a classic example of the conflict between history and heritage that David Lowenthal has recently described in a superb study, *Possessed by the Past* (1996).

Maier has little sympathy with most previous analyses of the Declaration, which tended to concentrate on the ideas and the philosophies that presumably lay behind its words. She doesn't bother with hermeneutics or attempt to refute Carl Becker, Morton White, and Garry Wills, the principal scholars who have written on the Declaration in this century. These scholars, like most students of the document, she writes, "examined the Declaration for the political ideas it expressed, and then jumped from its text to the more systematic treatises of eighteenth-century European writers." Instead, she simply bypasses their often ethereal discussions of political philosophy and descends directly to "the grubby world of eighteenth-century American politics," where she has spent much of her working life. It is in that political world, she says, that an accurate understanding of the origins of the Declaration can best be found.

It turns out that the Declaration is not so extraordinary after all, that Jefferson was not as original or as important as he is sometimes pictured in drafting it, and that we don't have to know about the ideas of Jean Jacques Burlamaqui or Francis Hutcheson to comprehend it. Maier is a historian through and through, and in her expert hands the Declaration is set in its proper historical context and becomes what it was in 1776: simply "a workaday document of the Second Continental Congress" and "one of many similar documents of the time in which Americans advocated, explained, and justified Independence." Her book is contextual history at its best.

Maier begins her account with the assembling of the Second Continental Congress in May of 1775, soon after the war between the colonists and Britain broke out in April at Lexington and Concord. The

Congress quickly became the first government of the United States, and "no doubt," she says, "the strangest government we have ever had." In essence the Congress replaced the British Crown in American political life, which is why it assumed an authority far beyond what the colonists had conceded to Parliament. As a substitute for the Crown, it set out to do all the things that the king had done in the colonies, from regulating Indian affairs to borrowing money to directing the army. The confusion and the heavy tasks of government often overwhelmed the several dozen delegates from the colonies who made up the Congress. Because Congress was the entire central government for the colonies, blending legislative, executive, and judicial functions, its members ended up deciding not only major issues of policy but also the most mundane matters of administration, including whether to pay the bill submitted by a doorkeeper for his services. With only a handful of clerks to help the delegates, it is amazing that anything got done.

When the war began in April 1775, Maier writes, most Americans still favored reconciliation with Great Britain. They said they were willing to remain within the British Empire but tied as separate colonies only to the king, with Parliament having no authority over them whatsoever. How the colonists arrived at this extraordinary conclusion, anticipating by nearly two centuries what became the commonwealth theory of the British Empire, is part of the fascinating story of the imperial debate that took place over the previous decade.

The colonists had begun the debate with Britain in 1765 by declaring their opposition to Parliament's Stamp Act, convinced that they could be taxed only by their own colonial representatives. At the same time, however, they did concede that Parliament had the right to regulate their trade, as it had done since the seventeenth century. The British responded with their assertion of the sovereignty of Parliament: that Parliament's authority was supreme, final, and indivisible. As the Declaratory Act of 1766 stated, it could bind the colonies "in all cases whatsoever." When the colonists continued to try to divide Parliament's authority, denying its

right to tax them but allowing its right to regulate their trade, the British government became exasperated. The colonists, the British apologists said, were either entirely under Parliament's authority or entirely outside it: there was no middle ground.

By 1773–74 many of the colonists had decided that if these were the choices, they were better off being wholly outside of Parliament's authority and connected to Britain only by their common allegiance to the king. But, of course, this did not explain why the colonists in the past had recognized Parliament's right to regulate their trade; the best the First Continental Congress could do in 1774 was to slip in a grant of power to Parliament to regulate their trade "from the necessity of the case." By 1775 many colonists had repudiated even that necessity, which is why James Wilson of Pennsylvania made the seemingly absurd suggestion that regulation of trade be made part of the king's prerogative powers; it seemed the only way of consistently denying Parliament's authority and still meaningfully remaining in a royal commercial empire.

In her recounting of the escalating imperial controversy, Maier does not have much sympathy for the British position. She concentrates on the detailed setting of the American side of the debate, and the British get short shrift. She dismisses the king as being "stubborn, not especially imaginative, and temperamentally disinclined to think through the careful arguments colonists posed," and describes British policy as persistently "wrongheaded." Perhaps a more extensive inquiry into the British position might have shifted her sympathies somewhat and made clearer why the British acted as they did. The British government after all was in desperate need of money to support its newly enlarged American empire and naturally looked to the colonists to give it some help. For nearly a decade the government had appeased the colonists and had backed away from one colonial protest after another until it felt it could retreat no more.

Although Maier does not describe the British with much depth, she more than makes up for this by her rich account of the American position. Her most important contribution to our understanding of the origins of

the Declaration is her long second chapter on "The 'Other' Declarations of Independence." In her research she uncovered at least ninety different declarations of independence that Americans in the colonies (later states) and localities adopted between April and July of 1776, most of which have been forgotten under the influence of our national obsession with the Continental Congress's Declaration of Independence. These declarations were issued by a wide variety of groups and institutions: Massachusetts town meetings, New York mechanics, Pennsylvania militiamen, Maryland and Virginia county conventions, and South Carolina grand juries. They were very much expressions of popular feeling from the bottom up. In fact, Maier believes that these "state and local 'declarations of Independence' offer the best opportunity to hear the voice of the people from the spring of 1776 that we are likely to get."

In persuasive detail Maier demonstrates that these many addresses and declarations had many precedents in English history, the most important being, of course, the English Declaration of Rights of 1688–89. The seventeenth-century English Declaration had a particular significance for Americans in 1776 because it not only formally ended the reign of James II but justified that outcome by making a series of accusations against the king. Many Americans, including Jefferson in his preamble for the Virginia constitution, used the English Declaration as a model and sought to bring the same kinds of charges against George III as had been brought against James II.

In all of their various declarations and resolutions on independence issued between April and July 1776, the Americans were self-consciously concerned, as their ancestors had been in 1689, to justify legally their break from the Crown. Although these documents often differed from one another in form and style, their contents were remarkably similar. They tended to cite the same brief set of oppressions to explain why independence from Britain was necessary. Although the provincial and local declarations usually singled out for scorn Parliament's claim to make laws to bind the colonists "in all cases whatsoever," they increasingly focused on

the actions of the king, the king being the only link many Americans still thought remained between the colonies and Great Britain. They indicted the king for rejecting their petitions, for waging war on them, for hiring German mercenaries, and for declaring that they were in a state of rebellion and out of the Crown's protection. In the end, the states and localities justified their separation from Britain by the natural laws of self-preservation and by the king's breaking of the presumed contract between ruler and people.

Although the central purpose of Maier's book is to explain the origins not of the Revolution but of the Declaration of Independence, she cannot help perceiving in these dozens of state and local resolutions and declarations the reasons why the Americans revolted from Great Britain in 1776. Although often legalistic in style, these documents were actually personal and historical in character; they showed how and why the men who drafted and adopted them had become converted to independence. "Nothing," she writes, "—certainly not the Declaration of Independence Congress set about editing on July 2—provides a better explanation of why the American people finally chose to leave the British Empire and to take up the reins of government themselves."

This is a remarkable statement, for it assumes an old-fashioned mode of historical explanation that most twentieth-century historians, from Charles Beard to Lewis Namier, have disparaged: namely, the view that formal public documents provide the best historical evidence of why people acted as they did. No doubt Maier's suggestion that the formal addresses and declarations of these years offer the fullest explanation for the Revolution is a healthy corrective in our current cynical age where apparently nothing can be taken at face value. But were there no other motivations, no other sources, for the Revolution than what Americans stated in these formal documents? George III, royal officials, and American Tories certainly thought there were many unspoken ambitions and desires lying behind the Revolutionary movement, and everything that we have learned about human psychology and latent material interests over the

past century and a half suggests that there may be some truth in what they said. Can we be sure, for example, that because the formal documents did not stress economic motives "the promise of economic freedom and expansion was never powerfully yoked to the cause of Independence"?

By assuming that the Americans always meant what they said in their many formal documents, Maier creates some awkwardness for herself. The colonists, for example, in their addresses and petitions to the British government in 1775 always stressed that as faithful subjects they had no intention of dissolving the imperial relationship and wanted nothing more than a just reconciliation with the mother country. By taking the Americans at their word and emphasizing their persistent loyalty and desires for reconciliation, Maier naturally finds that their eventual decision for independence must have been a "difficult" one. She tries to account for this difficulty by suggesting the colonists feared cutting loose from a nation whose values and institutions they had a strong inherited reverence for.

This means that she has to downplay Thomas Paine's *Common Sense,* published in January 1776, with its excited call for independence and its vicious assault on the British constitution. Her ninety provincial and local documents, she says, suggest that "Paine's influence was more modest than he claimed and than his more enthusiastic admirers assume." Then, however, Maier has to admit that much of Paine's case against monarchy had been made in the colonial press or pulpits over the previous six years— but not, of course, in any of the formal documents or declarations issued by the colonists in these years.

This discrepancy between what the formal public documents were saying and what other voices in the culture were saying is a problem that Maier, in her efforts to explain the Revolution, repeatedly stumbles over or evades. She finds, for example, that in the many state and local declarations "concern for American 'virtue,' so much emphasized by recent historians, was a distinctly minor theme." But, of course, it was not a minor theme for many other writers faced with the social and moral implications

of establishing republics. By concentrating almost exclusively on the formal public declarations of independence that necessarily tended to be consensus building in character, Maier has no way of accounting for the passionate revulsions and melioristic aspirations expressed in other kinds of documents.

But these difficulties in explaining the Revolution do not ultimately detract from Maier's main task of explaining the Declaration of Independence. In that task she has succeeded superbly. She has put together as complete and as accurate an account of how the Declaration was written as we are ever likely to get. She shows that the participants' later recollections are full of mistakes, and she demonstrates convincingly that the Declaration was not the work of a single talented writer but the product of many busy men working under very tight time constraints.

Only on June 11, 1776, did Congress appoint the drafting committee. Jefferson and John Adams dominated the committee, with Jefferson writing the initial draft, but the other committee members—Roger Sherman, Robert R. Livingston, and Benjamin Franklin—also made contributions. And most important, writes Maier, the Congress itself "by an act of group editing that has to be one of the great marvels of history" turned the committee's draft into a distinguished document.

Jefferson worked fast, drawing on the draft preamble for the Virginia constitution that he had just completed, which itself was based on the English Declaration of Rights of 1689, and on a preliminary version of the Virginia Declaration of Rights recently drafted by George Mason. Maier points out quite rightly that the eighteenth century had little of our modern striving for novelty or our aversion to imitation: "Achievement lay instead in the creative adaptation of preexisting models to different circumstances." So Jefferson had no inhibitions in borrowing from himself and others.

According to Maier, he would have benefited from paying more attention to the other declarations of independence, which had the good sense to realize that less is often better. To justify American independence,

Jefferson thought he had to cite as many injuries and usurpations that George III had inflicted on the colonists as he could. Some of his twenty-one charges against the king were so vague and obscure that his draft "left observers, then and now, scrambling to figure out what it was talking about." Most extraordinary was Jefferson's accusation that George III was solely responsible for the persistence of the slave trade, which, says Maier, Jefferson meant "to be the emotional climax of his case against the King." Adams later recalled that he thought that Jefferson's indictment of the king was "too personal" and "too passionate, too much like scolding, for so grave and solemn a document," but he made very few changes in the draft at the time. Maier is less deferential: she is sure that the more focused and more concise grassroots resolutions of the states and localities actually offered a more effective case for independence than Jefferson had.

Jefferson's preamble with its ringing phrases about equality and rights is what we today most remember and care about; in fact, the preamble alone is what has made the Declaration the most sacred of all American political documents. For this reason, modern scholars have tended to ignore the charges against the king and to focus on the preamble, treating it as high philosophy and looking for its sources in every conceivable corner of the intellectual world of eighteenth-century Europe. Maier knows better; she knows that the Declaration was not a philosophical but a political and constitutional document, and she finds the sources of its preamble in the writings of contemporary Americans, especially in George Mason's draft of the Virginia Declaration of Rights. There was nothing new, says Maier, in what Jefferson said. All of the sentiments that Jefferson so eloquently expressed—from "created equal" to "the pursuit of happiness"—were "absolutely conventional among Americans of his time."

On June 28, Congress received the committee's draft, and on July 2, after actually affirming that the colonies were free and independent states, it began revising it. It was not an easy time for editing documents. The British army had just landed on Staten Island, and the Congress had a

multitude of tasks to attend to, including deciding the wages and rum allowance that shipwrights sent to Lake Champlain would receive. We know nothing of how the members of Congress went about their editing, only the results. Congress eliminated fully a quarter of Jefferson's text, including his long outlandish passage on the slave trade, and generally moderated his harsh claims.

All in all, Maier believes that the members of Congress did a remarkable job of compressing and ,improving Jefferson's text. "By exercising their intelligence, political good sense, and a discerning sense of language, the delegates managed to make the Declaration at once more accurate and more consonant with the convictions of their constituents, and to enhance both its power and its eloquence." Jefferson, of course, never saw it that way. He was angry at the cuts and for the rest of his life insisted on the superiority of his original draft.

Maier devotes the final chapter of her book to the ways the Declaration developed in the half century or so following 1776 into the moral standard of the nation. At first, with independence established and with no need any longer to explain how and why British authority had ended, the document was all but forgotten. Indeed, Mason's draft of the Virginia Declaration of Rights seems to have had more impact on Revolutionary constitution makers than the Declaration of Independence. Certainly no one initially saw the Declaration as a classic statement of political principles. Only in the 1790s, with the emergence of the bitter partisan politics between the Federalists and the Jefferson-led Republicans, did the Declaration begin to be celebrated as a great founding document.

Because the Federalists dominated most local celebrations of the Fourth of July, the Republicans began holding their own celebrations marked by readings of the Declaration that emphasized Jefferson's role in its creation. Over the next several decades not only did Americans become increasingly familiar with the language of the Declaration, but they came to cherish that language to the point where they were willing to fight over who was responsible for it. By the early nineteenth century people were

much more interested in individual creativity and originality than they had been in the eighteenth century. Suddenly the authorship of the Declaration assumed an importance that it had not had earlier.

During the 1820s a new generation of Americans anxiously began recovering and preserving remnants of the Revolutionary past that seemed to be rapidly passing away. As one of the longest lived Revolutionaries, Jefferson was well aware of what was happening, and he actively fostered this new dedication to the past, particularly the new interest in the writing of the Declaration of Independence. He remained concerned with all aspects of the Declaration, and over the decades he wrote hundreds of letters in response to requests for details on its creation. Gradually he came to see his writing of the Declaration as a justification of his life's work; and in 1826, the last year of his life, he proposed that his tomb should list "Author of the Declaration of Independence" as the first of what he believed were his three great achievements, the others being his drafting of the Virginia Statute of Religious Freedom and his founding of the University of Virginia. By then Jefferson had come to realize that the Declaration had assumed a quasi-religious character and that small things, such as his writing desk, had become holy objects "like the relics of saints."

As Americans began sanctifying Jefferson and his Declaration, they increasingly concentrated on its preamble, particularly on the phrase "all men are created equal." Workers, farmers, and women's rights advocates began using the Declaration to justify their quests for equality and their opposition to the tyranny of others. The most powerful invocations of the Declaration, however, were made by the opponents of slavery who stressed what William Lloyd Garrison called the "horrible inconsistency" between the Declaration's professions of liberty and equality and America's continuance of slavery. This in turn provoked the defenders of slavery, like John C. Calhoun of South Carolina, to claim that there was "not a word of truth" in the Declaration's notion that all men were created equal. By the 1850s antislave politicians like Abraham Lincoln had come to believe

that the equality phrase in the Declaration was "the father of all moral principles" and the basic "axiom" of a free society. Maier admits that in many respects the Southern defenders of slavery often offered a more historically accurate understanding of the Declaration than did slavery's opponents. Lincoln's "version of what the founders meant," for example, "was full of wishful suppositions."

But whether it was bad history or not, Lincoln's appeal to equality in the Declaration as the moral standard for Americans was not, in Maier's convincing view, a single-handed sleight of hand foisted on the nation, as Willmoore Kendall, M. E. Bradford, and Garry Wills have argued; rather it was the natural consequence of the ways many Americans over the previous generation had used the ideal of equality to advance a variety of causes. Lincoln by himself no more gave the nation a new past than Jefferson by himself created the Declaration of Independence. The Declaration, Maier says, belongs to the whole culture that continually reinterprets it; "its meaning changes as new groups and new causes claim its mantle, constantly reopening the issue of what the nation's 'founding principles' demand." Of course, these changing meanings of the Declaration, like Lincoln's "wishful suppositions," constitute the heritage that distorts and violates the authentic history of the document that Maier, as a good critical historian, hopes to promote. To what extent should critical history try to undermine this kind of moralizing heritage that Maier analyzes? Her book raises the question but does not explicitly answer it.

In the last pages of her book, Maier's tone in criticizing the shrine in the National Archives becomes more openly strident and angry. Not only does the shrine have nothing whatsoever to do with the actual history of the Revolution, but it harms our ability to act in the present. "The symbolism is all wrong," she says; "it suggests a tradition locked in a glorious but dead past, reinforces the passive instincts of an anti-political age, and undercuts the acknowledgment and exercise of public responsibilities essential to the survival of the republic and its ideals." She wants us to realize that the vitality of the Declaration lies in our readiness to discuss its

implications and in our ongoing politics, "not in the mummified paper curiosities lying in state at the Archives," and "not in the worship of false gods who are at odds with our eighteenth-century origins."

This seems harsh. Can we have a civic religion without relics? Perhaps Maier ought to have a little more compassion for a people who lack common origins as well as most of the other ordinary attributes of nationhood. At the outset, she pointed out that "the original, signed texts of the Declaration of Independence and, to a lesser extent, the Constitution have become for the United States what Lenin's body was for the Soviet Union, a tangible remnant of the revolution to which its children can still cling." With the collapse of the Soviet Union, however, some Russians are now suggesting that Lenin should be finally buried. By contrast, it hardly seems a symbol of decadence or weakness that many Americans want to see the original texts of the documents whose principles and traditions hold them together. Surely no country's sense of itself as a cohesive nation is ever so strong that it can do without at least a few tangible symbols of identity and purpose. Paying homage to eloquently composed historical documents seems a rather innocuous way for people to maintain their heritage and affirm their nationhood. Instead of lamenting such symbolism, perhaps we ought to be glad that there are some Americans still drawn to seeing these remnants of our Revolution. And a good many of them, we may suspect, come to see them not in a spirit of abject veneration but just to get an idea of what they looked like when they were written.


## AFTERWORD

In her book Maier certainly exposed the tension that exists between history and heritage (or memory). She was so committed to critical contextual history—in getting the story of 1776 right—that she has no sympathy whatsoever with the symbolic memory that has grown up around

Jefferson over the past two centuries. She cannot tolerate the invented notion that Jefferson was the "author" of the Declaration, and she has little patience with what later generations of Americans have done in distorting the actual historical origins of the Declaration, in glossing, expanding, and changing its original historical meaning—in other words, creating the popular heritage that presently surrounds the Declaration. She describes all the ways subsequent generations embellished, misused, and refashioned the original historical character of the Declaration, and criticizes all of them. As we have seen, Maier even condemns Abraham Lincoln's use of the Declaration to condemn slavery as bad history. "Lincoln's view of the past . . . ," she writes, "was a product of political controversy, not research, and his version of what the founders meant was full of wishful suppositions."

Correcting the heritage that distorts and violates the authentic history of persons and documents in the past is presumably what critical historians are supposed to do. That may be appropriate when we are correcting obvious myths like the stories of Parson Weems about George Washington. But what about the uses that Lincoln and Martin Luther King, Jr., made of Jefferson and his statements about equality? By the precise standards of critical history, these uses were part of a false heritage that it is presumably the responsibility of historians to correct.

Yet these distorted heritages are precisely what many people want and perhaps need in order to keep the past alive and meaningful. Should we critical historians tamper with this popular memory? Can we really cut Jefferson and the other Founding Fathers loose from the present without losing something very valuable to the culture? Is it even possible to do so? Historian Nell Painter discovered this problem in presenting her revisionist and historically accurate portrait of the famous ex-slave and abolitionist preacher Sojourner Truth. Painter came to realize that audiences and readers did not want to hear about her revisions, however historically accurate they were, especially her evidence that Sojourner Truth never uttered the famous remark "A'n't I a woman?" And at the end of her book

*Sojourner Truth: A Life, a Symbol* (1996), Painter herself seems to concede that heritage is more important than history. "The symbol of Sojourner Truth," she says, "is stronger and more essential in our culture than the complicated historic person. . . . The symbol we require in our public life still triumphs over scholarship."

This was the message conveyed by the newspaper editor in the movie *The Man Who Shot Liberty Valance* (1962), who said, "When the legend becomes fact, print the legend." We haven't yet worked out the precise role of critical history in the culture.

# 14.

# COMPARATIVE HISTORY

*The Americas in the Age of Revolution, 1750–1850,*
by Lester D. Langley (New Haven: Yale University Press, 1997)

*The New York Review of Books,* November 20, 1997

H ISTORIANS HAVE BECOME more cosmopolitan these days. Many of them have broadened their horizons and have begun to escape from the traditional preoccupation with their own national pasts. Historians of the United States in particular have become increasingly defensive about their long-existing habit of interpreting America's past in terms of what is called exceptionalism. Indeed, some historians have come to think of American exceptionalism as a kind of bogey that must be exorcised from the American historical profession and indeed from the culture at large.

For these historians American exceptionalism has not meant merely that the United States has been different from other countries. All nations are different from one another, and all have unique histories. But Americans seem to have exaggerated their sense of uniqueness. They have tended to think of their nation not just as different but as specially or providentially blessed, as somehow free from the larger tendencies of history and the common fate of nations.

Since the late 1960s this traditional belief in American exceptionalism has eroded in a variety of ways. Many intellectuals have concluded that

the United States no longer has a divinely consecrated place in the vanguard of history. The country's history does not seem exceptional after all: the United States is not exempt from the constraints and contingencies of history. The conflict in Vietnam convinced many that the moral character of the United States was not different from that of other nations. Americans, it seemed, no longer had any uniquely transcendent part to play in the world in promoting liberty and democracy. At the same time, America's sense of difference from Europe, on which its exceptionalism was originally founded, has slowly disappeared as European nations have attained standards of living and degrees of freedom and democratic political stability that are equal to, if not higher than, those of the United States. Even the conservative celebrator of America Irving Kristol admits that America now is "a middle-aged nation," not all that different from the older nations of England and France. "American exceptionalism," he says, is virtually over. "We are now a world power, and a world power is not a 'city on a hill,' a 'light unto the nations'—phrases that, with every passing year, ring more hollow." For the first time in our history, we Americans are confronting the fact that the United States may be just another nation among nations without any special messianic destiny.

Without its sense of exceptionalism, American history is losing much of its former close ties to the nation. Throughout the Western world the traditional role of history was to promote a sense of nationhood. But with a weakening of nationalism and the development of more critical and less chauvinistic kinds of history over the past several decades, that role is changing. For the most part, history is no longer designed to inculcate patriotism, build a national identity, and turn immigrants into citizens. Instead, many historians have begun emphasizing racial, ethnic, and gender diversity, which has tended to dilute a unified sense of American identity. Some American intellectuals are even promoting a new intellectual globalism that seeks to transcend all national loyalties and even the idea of national citizenship. Some, such as the philosopher Martha Nussbaum, argue for a civic education that cultivates a citizenship of all

humanity, not of a particular nation. Since national identity is "a morally irrelevant characteristic," students should be taught that their "primary allegiance is to the community of human beings in the entire world."

Although these sorts of shifts in perspective may not be the only force explaining the growing cosmopolitanism of historians, there is no denying the recent broadening of historical scholarship. Historians of the United States no longer confine themselves to the nation's borders; they now increasingly see the past of the United States as part of the larger history of the Atlantic world, if not of the entire globe. Although the concept of an Atlantic civilization goes back at least to the eighteenth century, it was only in the Cold War years immediately following World War II that historians like R. R. Palmer and Jacques Godechot attempted to fill it out and develop it historically. Yet it is only in the past several decades that dozens of historians have begun to make the idea of America's involvement in a larger Atlantic world central to their work.

Many historians of colonial America, for example, no longer focus exclusively on the thirteen continental British colonies that became the United States in 1776. Many now place the history of the United States within the context of the whole Atlantic basin, including Western Europe, West Africa, the Caribbean and South America, and the rest of North America. See, for instance, *Atlantic America, 1492–1800*, the first volume of D. W. Meinig's *The Shaping of America* (1986), which seeks to set the history of the United States within the broadest possible geographical perspective. Subjects such as the history of the slave trade, slavery, and African American assimilation can no longer be understood within the confines of what became the continental United States. We now have to range from villages along the Gold Coast of Africa to the Cape Verde islands to Curaçao, Martinique, and Barbados to New Orleans, Saint Augustine, and the Chesapeake, dealing with the colonies and trade routes of five different European states in the Atlantic world.

Since George Bancroft wrote his ten-volume history in the early nine-

teenth century, historians of early America have investigated the American colonial past as a means of understanding the origins of the United States; now many of them study American colonial history as simply a vital part of the pan-Atlantic system in the premodern era. As nationhood has receded in importance, historians have become less interested in early America for its own sake and more for what it reveals about the ways premodern Western society became modern.

Perhaps the most important consequence of this broadened perspective for American colonial history has been its embrace of the peoples of Hispanic America. Some early American historians like Mathew Mulcahy and Russell R. Menard have called for entirely new conceptions of America's colonial past, new conceptions that would "think of colonial history as a history of all of the Americas." Many would now like to reintroduce the hemispheric perspective that historian Herbert E. Bolton tried and failed to make stick in the 1930s—a perspective that placed United States history in a comparative framework with Canada, Mexico, the Caribbean, and the countries of South America.

Some historians have argued that the history of Santa Fe in 1776 is just as important to American cultural identity as the history of Boston in 1776. As exaggerated as some of these proposals might at times appear, most are not the idle chatter of a few multicultural-minded historians. In fact, the Institute of Early American History and Culture in Williamsburg, the center for early American studies in America and the publisher of the leading journal in the field, the *William and Mary Quarterly*, announced in 1994 that it planned "to diversify its agenda" by reaching beyond its traditional commitment to study the British North American colonies in order to investigate the other peoples of the Atlantic world and especially those of Hispanic America. Early American historians now have concerns other than simply the origins of the United States.

With these expanded horizons and the weakening of the belief in American exceptionalism, early American historians in particular have

inevitably become more interested in comparing what happened in North America with what happened elsewhere in the Western Hemisphere. British America was not the only place in this hemisphere that experienced encounters between European colonizers and indigenous peoples or that imported African slaves or that broke away in revolt from a European imperial power.

The history of slavery and race relations in America and other parts of the Western Hemisphere has been the subject that has been most thoroughly and richly compared—beginning with Frank Tannenbaum's *Slave and Citizen: The Negro in the Americas* of 1946 and continuing up to the more recent comparative studies of both slavery and abolitionism by Stanley Elkins, David B. Davis, Herbert Klein, Eugene Genovese, Carl Degler, Seymour Drescher, and Robin Blackburn. Gradually, however, other experiences common to the Americas besides slavery are being studied and compared. The Johns Hopkins University has long had a Program in Atlantic History and Culture, and the John Carter Brown Library in Providence, the largest repository in the world of imprints dealing with the Americas in the colonial period, has recently established a Center for New World Comparative Studies.

Colonial historians of British America and Latin America are increasingly teaching joint comparative courses at various universities, and more and more of them are publishing works that compare developments in the two continents of the Western Hemisphere. Peggy Liss has written about the eighteenth-century networks of trade and ideas in *Atlantic Empires* (1983). Patricia Seed has compared *Ceremonies of Possession in Europe's Conquest of the New World, 1492–1640* (1995). Anthony Pagden, in his *Lords of All the World* (1995), has compared Spanish, French, and British ideologies of empire between 1500 and 1800. John H. Elliott, the Regius Professor of Modern History at Oxford, has launched a major large-scale comparison of Spain and Britain in the colonial Americas, of which several articles have appeared. And now Lester D. Langley has written a comparative

history of three revolutions in the Americas: the American Revolution in 1776, the 1791 slave revolt in the French Caribbean colony that became Haiti, and the prolonged Spanish-American struggle for independence that ended a half century later.

Langley, who is research professor of history at the University of Georgia, is the author of a half-dozen or so books on Central and South America, often in relation to the diplomatic policies of the United States. This, however, is his first full-scale attempt at comparative history, and it is one of the few comparisons of the eighteenth-century hemispheric revolutions ever made.

Writing comparative history is hard work. To compare his three revolutions Langley has had to read and digest hundreds of monographs in several languages, and then he has had to communicate all he found in some sort of comprehensible order. But how does one do this? How does one actually write comparative history? Political scientists and sociologists like John Dunn and Jack Goldstone are interested in comparing revolutions, but they have purposes distinct to their disciplines: they compare in order to compile generalizations about revolutionary social behavior, about the structural conditions that breed conflict and rebellion, which will presumably help them understand revolutions in the future. But historians have different purposes. They are interested not in making generalizations about social behavior for the future but in describing and explaining particular events in the past. How does comparative history help do this? The great French historian Marc Bloch once remarked that the comparative method was designed not to hunt out resemblances but to emphasize differences. But, of course, without resemblances there can be no meaningful comparison, even if that comparison eventually results in stressing differences.

Writing as a historian, Langley naturally tries to avoid generalizations about social behavior. Sometimes, however, he forgets his discipline and slips into asserting some sociological truths of his own, as when he says

"the true revolutionary can never admit of ambiguity or contradiction in the waging of the cause." But for the most part, as he says, he is less concerned with addressing structural matters of revolutionary causation and consequence than with "exploring the particularity" of each of his three revolutions. Consequently, he neatly divides his book into three parts and in each part presents a narrative of between sixty or seventy pages, outlining what he sees as the principal events and characteristics of each revolution. He presumably hopes that the juxtaposition of these brief narratives will illuminate and enrich our understanding of all three revolutions in a way that a description of each alone could not do. Unfortunately, his expectation is not borne out as successfully as he hoped.

The problem here is partly owing to his writing. Not only are his sometimes cryptic descriptions of the revolutions hard to follow, largely because he presumes that the reader already knows pretty much what happened, but the book itself is hard to read because of its clumsy prose and inadequate editing. It is marked throughout by dangling participles, shifting subjects, and ambiguous pronoun references. Langley also has the disconcerting habit of inserting quotations into his narrative without identifying for the reader whether they are the words of eighteenth-century participants or present-day historians.

Still, the problems of his comparative history go beyond simple matters of writing. Langley's first section deals with the American Revolution, which is described as "the revolution from above." It arose in a society that was very different from those in the other parts of the Western Hemisphere. The population in 1770 numbered a little over two million, 80 percent of whom were whites of European descent. There were about four hundred thousand black slaves, mostly located in the Southern colonies. The existence of mulattoes, mestizos, and other mixed races was scarcely acknowledged by Anglo-Americans in the mainland colonies. By 1770 the native Indians east of the Mississippi had been reduced in numbers to about one hundred thousand and had been relentlessly pushed to the edges of the expanding white settlements. (In Langley's book this kind of basic demo-

graphic data is absent or hard to come by; there is, for example, no entry for population in the index.)

Langley cites dozens of different works on the American Revolution, many with perspectives and arguments at odds with one another, but he somehow harmonizes them. He describes both the attempts of British officials in the 1760s and 1770s to overhaul the empire—partly by extracting tax revenues from the colonists—and the efforts of the patriot Whig elites to mobilize the American populace into resistance and eventually into revolution. He seems to believe that these elites were uncertain and apprehensive about the popular forces they were rallying; he makes much, for example, of the rioting and violence in the period leading up to the Revolution, which he thinks arose essentially as a result of poverty, even though eighteenth-century white Americans in general probably had the highest standard of living in the world.

At any rate, the Revolution set forth ideals of liberty and equality that had contagious effects in expanding political participation and in challenging traditional elite rule. In some parts of the country black slaves who fought the British were granted their freedom. Yet, Langley writes, because the Revolutionary leaders feared social disorder, they sought strenuously to limit the social forces unleashed by the Revolution and were largely successful in doing so. "The inequities in wealth that had characterized prerevolutionary British America remained." Their revolution thus became a "social revolution promised but left unfulfilled." By 1800 the Revolutionary leaders had no further need of a large professional army and could safely reduce the nation's military force to a small frontier constabulary. Because the people of the United States "had been mobilized for war, but the experience had not militarized society," they "escaped dictatorship or militarism" and the fate of the Latin American republics.

Langley next describes the Haitian Revolution, which he calls "the revolution from below." It began in 1790 on the French island colony of Saint Domingue with an uprising of free coloreds. The free coloreds, a

diverse group that numbered about thirty thousand and included French-educated planters, tradesmen, artisans, and small landowners, had been infected with French revolutionary principles and now demanded equality with whites. The whites numbered about forty thousand, but they were bitterly divided between the more prosperous *grands blancs* and the disorderly *petits blancs*. Beneath the whites and the free coloreds were half a million African slaves.

Neither the whites nor the free coloreds realized the extent to which their civil war was affecting the slaves. In August 1791 the slaves on the northern plains rose up, soon becoming a force of twelve thousand that began killing whites and destroying plantations. Brutal retaliation by the whites did not stop growing numbers of slaves from deserting the plantations. Confronted with this rebellion from below, French officials sought to forge an alliance between the whites and the free coloreds and sent six thousand troops to put down the rebellion. But the whites and free coloreds were so divided by factions that the fighting became worse and eventually spilled over into the Spanish portion of Hispaniola. With the end of the French monarchy and the outbreak of war between France and England in 1793, English forces invaded the island and soon became entangled in the brutal racial wars. Although the great ex-slave leader of the revolt, François-Dominique Toussaint L'Ouverture, tried to preserve a multiracial society, he could not contain the chaos that spiraled into the rebellion's eventual goal of eliminating both slavery and whites.

With the failure in 1803 of Napoléon's effort to recover the colony for France, Haiti joined the United States as the second independent state of the New World; but unlike the United States, Haiti succeeded in ending slavery and proclaiming racial equality at the moment of independence—achievements that prevented the United States from diplomatically recognizing the new republic until the time of the Civil War.

Although the Haitians had already endured more than a dozen years

of civil war and seen their land devastated and a third of their population killed, their miseries were not over. Toussaint's successors tried to conquer the Spanish portion of the island and warred among themselves for two decades. By the 1820s decades of rebellion and violence had left Haiti impoverished and militarized; yet because it was the only nation in world history ever created by slaves, it remained an inspiration to blacks in bondage everywhere in the New World.

In his third section Langley describes the many rebellions and wars of independence that broke out in Latin America in the aftermath of the American, French, and Haitian revolutions. Although there are points of similarity, in many crucial respects the Latin American colonial empire was very different from that of British North America. Out of a total population of 13.5 million in Latin America in 1800, there were 3.5 million whites, most of whom were American-born (creoles); there were only about 30,000 Spanish-born (*peninsulares*), who were sent out by the Crown to staff the offices of the imperial bureaucracy. Although many creoles managed to secure a share of these imperial offices, their local power remained dependent on the law and institutions radiating out from the Crown in Spain. Unlike the American politicians in the British colonies, these creole leaders in Latin America never developed popular representative institutions like the North American colonial assemblies that existed outside the imperial bureaucracy and contested its authority.

Yet the Latin American revolutions originated in circumstances similar to those that precipitated resistance and revolution in British North America; they were touched off by the attempts of Spanish officials both to tighten their control over and to raise revenues from their empire during the last third of the eighteenth century. Although the Spanish creole elites were as angry at the new taxes and the arbitrariness of the imperial reforms as the British-American patriots were, they were reluctant to resist imperial authority too directly and to move toward independence in

the relatively aggressive manner of the British-American leaders. Unlike the North American leaders, they were a minority amid a mass of mestizos, mulattoes, Indians, and slaves whose passions they feared exciting. Despite being inspired by the example of the successful North American revolution against imperial authority, they also knew from the experience of Haiti the dangers of arousing a revolution from below.

Yet Napoléon's invasion of Spain and his removal of the Spanish king from the throne in 1807–8 made change inevitable and aroused calls for independence. Still, the creoles hesitated. Liberators like Simón Bolívar and José de San Martín realized they could never win the struggle for independence without mobilizing the lower orders of slaves, Indians, and those of mixed descent; yet they also feared that the social consequences of such a mobilization might make the costs of independence too high. So the creole elites equivocated and took away privileges and rights even as they promised them, and repressed the lower orders even as they freed them.

By 1826 both Spain and Portugal were finally driven from the New World, with Spain retaining in America only the islands of Cuba and Puerto Rico. Seventeen Spanish-American states and Brazil achieved independence, but their revolution, says Langley, became "the revolution denied." The initial calls for liberty ended with desperate searches for authority. Successive Latin American leaders realized that they could contain the chaos and violence released by independence only by granting military authority to local chieftains or caudillos. Latin America, Bolívar concluded on the eve of his death, was "ungovernable." Order could be maintained only by force.

In a fourth part of his book, which is titled "The Revolutionary Legacy," Langley assesses the consequences of the various revolutions up to the mid-nineteenth century. Perhaps because he wants to expose the fiction of exceptionalism that Americans invented for themselves, he sometimes seems harsher in his judgments of the American Revolution

and the United States than he is of the other hemispheric revolutions and states. What troubles him especially (and many other historians these days) is the failure of the American Revolutionaries to abolish slavery entirely and to establish a truly democratic, equal, and pluralistic society. The Revolutionary leaders should have known better, but nevertheless they went ahead and "excluded women and minorities from any meaningful participation in political life." Langley seems implicitly to be suggesting some sort of utopian ideal against which he measures past American society. Thus he emphasizes "the persistence of impoverishment" and inequality in Jacksonian America. But one wonders: poor and unequal compared to what? To other nations in 1830? Or to the present? Or to what ought to be? Just how is comparative history supposed to work?

Langley doesn't see much good in what he calls Tocqueville's America. The market economy may have appeared to rest on voluntary labor, but it was "in actuality a subtler form of coercion" than the indentured servitude it had done away with. (He does concede, however, that the labor in the market economy was not as bad as slavery.) The political leaders were hypocritical and cynical: they made up myths to hide the sins and inequities of the society and set up political parties as a democratic sham, "the surest means of keeping government out of the hands of the vaunted common man." Yet most historians have asserted the contrary: that political parties, for all their failings, were the means by which America became the most democratic nation in the nineteenth-century world.

In Langley's view, the early American elites, including Jefferson, not only were deceitful in their treatment of the Indians but also hoodwinked the mass of whites about the western lands, which, Langley says, "disproportionately benefited the few"; the political leaders were able "to persuade the public that national expansion was for the people, not the developers." Apparently, Langley thinks that a few developers made killings in western lands at the expense of all those hundreds of thousands of

settlers and squatters—even though, in fact, most developers went bankrupt while the settlers steadily refused to pay what was asked for the lands and indeed eventually in 1862 pressured the government simply to give the land away.

Although Langley admits that the postrevolutionary United States was notably more successful than Haiti or Spanish America in integrating "disparate and conflictive social groups" into a common citizenry, he still finds fault with Jacksonian America for its exclusion of women, Indians, and blacks from the full benefits of the society. He suggests (no doubt correctly) that the Civil War might have been avoided if the U.S. leaders had behaved differently and abolished slavery everywhere and had compelled the society to live up to its revolutionary promises by including the dispossessed within its ranks. Langley seems to believe that both the North and South American leaders throughout the entire period had more freedom of choice than they in fact had. Only by minimizing the powerful cultural and other historical circumstances impinging on the political leaders can he accuse these leaders, as he does, of making "the wrong choices at independence." It is always easier in retrospect to know what went wrong.

No doubt Americans in the early nineteenth century wanted to exclude blacks and Indians from their society as a solution to the problems of racial mixture and assimilation. But the policies of excluding and removing different "others" were not improvisations of the moment; their cultural sources went way back in European and American history. Patricia Seed's comparative history of the different ways the European states took possession of the New World in the sixteenth and seventeenth centuries points out that from the very beginning of colonization in America, English culture tended to dispossess and exclude the non-English by building actual and psychological fences between people and by assuming that property belonged only to those who farmed and improved it. Such deeply rooted ethnocentric habits of mind were not eas-

ily overcome and were still very much present in Anglo-American culture two centuries later.

Comparative history, such as that in Seed's book, can help us see things that we otherwise might miss. But Langley doesn't clearly explain what he hoped his own comparative method would accomplish. He has told three stories one after another in all their particularity, but he has a great deal of trouble, especially in his painfully contorted introduction, in explaining what all these particularities add up to. He notes the importance of theory for comparative studies of revolution, but he realizes that any theory applied to these revolutions would be simplistic and would miss all "the nuances of the particular." He says that his revolutions are more easily described than explained. He repeatedly laments that virtually everything about these revolutions is too complicated, ambiguous, and chaotic for explanation, and none of the prevailing theories of revolution can encompass them. He puts forward some sort of "chaos theory," involving both "local disorder" and "creative adaptability," but then immediately dismisses it as "inadequate." In frustration he suggests the weather as a metaphor or model for the revolutions, both being predictable and unpredictable at the same time. Ultimately, however, Langley concludes that the only thing the revolutions "had in common was chaos and complexity," which meant that their dynamics did not follow a linear pattern. "What explained the character of these revolutions," he writes, "was their chaotic form." The leaders who realized this could adapt creatively and be successful. Washington, for example, "won the war in the Pennsylvania countryside because he adapted to its chaotic patterns." But Bolívar failed as a postrevolutionary leader because he could no longer survive in a chaotic world.

Contending that everything is too complex, ambiguous, and chaotic for simple coherent explanation is not what we usually expect from a historical account. Certainly writing comparative history is difficult, and Langley should be commended for the great efforts he has made. But in

this case the aims and methods of comparative history remain too vague and loosely defined. More than anything else, Langley's book suggests that if the revolutions in the hemisphere are to be compared, we need a clearer approach to their similarities and differences than anything we have had so far.

## AFTERWORD

In some sense all history writing is comparative. When writing about the past, historians live in the present and thus implicitly and necessarily compare that distant different past with their present. But comparing two different societies in the past with one another is another matter altogether and one not easily accomplished, at least not by historians. Social scientists, not historians, engage in most of the historical comparisons. Such social scientists are not interested in the particularities of the past; instead, they make comparisons of past behavior in order to generate theories or models that can be used to explain or predict behavior in present-day social situations.

Historians have other purposes for their comparisons, less grand, and more particular: they want to illuminate the details of roughly similar past phenomena by setting them side by side. This works best if the past societies or phenomena to be compared are not too different from one another or too distantly separated in time. A comparison of the Ottoman Empire in the fifteenth century with the British Empire in the eighteenth century, for example, is not very enlightening, at least for a historian: the societies being compared are too different and too far apart in time. The questions such a comparison generates are sociological, not historical: What is an empire? What is the nature of imperial bureaucracies? What makes an empire strong or weakens it?

But a comparison between the Spanish and British empires in the New World can be very enlightening. They both existed roughly at the same

time and had similar experiences. Since my review was written John Elliott has completed his magisterial work *Empires of the Atlantic World: Britain and Spain in America, 1492–1830* (2006). It is a work of history, not social science, so there are no theories or models to be found. Instead, Elliott has given us a wealth of detail that shakes up traditional perspectives and throws new light on old issues. It is a superb example of how comparative history ought to be written.

# 15.

# POSTMODERN HISTORY

*The Name of War: King Philip's War and the Origins of*
*American Identity* by Jill Lepore (New York: Knopf, 1998)

*The New York Review of Books*, April 9, 1998

O NE OF THE MOST important consequences of the upheaval in the writing of American history that has taken place over the past generation has been the new attention paid to the Indians. A century ago historians of early America scarcely acknowledged their existence. In the opening paragraphs of his essay in the first issue of the *American Historical Review* in 1895, Frederick Jackson Turner set forth his entire frontier thesis for understanding the origins of the United States, and the Indians had no place in it. For Turner, the New World the Europeans came to in the seventeenth century was "virgin soil," an "unexploited wilderness" out of which American distinctiveness was born. Indeed, wrote Turner, it was "the fact of unoccupied territory in America that sets the evolution of American and European institutions in contrast."

No historian of early America would write that way anymore. Through the efforts of a squadron of scholars, the Indians have made their presence felt in early America. During the past several decades works dealing with the native peoples of North America in the colonial period have multiplied dramatically. Since the 1960s the *William and Mary Quarterly*, the principal journal in the field of early American history, has increased its

publication of articles on Indians fivefold. Some of the best historians in the United States have been turning to the indigenous peoples as a subject of research, and books on Indians in early America have begun winning prestigious prizes.

Some of this recent interest in the native peoples of America has grown out of the natural tendencies of young scholars in the historical profession to look for new and fresh topics for research. Others, like Daniel K. Richter, see in the history of the Indians an excellent means of challenging "people to stand outside their comfortable . . . assumptions and to learn unpleasant lessons from their study of the past." A historian of this sort sees himself or herself as "a *critic* of culture" whose principle task is "to illuminate conditions of the present by casting a harsh light on previous experience," something not all that hard to do in the case of the Indians.

But perhaps most important in explaining this new interest in the Indians of early America have been the changing perspectives that many recent historians have brought to bear on America's colonial past. Early American historians today are not as interested in explaining the origins of America's peculiar national character as they used to be. Many of them have lost confidence in the traditional belief that the United States has a collective identity with common origins, and they have begun to look at early American history from vantage points beyond the nation, seeing in America's colonial past something other than the beginnings of the United States. Louis Hartz a generation ago saw what such a changed perspective might mean for Americans' conception of the Indian. The neglect of the Indian, he wrote, stemmed solely from the "interior perspectives" of historians like Frederick Jackson Turner. Since it was the fate of America as a nation "to destroy and exclude the Indian, life inside it has had a dwindling contact with him. How could he then be perceived? How could he be appreciated as a problem comparable to the rise of the 'common man' or the emergence of the trusts?" But of course, said Hartz, once American historians get outside the narrow confines of the nation, "the

very fact that the Indian was thus eliminated . . . becomes a matter of very great importance."

Most historians today deny that the Indian was ever in fact eliminated, but all would agree that the Indian's story has not been as well integrated into American history as it might have been. Until recently the Indians—when written about at all—have been treated as a side issue in frontier history or given only walk-on roles in the larger drama of American history. Rarely have they been seen as central participants in American history, even when, as in the seventeenth century, they dominated much of the landscape. Although some Indian scholars, like Calvin Martin, doubt that Western-style historical methods can ever accurately convey the Indians' past, many other Indian historians, like James Merrell, believe that a blending of ethnology and history can do the job. For the writing of Indian history, says Merrell, historians need only "borrow freely from other disciplines and examine all sorts of evidence to give voice to the historically silent." But not just to the historically silent. It turns out that the voices of the historically loquacious, like the Puritans of early New England, can benefit as well from free-wheeling, multidisciplinary scholarship. Jill Lepore's fascinating book on King Philip's War is a product of just such imaginative, wide-ranging scholarship.

Although King Philip's War is the most bloody and destructive war in the history of all the American people, it began simply enough. In late January 1675, John Sassamon, a Christian Indian who had recently warned the English colonists of a possible Indian uprising, died in mysterious circumstances. Three Wampanoags close to Philip, the Wampanoag ruler, were tried for the murder of Sassamon and found guilty, and in June 1675 they were executed by Plymouth Colony. The executions touched off Indian attacks on English settlements that quickly escalated into a ferocious conflict that spread throughout large parts of southern New England. By the time Philip was shot fourteen months later in August 1676, thousands of people had been killed, both English and natives.

Indeed, the war inflicted greater casualties in proportion to population

than any other war in American history. By August 1676 twenty-five English towns, more than half of all the English communities in New England, had been destroyed, and the line of English settlement had been pushed back almost to the coast. English efforts to colonize New England over half a century were nearly wiped out. The Indian losses were even greater. Not only were thousands killed by war, starvation, or disease, but thousands more were sold to the West Indies as slaves. Even Christian Indians who had been loyal to the English were not spared. Most were removed from their "praying towns" and imprisoned on barren islands, where many died of cold and hunger. King Philip's War, concludes Lepore, "proved to be not only the most fatal war in all of American history but also one of the most merciless."

Lepore's book is not a conventional narrative history of the war. To be sure, it contains a four-page chronology of the war and here and there dwells on some of its particular incidents. But the book neither tells the story of the war nor tries to analyze systematically causes and consequences. Instead, Lepore offers us a meditation on the war, a series of reflections and speculations on what the war meant not only for the English and the Indians of the seventeenth century but also for their heirs in the nineteenth and twentieth centuries.

If there can be such a thing as postmodern history, perhaps this book can be best understood as an example of it. In the new postmodern world historians do not recount events and tell stories. Instead, they muse and ponder over the stories and accounts of events that others have told, or in the case of the Indians, have not told. In Lepore's history the writing about the war became as important as the waging of it. As she says, "War is a contest of words as much as it is a contest of wounds."

In this sort of postmodern history, culture becomes everything, and political, social, and economic forces do not count for much. Lepore never really explains why the Indians rose up in rebellion when they did. She tells us nothing about the development of the Puritans' economy in the several decades of settlement preceding the war and never mentions the

extent to which the English were exploiting Indian labor, in many cases bonded Indian labor. Nor does she emphasize the fact that this was not a war of whites against Indians but one in which whites and their Indian allies fought Indians; indeed, on a per capita basis more Indians than Puritan soldiers fought to put down Philip's rebellion.

Instead of a traditional historical account of the war, Lepore reflects on the ways people wrote about it. Hers is a history sparing of events but rich in imagination, in moral ruminations over the meaning and justice of war, and in literary and cultural theory. Indeed, rarely has a work of history stressed the dependence of reality on texts as much as this one. Lepore is less interested in happenings than in their symbolic meaning. Metaphors and images overwhelm simple statements of fact, and nothing is as it may seem on the surface. Because Lepore believes that King Philip's War was very much about language and suggests many sorts of allegories, in some sense, she says, it has never ended. "In other times, in other places, its painful wounds would be reopened, its vicious words spoken again."

Lepore spends a half-dozen pages in the preface explaining why she calls the conflict King Philip's War. This is no easy matter, since that title is, as scholars say these days, much "contested." Some think it should be called a Puritan Conquest. Others want to call it Metacom's Rebellion, which more accurately refers to Philip by his Algonquian name and more properly celebrates Indian resistance. Besides, Philip was not a king but a sachem. "War" is the most disputed of the terms. Even some of the English colonists, as the Puritan historian William Hubbard declared in 1677, thought that the "Massacres" and "barbarous inhumane Outrages" of the conflict were too base and ignoble to deserve "the Name of a War." As a recognition of "the importance of language" in understanding war, Lepore has used Hubbard's phrase as a title for her "own set of words about war."

Lepore divides her book into four parts—"Language," "War," "Bondage," and "Memory"—which define her themes of analysis and meditation.

Part One examines why so many colonists wrote so much
about King Philip's War while New England's Algonquians
wrote so little. . . . Part Two traces how boundaries were drawn
during King Philip's War, both on the physical landscape
and on the landscapes of the human body, and how the war's
cruelties were explained and justified by both sides, especially
in religious terms. Part Three contrasts New Englanders'
differing experiences of bondage during the war: captivity,
confinement, slavery. Last, Part Four analyzes how subsequent
generations of Americans have remembered King Philip's War,
most notably through *Metamora, Or, the Last of the Wampanoags,* a
wildly popular play that was performed in theaters across
America in the 1830s and 1840s.

Lepore begins her book with the Reverend William Hubbard's graphic
account of a captured Narragansett Indian being tortured by some
Mohegan Indians, who were allies of the English in the war. As Englishmen
watched, the Mohegans formed a great circle around the Narragansett and
then slowly cut off each of his fingers and toes, forcing him all the while
to sing and dance, and then they broke his legs, before finally knocking
out his brains. Lepore spends a lot of time with this gruesome scene, ana-
lyzing its implications. She correctly points out that the English prided
themselves on their gentleness in contrast to the cruel Spanish and that
some of them worried constantly about degenerating into savagery.
Nevertheless, without any evidence from Hubbard's account—indeed,
Hubbard specifically says that the English were "not delighted in blood"—
Lepore somehow convinces herself that the English spectators found the
suffering of the tortured Indian "sublimely satisfying."

It is entirely plausible, of course, that some of the English enjoyed
watching the Indian being tortured; the Narragansett after all had bragged
of killing nineteen of their countrymen. Moreover, the incident occurred
a year after the war had begun, and the English had been severely brutal-

ized by the ferocity of the fighting. Certainly, some of them committed more terrible atrocities than those committed by the Indians. Yet, as brutal and cruel as the English were during the war, they, or at least their ministers and leaders, did not condone torture of the sort Lepore describes. Indeed, that was the point Hubbard was trying to make in describing the scene.

Yet Lepore has decided that since "watching is the chief sport" of torture, the English must have enjoyed it. Only if the English enjoyed the spectacle would they jeopardize their identity as "civilized" men. And since the Puritans' worrying about losing their Englishness is a major theme of her book, it is important for her argument that the English relish such "savage" pleasures. She does concede that the English expressed disgust with the torturing, "but," she says, "the other side of disgust is desire, and, despite protestations to the contrary, clearly the English feel that too. . . . While they may find it painful to watch as a young man has his fingers sawed off, they also find it pleasurable."

As evidence for this unverifiable conclusion, Lepore cites not seventeenth-century materials but literary critic Stephen Greenblatt, who believes that disgust and "bourgeois desire" are related. Indeed, in order to analyze the war she draws on literary critics like Greenblatt and Elaine Scarry for many of the theories that she uses in place of traditional sorts of historical evidence.

Beginning a chapter with the thick description of an exemplary anecdote and then imaginatively teasing out its cultural implications is Lepore's usual technique. Her writing is always clear—mercifully she avoids the jargon of literary criticism—and many of her ruminations are fascinating and informative. Sometimes, however, she seems to carry on her musing too long. For example, on the question of whether or not John Sassamon, whose death touched off the war, was actually murdered, Lepore begins with the process by which historians usually reach conclusions. She examines the surviving evidence and weighs alternatives, finally making judgments about what happened. But after proceeding in a straightforward

fashion through the case, Lepore decides that we cannot tell who killed Sassamon. Thus, she writes, we ought to forget about the murderer and instead investigate the motive. But then she finds that the exact motive is unclear and, in fact, "may not matter." What really killed him was his status as a Christian convert and cultural mediator between the Indians and the English. "In a sense, literacy killed John Sassamon." She then spends the rest of the chapter explaining what she means by this literary explanation.

In doing so, Lepore certainly has many texts to interpret. Within eight years after the war began in 1675, the Puritans had written twenty-one different accounts of the conflict, many published in more than one edition. But since the Indians had no written language, they wrote nothing; and this is a problem. If the war was very much a war of words, Lepore asks, "Can it ever be a fair fight when only one side has access to those perfect instruments of empire, pens, paper, and printing presses?" In place of history, however, the Indians did have myths, and these oral myths, Lepore suggests, may be just as good and reliable as the constructed histories of the Europeans in preserving the past. Of course, some Indians did learn to read and write, but by acquiring literacy they lost their native language and culture and thus their Indianness. So one of the consequences of literacy, muses Lepore, may be "the death of those who acquire it." Therefore, it makes little sense, Lepore writes, to explain the native culture's "lack of written history by simply pointing to its attachment to mythical thinking." With death by literacy staring them in the face, the Indians had good reason not to write.

Lepore shows some sympathy for the extraordinary efforts of Puritan minister John Eliot to translate the Bible and other documents into a written version of Massachusett, the oral Algonquian language, in order to convert the Indians to Christianity. Eliot even frantically tried to convert Philip himself. But Sassamon was his most important convert, and Sassamon's literacy, which gave him the ability to move between both cultures, was his undoing. One rumor had Sassamon murdered by Philip

because he wrote out Philip's will and distorted the sachem's intentions. "While it may or may not be true," the story still suggests that the Wampanoags regarded Sassamon's literacy as mysterious and dangerous. "His life, and his death, serve as a metaphor for tensions that would prove fatal to the thousands of literate and nonliterate Indians who died in King Philip's War." If Sassamon had lived, Lepore speculates, he might have written his own history of the war. "On the other hand, he might not have." Maybe he "did in fact lack the kind of 'historical consciousness' that anthropologists have commonly attributed to literate peoples." "Frustratingly," she concludes, "we will never know what kind of a writer John Sassamon might have been."

Thus Lepore's analyses go, moving back and forth on the one hand, then on the other, debating with herself, suggesting alternatives and then dismissing them, pondering, speculating, and ruminating over what can or cannot be known and what cultural theory tells us. The conclusions she reaches—often that the evidence is too scanty to know anything for sure—are in many cases sound and balanced. But she is not interested in telling us her conclusions; she wants us to see, in all of its uncertainty and indeterminacy, the process of how she arrives at them. So it is not just war that is a contest of words; it is history writing too.

Although Lepore starts by emphasizing just how much some of the English wrote about the war, she later says she is more impressed with the fact that most of them wrote very little. Apparently, most felt incapable of describing the devastation of the conflict; their pain could not be expressed in language, although Lepore herself has no trouble in this respect. She finds a number of words in the English writings—"paper and books and pens and ink"—that were sometimes used metaphorically and acted "as measurements of pain and evil." The image of "blood as ink" was crucial. But ultimately only Elaine Scarry's theory about what pain does to language—"either it remains inarticulate or else the moment it first becomes articulate it silences all else"—could help Lepore resolve

"the incongruity between how much some colonists wrote about King Philip's War and how little others wrote."

The "real silence" was, of course, that of the Algonquians, who had no written language. Lepore imagines that the colonists must have been worried about what the Indians might say about the war. "Even while the English lamented their helplessness against Indian attacks," she suggests, "they took comfort in the knowledge that they controlled the pens and printing presses. . . . If war is a contest of both injuries and interpretation, the English made sure that they won the latter, even when the former was not yet assured."

When Lepore gets to the actual cruelty and bloodshed of the war, she becomes more and more excited about metaphorical speech and actions by both settlers and Indians and how literary theory can interpret them. She begins a chapter, as usual, with an exemplary anecdote, in this case with a description of a bloody Indian attack on the household of Thomas Wakely in which Wakely's house was burned, most of his family killed, and the rest taken captive. She suggests that Wakely might have saved his family if he had been willing to leave his house. But he was "too attached to his property to abandon it." It seems he had too much of that typical bourgeois attachment to possessions to know what was good for him.

In fact, says Lepore, the English tended to measure their losses by counting not just people but also property and possessions. Although Lepore concedes that the English had plenty of good practical reasons to count their cattle, crops, and houses among their losses, she suggests that the real reason was their fear of losing their cultural identity—their possessions presumably being what ultimately separated them from the Indians. But from the evidence Lepore presents, it was the Indians who should have been frightened of losing their identity. Although Lepore believes that the "Algonquians had always celebrated their detachment from goods and property," they were certainly interested in acquiring at every opportunity English blankets, clothing, hardware, and furniture.

Lepore makes a great deal of what she calls "the metaphor of naked-ness." The Indians stripped the bodies of the English naked, and although this kind of pillaging of bodies was common in the Thirty Years' War and in the English Civil War, Lepore nevertheless sees it as the stripping away of the marks of civilization and turning the English into barbarians. So when neighbors described a bloodied, severely wounded Englishwoman who had been stripped naked and partially scalped as "a frightful spectacle," they were responding not just to the woman's physical appearance but also to the fact that "she had been shorn of all emblems of piety, civility, and Englishness."

But these mutilated English bodies were not just bodies; modern cultural theory helps us see that they stood for English property as well. "Bodies were defined in relationship to houses, but houses, too, were metaphorical bodies." Thus, Lepore contends, nearly any attack on a house "could be understood metaphorically as an assault on the human body." The English who stood in doorways or ventured out of their houses during an Indian attack were often easy victims. "Open doors, then, could be like wounds on the body, the people spilling out like blood."

Apparently realizing that she may have carried her metaphor of bodies and houses too far, Lepore admits that houses did offer "very real protection" during Indian attacks. So Thomas Wakely may not have been so foolish and so bourgeois in staying in his house. Yet in the end Lepore cannot give up her notion that it was Wakely's cultural identity that kept him from fleeing. "Separated from his property, Thomas Wakely would no longer be Thomas Wakely, farmer, no longer Thomas Wakely, Englishman."

Englishmen may have understood the symbolic importance of their property, but Lepore believes they were not adept at reading the symbolic language of the Indians. She especially indicts the Puritans for being "unwilling or unable to place Indian 'cruelties' within the broader context of Algonquian culture." They should have known better, but then they did not have, as Lepore does, anthropologist Mary Douglas to help them to understand the ritualistic character of the Indians' atrocities.

"Algonquian attacks and Algonquian tortures were not random or arbitrary," writes Lepore. "On the contrary, they were deliberate and deeply symbolic." She gives as one example their burying of English captives alive accompanied by the taunt: "You English since you came into this Countrey have grown exceedingly above the Ground, let us now see how you will grow when Planted into the Ground." If the Puritans had possessed any sort of cultural sensitivity, says Lepore, they would have seen examples of such atrocities "as partial explanations for what had provoked the Indians to wage war." But the Puritans, obsessed with their own sins, ignored the symbolic meaning of these practices. "Busily interpreting Indian actions as messages from God, New England's colonists," says Lepore, "utterly failed to see Indian actions as messages from *Indians,* or even simply to pay attention to Indian explanations for the war."

When Lepore comes to indict the English for selling captured Indians into slavery in the Caribbean, she allows the modern sensibilities that infuse her study to get out of hand. Selling prisoners of war into slavery or servitude was a common practice in the seventeenth century. There were no POW camps, and armies often dealt with masses of prisoners by recruiting them into their own ranks or selling them into bondage. Although the Puritans' actions were not all that unusual and, indeed, were seen by them as merciful, Lepore can see them only in modern racial terms. Since "Indians could be enslaved, while English people could not," the enslavement of the Indians "must be considered as a critical step in the evolution toward an increasingly racialized ideology of the differences between Europeans and Indians. . . . Only because Indians are somehow less than human can they be fully enslaved in a way Europeans never could." She never mentions the fact that during the English Civil War the English likewise sold Scottish and Irish prisoners into bondage in the West Indies. It was a cruel and brutal age, and human life was a great deal cheaper than it is for us today.

Even her account of the Puritans' frightened confinement of the Christian Indians to isolated islands seems lacking in perspective. It is

worth recalling that supposedly enlightened twentieth-century Americans interned American citizens of Japanese ancestry in World War II at a time when the threat of national survival was no way comparable to that faced by the English colonists in 1675 and 1676.

One senses that Lepore wants to be fair in her judgments of Puritan and Indian behavior, but understandably her sympathies lie with the Indians. Both sides, for example, beheaded their victims and displayed the heads on poles (a common practice in European wars as well); but "unlike its English counterpart, the Algonquian practice of decapitation had religious significance," which presumably made it more defensible.

What in the end seems extraordinary about the Puritans' behavior is not their harsh treatment of the Indians but their continual agonizing and worrying about that treatment. Would that the Puritans in England had agonized as much about their savage treatment of the Irish during the Civil War. In 1644 Parliament passed an ordinance condemning to death all Irish rebels captured in England. As one historian has recently pointed out, "Throughout King Philip's War, the Puritans would never reach that point with the Indians."* Of course, in our present eyes, given what happened to the Indians in America, no amount of contextual history writing can ever morally justify the Puritans' behavior.

In her final section on memory Lepore describes the different ways subsequent Americans have remembered the war. Although by the end of the eighteenth century many white Americans had assumed that the Indians had vanished, they had not. "Instead they became increasingly integrated into the wider colonial community," many of them intermarrying with free blacks, and forming a "new Indian identity." Yet white Americans' sense that the Indians were no longer present in the Northeast gave them the security to romanticize the native peoples. They were free even to adopt some attributes of Indianness in order to assert their cul-

---

* James Drake, "Restraining Atrocity: The Conduct of King Philip's War," *New England Quarterly* 70 (1997): 50.

tural independence from the decadence of the Old World. In the past, white Americans had seen the Indians as barbarians threatening their civility; now they saw them as natural beings free from the artificial restraints and refinements of polished life. By the early nineteenth century Americans like Washington Irving were actually celebrating King Philip as a liberty-loving revolutionary. It was the famous actor Edwin Forrest in the play *Metamora,* however, who was most responsible for turning Philip into a popular American hero. For two decades in the 1830s and 1840s, his portrayal of the "Last of the Wampanoags" dominated the American theater. For twenty-five years only two seasons in Philadelphia were without a performance of *Metamora.*

As popular as Forrest's performances were, however, when he played before people who had a vested interest in removing the Indians, as was the case in Georgia in 1831, he was not at all well received. Not that *Metamora* was meant to be an indictment of the 1830s removal of the Indians to lands west of the Mississippi. Lepore argues that even those New Englanders who opposed Indian removal and applauded Forrest's play only did so because the Indians seemed to be no longer part of their lives and no longer mattered to them. Thus "*Metamora* served as an important vehicle by which white Americans came to understand Indian removal as inevitable, and Philip, newly heroized, became a central figure in the search for an American identity and an American past."

In time, the New England native peoples themselves, some of whom had earlier passed as either white or black, began "to reassert their tribal identities, and increasingly, to think of themselves as 'Indians,'" a process that has continued up to the present. In recent decades the various New England tribes have pressed for federal recognition and for the return of lost tribal lands; the success of some of them has led to their running gambling casinos and accumulating massive amounts of wealth. At the same time, many of the Indians have continued the contest over the meaning of King Philip's War that began over three centuries ago. In 1993 in a commemoration of the Great Swamp fight in which hundreds of Indians

were massacred, a Narragansett tribal historian declared, "We are Narragansetts first, and we are Americans when it is convenient." Lepore sees this statement as an attempt by the present-day Indians of New England "to preserve their Indianness as fiercely as seventeenth-century colonists once struggled to preserve their Englishness." American history turns out to be one long story of different peoples' struggling to identify themselves.

## AFTERWORD

As I suggested in the review, postmodern history is meditative and self-reflective history. It often tells us more about the historian than the events he or she is presumably recounting. Jill Lepore is an excellent stylist, and she has emerged in the past decade as a major American historian and a writer for *The New Yorker*. Perhaps she is the ideal historian for our postmodern era.

# 16.

# SATIRICAL HISTORY

*The Fabulous History of the Dismal Swamp Company:*
*A Story of George Washington's Times*
by Charles Royster (New York: Knopf, 1999)

*William and Mary Quarterly,* 3d Ser., 57 (2000)

I N THE EIGHTEENTH CENTURY the Dismal Swamp comprised a half
million acres lying between the lower James River in Virginia and
Albemarle Sound in North Carolina. Two hundred years later the swamp
had considerably shrunk in size and had become something of a tourist
attraction. Early in the twentieth century a tourist entering the Dismal
Swamp asked her guide why a swamp so filled with color, sunshine, and
bird calls was named "dismal." "There's more to it than shows just at first,
ma'am," the guide answered. "There are more sad stories about this swamp
than all the sunshine can make bright."

Charles Royster, professor of history at Louisiana State, knows more
of these sad stories than anyone, and in this strange and wonderful book
he has put together many of them from the eighteenth century for our
edification and entertainment. Most of these stories deal with the share-
holders of the eighteenth-century Dismal Swamp Company and their
relations and connections, and most of the stories are indeed sad. Although
these stories focus on Virginia and the Dismal Swamp, they range over the
entire Atlantic world: from Antigua to the Gold Coast of Africa, from the

Ohio Valley to London. And they span the era roughly coinciding with George Washington's life: from the first third of the eighteenth century to the very beginning of the nineteenth. Although this long Revolutionary era is one of the most written-about periods in American history, no history of the period like this one has ever appeared before. This history of the Dismal Swamp Company is truly fabulous—astonishing and barely believable—and it is told by Royster in the most remarkable manner. The stories of the Dismal Swamp may be sad, but Royster often makes them seem funny, at times even hilarious. There is nothing quite like this book for the eighteenth-century Virginia aristocracy; indeed, there is nothing quite like it in all American history writing.

Royster begins his history with William Byrd, who first conceived of doing something with the Dismal Swamp in his *History of the Dividing Line* in 1728. Byrd was confident that the huge swamp could be drained and made profitable without too much difficulty. Finance a company for ten years with an investment of four thousand pounds, he wrote. Start with ten slaves to dig ditches, cut down trees, make boards and shingles, grow rice and corn and hemp, and tend cattle. The slaves would feed themselves and breed, and with their profits more slaves could be bought. Byrd had "no doubt in the world" that once drained and cleared, the Dismal Swamp could become as rich as any soil in Virginia. "From all which we may safely conclude," wrote Byrd, "that each share will then be worth more than Ten times the value of the original subscription, besides the unspeakable Benefit it will prove to the Publick."

This was the dream of the Dismal Swamp, and such "Schemes of Gain" enchanted more than one eighteenth-century Virginian planter, including George Washington. From a very early age Washington was impressed with the Byrds and the Carters and the question of "how the greatest Estates we have in this colony were made." "Was it not," he asked, "by taking up & purchasing at very low rates the rich back Lands which were thought nothing in those days, but are now the most valuable lands we possess?" His answer: "Undoubtedly it was." Washington wanted land,

and he spent much of his life acquiring tens of thousands of acres in the West. But he especially had his eye on the potentialities of the Dismal Swamp. Although local people in both Virginia and North Carolina thought that the swamp was "a low sunken Morass, not fit for any of the purposes of Agriculture," Washington felt certain that it was "excessive Rich" and would "in time become the most valuable property in this Country."

Others agreed, and in 1763 twelve partners, including Washington and some of the most important men in Virginia—William Nelson, Thomas Nelson, Thomas Walker, Fielding Lewis, and speaker of the house and treasurer John Robinson, among others—formed the Dismal Swamp Company in order to drain and develop this great morass. These original partners and those to whom they subsequently resigned, transferred, bequeathed, or sold their shares in the company over the next three-quarters of a century are the main characters who make up Royster's remarkable series of stories. But there are many supporting characters as well who were connected in some way to the investors. Thus Royster is able to expand his cast of characters to include many fascinating figures on both sides of the Atlantic; he especially enjoys describing the roles of those like Robert Morris and James Wilson, who ended their lives in ruinous debts. Although the company never fulfilled its promise of great profits, dozens of hopeful speculators, including even Thomas Jefferson, who rarely ever speculated in anything, continued decade after decade to pour money into the scheme until the company finally collapsed in 1814.

Royster's stories almost exclusively concern the vicissitudes of the private lives and day-to-day private events of his characters: their births, marriages, speculations, sicknesses, wills, deaths, and suits at law. Public events like the Stamp Act, the Revolutionary War, and the formation of the Constitution remain very much in the background. And when these public events touch the lives of his characters, they have little of the impact we normally expect. The Revolutionary War, for example, is largely seen, in the words of a London merchant, as "a good Opportunity for

Business to People who are wise and skillful enough to keep their Affairs within their power."

During the past several decades the new social historians have begun stressing the private lives of people at the expense of the great headline events. Royster seems to be saying that if it is social history that is wanted, then this is it with a vengeance. Never before have the intimate lives of so many of the first families of eighteenth-century Virginia been so richly described and dissected. The book is a tour de force of historical imagination and research. Royster tells us about the size and furnishings of their houses, the lands and slaves they held, the portraits they had painted, the dowries they offered, the bills of exchange they had protested, and the incredibly entangled webs of kinsmen and relations they created through blood and marriage. As one new bride, arriving in Virginia from Philadelphia in 1761, wrote to her sister: "They are all Brothers, Sisters, or Cousins; so that if you use one person in the Colony ill, you affront all."

But Royster aims to do more than reveal the private lives of the Virginia aristocracy. He uses his stories to expose the extraordinary culture and behavior of these first families of Virginia: their soaring dreams and dashed hopes, their pretensions and follies, their many bankruptcies, their remarkable number of suicides, and even their occasional murders. We always knew that the eighteenth-century Anglo-American world was a world of financial revolutions, of banks and speculation, and fortunes made and lost. (An eighteenth-century English advice manual titled *Every Man His Own Broker* went through at least six editions by 1765.) But in Royster's history the daily preoccupations of people with their private interests are emphasized as never before.

Maybe this was the way most people then, as now, lived their lives, paying little attention to the headline events that dominate most history books. Certainly reading Royster one would scarcely realize that this aristocracy ever much cared about the political principles of liberty, virtue, and independence that they so often talked about. All that mattered to these aristocrats, Royster implies, was acquiring land, making a for-

tune, consuming conspicuously, and establishing dynasties. So the House of Burgesses' disagreement with the royal governor in 1769 over Parliament's power to tax the colonists, in which Washington took the lead, did not prevent Washington from trying at the same time to persuade the governor to give to the French and Indian War veterans two hundred thousand acres along the Ohio River. As Royster mischievously points out, Washington had a "scheme" in which he hoped to buy, at the cheapest possible rate, many of the veterans' grants without the veterans' knowing who was actually making the purchase.

This Virginia aristocratic world that Royster describes should be appalling. It is, after all, a world of corruption and cronyism, a world of shady deals and unscrupulous bargains in which everyone had his price— a world, in the words of a visiting English clergyman, of "extravagance, ostentation, and a disregard of economy." The "maxims so generally embraced" in Virginia, declared Robert Beverly in 1761, were "being in Debt & making great Promises for the future."

But in Royster's imaginative hands this world is not appalling at all. It is funny, absurd, and at times even hilarious. Royster tells his stories and describes his characters without anger or venom. There are lots of nice satiric touches and some inside jokes. Royster, for example, points out that Williamsburg after 1780, when it was no longer the Virginia state capital, rapidly decayed and became dull. "Even so, a Virginian who reluctantly followed her husband to the Mississippi Valley wrote home: 'Williams[bur]g is Paris compared to Baton Rouge,'" which, of course, is where Royster presently lives.

Royster is amused by everything. He is the sly observer who enjoys recounting how dishonest, weird, and hypocritical that eighteenth-century world was. He tell us that Alexander Macaulay, one of the managers of the Dismal Swamp Company, had a nasty habit of withdrawing funds from the company for his own use. In 1796 the managers met and "declared that no single partner—meaning Alexander Macaulay—would be allowed to draw money from the company's assets. Macaulay signed

the minutes. Three weeks later, he made his largest withdrawal, more than $8,000." In a like manner, when Royster tells us about Patrick Henry's seditious speech during the Parsons' Cause, a trial in 1763 in which ministers of the Church of England tried to recover back pay, he highlights Henry's explanation that "his sole view in engaging in the cause, and saying what he had, was to render himself popular." Then he deadpans: "Shortly after the trial, Patrick Henry was elected to the House of Burgesses." So too does Royster describe the flamboyant behavior of John Wilkes in the 1760s as having to do less about liberty and more about Wilkes's enjoying the ferment he stimulated. "He was an incomparable comedian in all he said or did," wrote Sir Nathaniel William Wraxall of Wilkes, "and he seemed to consider human life itself as a mere comedy." One could say the same about Royster. Ultimately, it is Royster's comic style that makes this history so fascinating, that keeps it from being simply a sordid tale of greed and failure.

It is a style that reminds one of Evelyn Waugh, the Waugh of the early comic novels. Indeed, this is a history of the eighteenth-century Virginia aristocracy as Waugh might have written it. There is the same view of an aristocratic world gone slightly mad; the same concentration on the incongruities and absurdities of human behavior; the same ambiguous detachment toward the characters in the story; the same deadpan descriptions of bizarre happenings; the same mordant irony, and the same humorous treatment of the most appalling incidents and circumstances. So Royster, after recounting the complicated problems government contractor Anthony Bacon had with the Mayne brothers—one of whom, Sir William, was his critic, the other, Robert, a fellow war contractor—concludes with a straight face that "Bacon had no need to worry about what Sir William Mayne might say. Later in the war, Robert Mayne went bankrupt and killed himself." So too Royster describes the sloop *Expedition,* two days out of Senegal in 1770 with 110 slaves on board, beginning to take on water. The *Expedition* hailed a passing sloop, the *James,* which agreed to take on board the crew of the *Expedition.* The *James* then sailed on leaving behind chained

Africans in a sinking sloop. After the *James* arrived several weeks later in Barbados, Royster tells us that the owner of the *Expedition* was able to recover thirty-two hundred pounds insurance on the sloop and her cargo. The owner, writes Royster dryly, "thought this sum 'full as much as they could have produced if they had arrived at market.'"

In its merciless but humorous dissection of social folly and decadence, this book is as close to a Waugh-like version of history as we are ever likely to get. It is, of course, not in any way an objective or balanced history of the eighteenth-century Virginia aristocracy, any more than Waugh's comic novels about the British aristocracy in the 1930s were objective and balanced. But it leaves an impression that is hard to forget. Some readers have concluded that Royster's history of the Dismal Swamp Company does not have a point. But they are wrong.

## AFTERWORD

I was reading some of Evelyn Waugh's 1930s satirical novels of the English aristocracy, such as *A Handful of Dust* and *Vile Bodies,* when I was reviewing Royster's book and was immediately struck by the similarity. I don't think Royster was influenced by Waugh; he simply has an outlook on the world similar to Waugh's. Royster is a distinguished historian with a number of superb studies on war and soldiers to his credit. But none of his previous works is quite as satirical and as comically bleak as this one. There is no other historian in the country who could have written this book.

# 17.

# MULTICULTURAL HISTORY

*Becoming America: The Revolution Before 1776*
by Jon Butler (Cambridge: Harvard University Press, 2000)

*The New Republic,* June 12, 2000

R EVOLUTIONS DO NOT just happen. They are the consequence of changing social, political, and cultural circumstances over a long period of time. This sensible proposition is the central theme of Jon Butler's book. According to Butler, professor of history and American and religious studies at Yale, American colonial society between 1680 and 1770 was dramatically transformed. During this period the small, primitive, and largely English settlements scattered along the North American coast became complicated and sophisticated societies. Enormous social, economic, political, and cultural changes in these decades "created a distinctly modern, and, ultimately, 'American' society in Britain's mainland colonies."

Indeed, almost everything that came to constitute American society at the time of the Revolution was a product of developments in the eighteenth century, not the seventeenth century. In 1680 most European settlers were English; but, as Butler observes, "by 1770 Britain's mainland settlements contained a polyglot population of English, Scots, Germans, Dutch, Swiss, French, and Africans." During the eighteenth century large numbers of black Africans had been brought as slaves into all the colonies, but especially into the colonies of the South. Farmers of various sorts had

become involved in international market economies. By the eve of the Revolution, merchants and planters amassed and displayed wealth to a degree that their seventeenth-century predecessors could not have imagined possible. "Complex, sophisticated politics replaced the rudimentary political mechanisms typical of the seventeenth-century colonies." New patterns of production and consumption arose, and a vigorous religious pluralism replaced the traditional state-supported religious orthodoxies of the past.

By 1770, Butler says, America had become "the first modern society" in the world. He admits that some characteristics of modernity were lacking in Britain's eighteenth-century mainland colonies: they were never very urban, and they did not experience the massive technological changes of the nineteenth century. In most other measures of modernity, however, Butler believes the eighteenth-century colonists came to know what being modern meant. They developed trans-Atlantic and international economies. They created the beginnings of large-scale participatory politics. They demonstrated "the modern penchant for power, control and authority over both humanity and nature that brooked few limitations or questions about their propriety." And, most important to Butler, they displayed a racial, ethnic, and religious diversity unmatched anywhere in the early modern world.

Of course, Butler concedes that America would become much more modern in the decades following the American Revolution. Slavery would become more devastating; politics would become more democratic; and the society would become more diverse, urban, and industrialized. "Still," says Butler, "the transformations between 1680 and 1770 carried a unique importance." The colonists of this period "created the America that fought the Revolution of 1776 and gave the new nation much of its essential identity."

Until recently, as Butler correctly points out, historians paid relatively little attention to the period between 1680 and the beginnings of the American Revolution. Owing to the lack of sufficient monographs in the

period, attempts by historians to write synthetic histories of the eighteenth century have generally failed. Despite attempts by several historians, the distinguished *History of the South*, for example, still lacks a volume for the period between 1689 and 1763, the only period of southern history that is missing from the series.

Until a few decades ago, moreover, many historians of colonial America believed that the meaning of America could be exclusively located in the minds of the Puritans of early seventeenth-century New England. Colonial historians sometimes dealt with the founding of Jamestown in 1607 and the origins of Virginia, but they never gave the South, especially the southern colonies beyond Virginia, the attention they lavished on New England. The middle colonies—New York, New Jersey, and Pennsylvania—whose histories covered the period 1680–1760, were the most neglected of all. After recording the initial settlements and perhaps dealing with the Salem witchcraft craze of 1692, historians of early America tended to skip rather quickly through the rest of colonial history, until they got to the decades leading up to the American Revolution. The result was a telescoped and foreshortened history of early America: from the Puritans to the Revolution in a single bound.

All this has changed in the past several decades. Historians have not only explored the entire seventeenth-century Chesapeake in rich detail, recovering a world that we scarcely knew existed, but at long last they have also begun to give us sophisticated histories of the other colonies in the late seventeenth and early eighteenth centuries. The neglected period, from 1680 to 1760, is no longer quite so neglected. We have learned about politics and economy in the Carolinas, about religion and ethnic conflict in the middle colonies, and about the native Indians and immigration and the development of slavery in all of British North America.

There has occurred a virtual explosion of writings about colonial America. According to Bernard Bailyn, the historian who over the past generation has dominated the period as much as any single scholar could,

early American history in the past fifty years has experienced a "creative ferment of scholarship," resulting in "a wealth of research and writing concentrated on a relatively short period of time that is perhaps unique in western historiography." Since the colonial period has few of the headline political events of the national period—no presidential elections, no congresses, no supreme court decisions—it was especially receptive to the new social and cultural histories that have tended to engross history writing over the past three or four decades.

Colonial historians found themselves freer than historians of the national period to concentrate on long-term social and cultural developments that cut through the headline events and political institutions that tended to preoccupy historians of the national period. It is not surprising, therefore, that the modern study of American demographic and family history began first in the colonial period, or that one of the earliest studies of American attitudes toward death concentrated on the colonial period. Unlike historians of the national period, who generally concentrate on a decade or two, colonial historians were used to dealing with long sweeps of time, and therefore they found the new social and cultural history of the past several decades especially attractive.

Under these new conditions, articles and books on early American history have poured from the presses in ever-increasing volume, to the point where their numbers can easily overwhelm anyone trying to deal with them. For this reason alone, we must congratulate Butler for his attempt to bring under control this profusion of scholarship and to make sense of it in fewer than 250 pages. His book is a tour de force of synthesis. He has organized his book not chronologically but thematically, under five subjects—"Peoples," "Economy," "Politics," "Things Material," and "Things Spiritual"—and has devoted a chapter to each. A final chapter, titled "1776," attempts to relate everything to the Revolution.

Early modern Europe was a society in motion, and many Europeans were used to people of all sorts coming and going everywhere. But no

European country, not even the Netherlands, which contained a wide variety of peoples, experienced the movement and diversity that transformed Britain's mainland colonies between 1680 and 1760. During the first half dozen decades or so of colonization in the seventeenth century, England's North American settlements had remained relatively simple and primitive societies. There was little ethnic diversity. Nearly 90 percent of the tens of thousands of European immigrants to these early colonies were English. Their hold on the continent was far from secure, and they often struggled in orgies of blood and violence to maintain themselves against the natives, who originally outnumbered the early European settlers, in some areas by as many as ten to one.

In the eight or nine decades after 1680, however, all this changed. The Indians saw their numbers drastically reduced, and many of the remaining natives were pushed westward. In the southern colonies, the Indian population declined from about two hundred thousand to fewer than sixty thousand. Not only were the numbers of separate tribal groups east of the Mississippi reduced by half in the course of the eighteenth century, but in all the mainland colonies, writes Butler, "whole Indian cultures disappeared." At the same time, the European population expanded by leaps and bounds, from fewer than two hundred thousand people in 1690 to over two million by 1770.

These mainland colonists became an ever more important proportion of the British Empire. In 1700 there was only one colonist for every twenty inhabitants of Britain and Ireland combined. By 1770 this ratio had become one to five. This rapidly growing colonial population, which was probably multiplying faster than any part of the Western world, was fueled not only by natural reproduction but by the immigration of tens of thousands of a wide variety of Europeans, most of whom were no longer English. In fact, "the British mainland colonies became a haven for non-English Europeans," creating a mixture of peoples that was unique in the colonial world.

But it was not the Europeans who constituted the largest group of

arrivals in the British colonies in the decades after 1680. The most numerous addition of peoples by far was the 250,000 African slaves forcibly
brought from the Caribbean or directly from Africa. Their numbers,
Butler notes, "outstripped all European immigrants combined." Befitting
their importance to the multihued society that America became, these
Africans receive nearly one-third of the pages Butler devotes to this initial
chapter. Indeed, in all his chapters Butler devotes a good deal of time to
describing the latest rich scholarly findings on both African slaves and
native Indians, understandably so, even when these findings do not always
fit his larger argument.

In his chapter on the economy, Butler sees the British mainland colonies between 1680 and 1770 soaring with unprecedented growth in every
direction. The economy grew faster than the population and became more
various and complex. More and more Americans began selling more and
more produce abroad, which in turn allowed them to buy an increasing
array of consumer goods. Most farmers may have been largely subsistence
farmers in the seventeenth century, but by 1760, argues Butler, in defiance
of the views of some historians, most farmers in most colonies had become "commercial farmers" to one degree or another.

This chapter, like the others in Butler's book, is a model of synthesis.
He has extracted information from a remarkable number of articles and
monographs, and has put it all together in a compelling and readable form.
His assessments and judgments are generally balanced and sensible as he
reconciles the different views of historians. The only major omission in
his discussion of the colonial economy is his neglect of paper money, one
of the most innovative devices the colonists used to carry on their trade.
Lacking the Bank of England, the colonists were compelled to create
government-issued bills of credit and land bank notes as instruments of
exchange and sources of small-scale investments.

Butler's chapter on colonial politics is less authoritative and convincing, mainly because he assumes that politics can exist only where there
are elections, a very presentist viewpoint. But local officials, outside of

New England, were usually appointed, not elected, and so Butler concludes that most of the vigorous and significant political activity took place at the level of the provincial assembly rather than at the level of the local town or county. Perhaps. But most provincial politics involved local issues and almost all of the day-to-day governing of people took place in town meetings and county courts. Provincial legislatures did not legislate in any modern sense, and provincial governors did not have legislative programs. Most of the legislatures' activities were private, local, and adjudicative. Given the large number of men eligible to vote in provincial elections, Butler is bewildered by how few actually did vote—"an anomaly," he says, "in a society so otherwise aggressive and demanding." Yet it was an anomaly only if one assumes that colonial politics was modern. It was not modern, not yet at least, though it was becoming so.

Unfortunately, Butler treats the period 1680–1770 too much like a single unit, and thus he cannot always deal adequately with the extraordinary political changes taking place over these decades, especially in the colonists' relationship to the empire. His astonishing description of the colonial agents in London as emissaries who "revealed the empire's utter centrality in colonial life" not only exaggerates the agents' role as "a principal avenue for articulating colonial sentiment at the hub," it also ignores changes in that role through time. The colonists used many other informal avenues of influence in London besides the agents, they appointed better men as agents in the seventeenth century than in the eighteenth, and they found the effectiveness of the agents declining drastically in the decade prior to the Revolution.

In his treatment of "Things Material," Butler becomes much bolder and more patriotic. He is more eager to stress that colonial society had become "significantly different from either Britain or continental Europe" and more "American." Indeed, he endorses the presently much-maligned notion of American "exceptionalism." Not only were the better-fed colonists on average three inches taller than their British cousins, but in the

course of the eighteenth century they "created an increasingly distinctive secular material culture." They built houses and furnishings in their own distinctive styles, and they developed crafts that fused Old World and New World materials and fashions in innovative ways. Indeed, Butler contends that colonial craftsmen easily equaled and sometimes surpassed their provincial counterparts in Britain. He goes so far as to suggest that the Americans' preference for simpler and plainer styles in housing, furniture, and objects was merely a matter of their having better aesthetic taste than the ornate-loving British aristocracy. Was Washington's mixing of sand in the paint on the façade of Mount Vernon, designed to simulate stone, an example of this superior taste?

In his chapter on "Things Spiritual" Butler repeats much of his earlier and pungently argued book on the Christianizing of early America, *Awash in a Sea of Faith,* which appeared in 1990. Although he mainly wants to emphasize the ways in which eighteenth-century Americans developed distinctive religious patterns, he continues to contend that the Great Awakening was not as important as most historians believe it was. In fact, he refrains from using the term and instead talks about evangelical revivals, which, he says, contrary to general opinion, then and now, "embraced relatively conservative rather than egalitarian or radical tendencies."

In his final chapter, "1776," Butler is at pains to deny that all of the dynamic developments of the eighteenth-century colonies caused the American Revolution or made it inevitable. The Revolution, he says, was essentially a product of political events in 1763–76. Still, he cannot help but believe that all the social, political, and cultural transformations that he has described had a decisive influence on the character of the Revolution. Indeed, he says that all those transformations had made American society "the first modern society," and the Revolution thus became "the first modern revolution, *the* model for the French Revolution of 1789 and subsequently for so many nineteenth- and twentieth-century revolutions."

This is quite a claim, and I quite agree with it. But in what ways was eighteenth-century America the first modern society and the Revolution the first modern revolution? Butler believes that the Revolution "lacked dominant elements found in revolutions since." Class differences, he says, did not drive the Revolution as they did the French, Russian, and Chinese revolutions. Maybe there were not the class conflicts of other revolutions, but there were serious social antagonisms everywhere that propelled events. Nor, Butler writes, was there a single, cohesive ideology comparable to modern Marxism. Again, maybe the republicanism of the American and French revolutions was not as single and cohesive as Marxism, but it was a powerful and coherent ideology and just as radical for the eighteenth century as Marxism would be for the nineteenth.

Still, even without these modern elements he thinks the American Revolution was modern, and it was modern because American society was modern. On the face of it, this seems a dubious claim. Many readers familiar with the period might naturally assume that Britain was the most modern of societies in the eighteenth century. After all, it had undergone a financial and commercial revolution and was already advanced in industrializing itself. It had London, the largest city in Europe, and a half dozen other burgeoning manufacturing centers each with over thirty thousand people. America, by contrast, remained overwhelmingly agricultural and rural. In 1760 its largest city, Philadelphia, had only about twenty thousand people. Despite all the economic development that Butler emphasizes, the colonies were still remarkably underdeveloped compared to the mother country. America had no Bank of England, no stock markets, no large-scale manufacturing, and few urban centers that could compare with those in Britain. Whatever the extent of its domestic and international commerce, it differed from Britain's by orders of magnitude. In its artistic and cultural achievements, America was all promise and little or no substance.

Since many readers might think that Britain, and not America, was the most modern society in the eighteenth century, Butler tries at various

points to stress American comparability with Britain. It is true, he admits, that the colonists did not develop large urban areas, but he suggests that "as early as 1720 cities of real urban complexity emerged from the meanest and simplest of towns." America may not have had the extensive manufacturing of Great Britain, but the craft trades in the colonies "compared favorably in breadth and possibly in depth with those found in Britain." Of course, Butler concedes that American artisans sometimes produced things in imitation of British styles, but just as often they revealed a "plenteous vigor, imagination, and a protean independence."

So eager is Butler to demonstrate the cultural precociousness of the colonists that he cites the Tuesday Club of Maryland, a small polite association active between 1745 and 1756, as something that "epitomized the artisanal, political, and literary creativity that could pour out from the colonies by the 1740s." He overlooks the fact that the Scottish physician and immigrant who founded the club did so because of his discovery upon his arrival in Maryland that its society was "Barbarous and desolate" in contrast to that of Edinburgh.

Butler believes that America was finally more modern than Britain for a different reason: its remarkable mixture of peoples. He seems to think that modernity lies mainly in social and religious diversity. Perhaps that is so today. But what about the late eighteenth century? It is true that American leaders often marveled at the mixture of Europeans in their society; yet what impressed them was not the multicultural diversity of these different peoples, but rather their remarkable acculturation and assimilation into one people. John Jay lived in New York City, the most ethnically and religiously diverse place in all America, and was himself three-eighths French and five-eighths Dutch, without any English ancestry; and yet Jay could declare with a straight face in *Federalist* No. 2, that

> Providence has been pleased to give this one connected
> country to one united people—a people descended from the

same ancestors, speaking the same language, professing the
same religion, attached to the same principles of government,
very similar in their manners and customs and who, by their
joint counsels, arms, and efforts . . . have nobly established
general liberty and independence.

The Revolutionary leaders' idea of a modern state, shared by enlightened British, French, and German eighteenth-century reformers as well,
was a polity that was characterized by homogeneity, not one that was
fractured by differences of language, ethnicity, and religion.

Much of Europe in the eighteenth century was still a patchwork of
small duchies, principalities, and city-states—nearly 350 of them. Even
those nation-states that had begun consolidating were not yet very secure or homogeneous. England had struggled for centuries to bring
Wales and Scotland under its control and had only in the Act of Union
in 1707 created the entity known as Great Britain. The ancien régime of
eighteenth-century France was a still a hodgepodge of provinces and
diverse peoples and by modern standards scarcely a single nation at all.
Spain had just recently begun assimilating the kingdoms of Castile and
Aragon into a single state, but the Basque provinces and Navarre still
maintained an extraordinary degree of independence from the central
monarchy.

European reformers everywhere wanted to eliminate these differences within their national boundaries and to bind the people of their
state together in a common culture. The American Revolutionaries were
no different. They thought that Americans had become the most enlightened people in the world precisely because they had done away with the
various peasant customs, craft holidays, and primitive peculiarities—
the morris dances, the charivaries, the bear baiting, and other folk
practices—that characterized the societies of the Old World. Americans
seemed to be more of a single people than the nations of Europe.

Nothing made enlightened eighteenth-century Americans prouder than the fact that most people in America spoke English and could understand one another from Maine to Georgia. That this was not true in the European nations was one of the great laments of enlightened reformers there. A Yorkshireman could not be understood in Somerset and vice versa. No task facing the French Revolutionaries was more formidable than overcoming the fact that the majority of people in France did not speak French.

The republicanism of the Revolutionaries put a premium on the homogeneity and the cohesiveness of their society. Monarchies could comprehend large territories and composite kingdoms and people with diverse interests and ethnicities. Monarchies had their unitary authority, kingly honors and patronage, hereditary aristocracies, established national churches, and standing armies to hold their diverse societies together. Republics had none of these adhesive elements. Republics were supposed to rely for cohesion on the moral qualities of their people: their virtue and their natural sociability. Republicanism created citizens, and citizens were all equal to one another. In fact, it was this emphasis on republican homogeneity and equal citizenship that drove the American Revolutionaries to exclude both blacks and Indians as citizens from the new republican nation-state they were trying to establish. It was for the same reason that conventional wisdom, made famous by Montesquieu, dictated that republics should be small in size and similar in character.

At the time of the Revolution, even religious diversity itself was not yet generally regarded as a good thing. To be sure, liberty of conscience was everywhere highly valued, but differences of religion were accepted only insofar as they made toleration and freedom of conscience possible. Many enlightened reformers, such as Jefferson and Madison, did greatly appreciate religious diversity, but they did so only because they realized that the more numerous the religious sects, the more likely those sects would want the state neutralized in religious matters. This in turn would

allow secular reformers like themselves to set public policy free of religious interference. But ultimately even many of these secular reformers and deists yearned for a homogeneous society, as Jefferson did, in which all Americans might become Unitarians.

Butler ignores all these republican concerns. He can see only "the broad ethnic and religious heterogeneity that would typify America and so many modern societies throughout the nineteenth and twentieth centuries." He concedes that for a while the Revolutionary impulse and its preoccupation with British Whig political ideology "reduced the potential impact of ethnic and national pluralism in America." Even with this concession, however, Butler underestimates the degree to which the Americans' law and culture remained essentially British even after the Revolution. His mistake is perhaps understandable, since he grossly miscalculates the percentage of people of British heritage in America. Butler has the British composing only a third of all inhabitants in 1770, when, in fact, even by 1790 the English and Scots together continued to make up over 60 percent of all Americans, including African Americans.

In his efforts to demonstrate the ways in which the modernity of eighteenth-century American society dictated much of the character of the Revolution, Butler sometimes gets things backward. American developments between 1680 and the Revolution, he says, had created "aggressive, willful, modern societies far more self-sufficient and self-directing than anyone ever managed they could be or would be." These new modern societies had "modernity's confidence in its mastery of the world and of individual and collective lives," especially of the lives of Africans and Indians. Butler seems to believe that the "moral blindness" that led to the further reduction of the Indians and the continued enslavement of Africans "reflected the hubris born of modernity's material and technological fertility and wide-reaching political authority." But, in fact, it was modernity, reflected in the ideals of the American Revolution, that for the

first time on a large scale morally condemned Americans' treatment of the Indians and Africans. However brutally white Americans treated Indians and Africans in the decades following the Revolution, and no one can deny the brutality, their mistreatment was denounced as a moral evil by more and more Americans in ways that had not been done in premodern times.

In the end, Butler is unable to connect in a satisfactory or convincing manner his first modern society with his first modern revolution. He realizes that the relationship is "complex, not simple or automatic." He correctly assumes that the Revolution built heavily on the past. It could not have occurred without all the transformations he has earlier described, and it did not, and could not, sweep away the society that made it. But Butler seems unwilling to admit that white Americans in 1776 had any real grievances with their society and any real desires for substantial social and political reform.

He never recaptures the tension in eighteenth-century American society, the ways it looked backward and forward at the same time. It was still a small-scale, underdeveloped society very much dominated by expectations of dependency and personal relationships. But it was also a dynamic, remarkably egalitarian society that lacked sufficient personal influence and patronage power to fulfill these expectations. Consequently, the connectedness of colonial society—its capacity to bind one person to another—was exceedingly fragile and vulnerable to continual challenge. The Revolution offered the decisive opportunity for challenge and change.

What ultimately made the American Revolution modern was not simply that it created a republic but that it changed the way people related one to another. Americans became modern not because they were diverse in origins and religions, but because they came to believe that all citizens were equal and independent and that all authority had to be earned by achievement and based on consent. Butler in his rich and read-

able book never quite explains why they should have come to believe in these ideals.

## AFTERWORD

This otherwise excellent book is ultimately marred by the present-mindedness of its author. It is, of course, impossible for a historian to escape entirely from his present, but it is essential to try. Whenever something such as multiculturalism comes to dominate our contemporary discourse, we ought to be suspicious of any attempt to read it back into the past.

# 18.

# HISTORY AND MYTH

*Inheriting the Revolution: The First Generation of Americans*
by Joyce Appleby
(Cambridge:: Harvard University Press, 2000)

*The New York Review of Books,* June 29, 2000

W E ARE OFTEN told that the baby boomers, that is, those born in the two decades or so following World War II, have brought about the greatest transformation of political, social, and cultural life in American history. Ever since this generation came of age in the 1960s and 1970s, it has involved America in a multitude of radical changes allegedly unmatched by the experience of any previous generation of Americans— changes in politics, civil rights, race relations, sexual habits, family life, women's roles, cultural attitudes. All these changes, according to many, have resulted in a series of challenges to our traditional identity as an optimistic, enterprising, and progressive nation.

But maybe this baby-boomer generation is not unique after all. If we read Joyce Appleby's new book, we might conclude that at least one earlier generation, the first generation—those born in the two decades or so following the Declaration of Independence—participated in an equally radical, or perhaps even more radical, transformation of American society and culture. In fact, according to Appleby, the changes brought about by

this first generation created much of the very traditional national identity that is presently being challenged.

This first generation, says Appleby, experienced a pace of change that no earlier Americans had ever experienced. Indeed, in less than a half century following the Declaration of Independence, Americans moved "from the end of traditional society—'the world we have lost'—to the social framework we are still living with." The Revolution released powerful popular forces that had existed just beneath the surface of colonial life, and once released, these forces overwhelmed and destroyed much of the colonists' world. This destruction, says Appleby, "forced the members of this generation to move forward on their own, a necessity that set them apart from earlier and later cohorts."

Not only did they, or at least the northerners among them, radically democratize politics and create a liberal, commercial, or capitalist market society of unparalleled scope and social influence, but they also constructed the peculiar national identity of autonomous and enterprising individuals that came to characterize Americans through much of their history. In other words, this powerful first generation, precisely because it was first, advanced an interpretation of the collective meaning of American democracy that made it difficult for the people of subsequent generations to set forth other identities and other meanings of America. As a result of Appleby's book we now know better where America's exceptional liberal consensus came from.

To put together her story of this first generation, Appleby scoured a variety of sources about the individuals who made up what she calls "my cohort." She read all she could find about thousands of individuals— famous and obscure, men and women, rich and poor, northerners and southerners, immigrants and old stock, blacks and Indians. Her most important source was the extraordinarily large number of autobiographies written by the men and women of her cohort. She counted nearly four hundred of which she says she read two hundred. Her "witnesses," as she calls these two hundred, were "those who did something in public—started

a business, invented a useful object, settled a town, organized a movement, ran for office, formed an association, or wrote for publication, if only an autobiography."

After a lengthy introduction, Appleby has seven chapters, each focusing on separate themes: responding to the Revolutionary tradition, enterprise, careers, distinctions, intimate relations, reform, and a new national identity. The book is thus not a narrative history of this first generation, but rather a series of analyses of these particular themes, culminating in the creation of a new American identity dedicated to individualism and free enterprise. Because Appleby often does not date the anecdotes and events she relates, it is not always easy to know when something is taking place within the thirty- or forty-year period she is dealing with. Thus readers who do not know the history of these decades between 1790 and 1830 very well may find it difficult to know the setting of what is happening.

Since Appleby does not describe in any detail what the old order was like, we pretty much have to take her word for the extent of change that took place during this first generation. Mostly what she offers us are a few brief phrases, such as "traditional hierarchies" or "old elite traditions" or "the old colonial social structure." The closest she comes in describing this old order is her short account of a patronage-dominated colonial world in which people had few choices of career or occupation.

Moreover, Appleby never fully explains why these remarkable changes took place when they did. Much of the time she seems to attribute everything to Thomas Jefferson. It was Jefferson's election in 1800 above all, she writes, that broke the Federalist identification between social and political authority and created the liberal and democratic society that emerged in the succeeding decades. Among early American historians Appleby has been one of the most important celebrators of Jefferson's role in American history. Not that she is unaware of Jefferson's dark side, his aversion to black Americans, and his expansionist policies that proved deadly for the native Indians in the West. Indeed, she recog-

nizes that the conservative Federalists were far more opposed to slavery and protective of African American and Indian rights than were the Jeffersonian Republicans. Still, she says, it was Jefferson and his supporters who were most responsible for democratizing American politics and commercializing the United States.

Sometimes, realizing perhaps that she may be attributing too much to Jefferson's election itself, she suggests that there were powerful long-existing demographic and economic forces that made inevitable the defeat of the Federalists' hierarchy and their plans for an integrated centralized European-like fiscal-military state. Here and there she suggests that it was the Revolution and its "tendencies" that actually challenged and subverted the older hierarchies and released the deep-lying social forces. Perhaps we might even see Jefferson's election itself as a consequence of those "tendencies."

Appleby's writing can be elegant at times, but it also can be hard going, with too many piled-up participles and subordinate clauses slowing down the flow of her prose. Sometimes too her passion for unusual images becomes strained or awkward, as when "economic failure and sectional dissension pushed the melody of many individuals into a minor key," or when women's "avenues to grace became highways to close bonds with those sharing their communion." Her citations and endnotes are often erratic: well-known information gets cited while important quotations are left undocumented.

Despite all of Appleby's remarkably detailed coverage of the society and the culture of this first generation, she ignores important themes or treats them superficially. There is almost nothing on the development of political parties and the emergence of the Jacksonian Democratic Party in the 1820s as the radically new model of a modern party. And there is nothing on the Revolutionary dream of America's becoming the world's leader in the arts and sciences and the struggle of the first generation in trying to realize that dream. For Appleby, Samuel F. B. Morse was simply someone who "pursued his career as an artist while applying himself to

inventions like the telegraph"; she ignores the fact that artists like Morse turned to inventing things only when their high-minded artistic aspirations were dismissed by a philistine commercial world. Appleby mentions the courts and the common law only to dismiss them as instruments for sustaining patriarchy in the home and workplace. Nowhere does she acknowledge the important role of judges in adapting the common law to help create the new commercial world of her first generation.

Still, despite these omissions, Appleby has painted a remarkably broad and rich portrait of early nineteenth-century society. It was above all a society very much on the move. Annual sales of western land increased from a hundred thousand acres in the 1790s to half a million after 1800, and farms multiplied at a rate unmatched since the original settlements. Tens of thousands of ordinary folk pulled up stakes in the East and moved westward, occupying more territory in a single generation than had been occupied in the 150 years of colonial history. Between 1800 and 1820, the trans-Appalachian population grew from a third of a million to more than two million. "Never again," Appleby writes, "would so large a portion of the nation live in new settlements." And, she says with some understandable awe, "there must have been something wondrous growing up" in these new settlements in the wilderness.

As the old colonial society fell apart, men and women scattered in all directions, and tens of thousands of "young people found their ways to opportunity." Choices and occupations of all sorts emerged and multiplied: in writing, publishing, journalism, school teaching, law, politics, medicine, civil engineering, painting, and preaching. To follow "the careers of those in the first generation," writes Appleby, "is to watch the sprawling American middle class materialize, summoned into existence by political independence, thickening trade connections, and religious revivals, all tied together by print." Reading became a necessity of life and a principal activity of nation building. Northern Americans became one of the most, if not the most, literate people in the world. Printers, publishers, and booksellers all doubled in number in the first decade of the nine-

teenth century. By 1810 Americans were buying twenty-four million copies of newspapers annually, the largest aggregate circulation of any country in the world.

Not only did lawyers multiply and come to dominate the increasing numbers of political offices, but preachers sprang up everywhere, no longer needing the college education and the credentials of their colonial predecessors. The revivalist movements of these years—called the Second Great Awakening—undermined the old established religious orders of Congregationalists and Anglicans and created a new and uniquely voluntary religious world dominated by evangelical Methodists and Baptists. Francis Asbury, the founding bishop of the American Methodist Church, estimated that in 1811 alone over three million Americans attended revivalist camp meetings. Evangelical preachers, says Appleby in one of her many mixed images, "unleashed a torrent of zeal among a full quarter of the adult population," not only among white men and women but African Americans as well. Out of the conversions of tens of thousands of newborn Christians caught up in the turmoil of these years emerged "a recognizable American type, . . . confined to a substantial minority of men and women, but powerful beyond its numbers because it involved a mastery of self and a prompting to good works." These evangelical Christians were "earnest, intrusive, passionate, and disciplined," and they "eagerly made their affirmations those of the nation at large."

Within two decades or so, Appleby writes, the revivalists transformed American civil society. Not only did they form proliferating numbers of churches and sects, many of them, like the Disciples of Christ and the Mormons, had no European roots whatsoever; but together with other reformers they also created thousands of other kinds of voluntary associations dedicated to everything from antislavery to temperance reform. Out of the dismantling of the traditional hierarchical society, writes Appleby, emerged a new democratic citizen: "the assertive individual who bends every effort to make his own way, both socially and intellectu-

ally, and reads his own reform as a sign of the possibilities for society at large."

Even more significant in creating this new vibrant society was the explosion of commercial activities in the North. In an important sense these commercial activities—the beginnings of capitalism—lie at the heart of Appleby's book. Several decades ago Appleby took on the task of refuting the so-called "republican synthesis," the historical interpretation most closely associated with the work of J. G. A. Pocock that contended that the United States was born in a mood of nostalgia for a lost classical world. In the world according to Pocock, Jefferson was no longer seen as a progressive reader of Locke leading America into its individualistic future; instead, he became a backward follower of the English Tory Bolingbroke, obsessed with virtue and corruption and fearful of new commercial developments.

In a series of important articles and in her book *Capitalism and a New Social Order: The Republican Vision of the 1790s* (1984), Appleby almost single-handedly rescued the liberal Jefferson from this "republican synthesis." Realizing that this synthesis could never explain the emergence of the liberal, individualistic, commercial, and interest-ridden world of early nineteenth-century America, Appleby simply denied its applicability to the main currents of eighteenth-century American social and economic life. She argued that most eighteenth-century American farmers had already become individualistic and commercial-minded, so much so that their commercial liberalism soon became part of the nation's understanding of itself. The spokesman for the mass of these American farmers was Jefferson. He and his followers, said Appleby, envisioned a new liberal economic order of competing enterprising individuals that eventually became America's ideology. Now in this new book Appleby seeks to detail the various ways in which this ideology of liberalism came to dominate early nineteenth-century American culture.

Capitalism, according to Appleby, was created by the commercial ac-

tivities of ordinary Americans. In their strenuous efforts to turn their talents and energy into cash, writes Appleby in one of her less elegant similes, "enterprising men knocked against enterprising men like so many billiard balls." It was not Hamilton's financial policies and the investments of wealthy elites that explain America's commercial growth in these years. It was the willingness of "ordinary men and women . . . to move, to innovate, to accept paper money, and to switch from homemade goods once commercial ones were available" that accounts for "the expansion of farming, commerce, credit, and information." To the surprise of European observers, American farmers did not resemble Old World peasants; they were commercial-minded entrepreneurs who were eager to abandon their land and move on to wherever profits were to be made.

But the truly remarkable sources of America's early nineteenth-century commercial boom, says Appleby, were "the boot-strap manufacturing ventures that proliferated in the rural North. . . . Mechanics, tradesmen, and farmers with little or no capital turned their brains and hands to making something new." Bright young middling men from obscure backgrounds, like Peter Cooper and Amasa Goodyear, were able to take advantage of America's unique conditions and opportunities to become successful businessmen. Novelty and inventiveness became their watchwords. Because American labor was expensive compared to European labor, these hustling entrepreneurs were eager to develop machines and tools to enhance productivity. They were risk takers as well, showing "a surprising willingness to venture outside the realm of their experience." Everywhere in the North manufacturing swiftly "passed from an artisanal phase to a commercial one," and America's internal market became "the largest in the world."

All these commercial farmers and small businessmen needed credit, lots of it, and they found it in the hundreds of state-chartered banks that sprang up everywhere in the North. Nothing like this democratization of credit existed anywhere else in the world. In 1813, New Hampshire, "a small state undistinguished for wealth in any category," had ten banks in six dif-

ferent towns, four of them in Portsmouth, a town of fewer than six thousand people. Not only did these banks offer local savers opportunities for investment, but they became the principal source of "currency—welcome, unregulated, and amazingly good at flooding the nation with notes."

"With economic pursuits that had previously been regulated now open to all comers, the economy," writes Appleby, "could be construed as voluntary, free, even natural." This, she contends, "seemed to confirm the most potent ideological legacy of this era: the idea of a natural harmony of interests mediated by natural economic laws." Americans convinced themselves that government had little or nothing to do with these economic activities. It was all free enterprise. Democracy and capitalism grew up together. "Conservatives then," she writes, "were not proto-industrialists, but defenders of obsolete cultural traditions. Competition, far from being associated with grinding the face of the poor, stirred up hopes of advancement in ordinary men and women, who vigorously rejected the aristocratic notion of natural inequality."

Appleby's book contains some of the most celebratory accounts of early American get-up-and-go that one can find in today's historical literature. But were these expansive accounts accurate depictions of reality? Were large numbers of Americans really participating in this explosion of capitalism? Appleby believes that "interpreting reality is the most serious intellectual activity people take part in, but that the process of interpretation—both individual and collective—is always prompted by outside events." Presumably she means by "outside events" the social reality itself, the day-to-day experience of people in the world. Appleby contends that it was her cohort of mostly successful northern white men who constructed America's national identity as an enterprising and innovative people. And this collective identity, "expressed in universal terms," was so dominant that it threw "other people into the shadows of national consciousness" and "obscured for decades to come the varieties of identities and affinities with the nation." Appleby seems uncertain about how far she should go in claiming that this national identity re-

flected social reality. She does not want to commit the sin of "homogenizing the experience of diverse groups," but at the same time she cannot help writing about her cohort in collective and "essentialist" terms, especially since it had sufficient power to create America's understanding of itself for decades to come. And her first generation did, after all, create capitalism in America.

From the beginning of the twentieth century "dissenting historians," as Appleby pointed out in an earlier work written with two colleagues, have always opposed "the conflation of democracy and free enterprise."* But she herself has never been reluctant to link capitalism with ordinary people, with democracy, and with its spokesman Jefferson—even in the face of a historical profession not all that eager to accept that linkage. Many historians want to believe that capitalism was created and sustained by narrow elites and profit-seeking capitalists—Hamilton and his moneyed men, for example. They do not like to see any connection between democracy, which is a good thing, and capitalism, which presumably is not such a good thing. Although Appleby is not necessarily celebrating this linkage, she has been committed to it for decades; and as a good historian she cannot help describing it in the same exultant terms that many of her characters in her period used. Of course, she often prefaces her many anecdotes and success stories with reminders about the harm done and the people left behind. She pauses to tell us of the plight of the Indians, of women, and of African Americans. She points out that many people went bankrupt and many were hurt by the rapid growth of commerce. But her general thrust is celebratory.

Thus Appleby emphasizes capitalism's "creative destruction" of older stable ways of life. Hundreds and thousands of talented young middling white men uprooted themselves and took risks and "turned themselves into agents of change." Their extraordinary entrepreneurial activities gave

---

* Joyce Appleby, Lynn Hunt, and Margaret Jacob, *Telling the Truth About History* (New York: W. W. Norton, 1994), 148.

free enterprise its good reputation in America—it was "the freedom to innovate, to aspire, to seek a range of individual satisfactions in the market. . . . To fail to mark this feature of the early republic is to obscure a very important element in American history: the creation of a popular, entrepreneurial culture that permeated all aspects of American society." Commerce, says Appleby, was not a divisive force for Americans but "the carrier of progress for an energetic, disciplined, self-reliant people."

Much of this praise of commerce and capitalism comes from the peculiar sources that Appleby has relied upon: the several hundred autobiographies, many of them written by successful businessmen who were proud of pulling themselves up by their own bootstraps. Of course, they often failed during their lifetimes, sometimes more than once, but they recovered and persevered and prospered. They were stories of success, and they had an inordinate influence on America's sense of itself.

Much of Appleby's book is not new. Other historians have emphasized the radical changes in American society and culture caused by the American Revolution. But what ultimately makes Appleby's book more than a mere collection of interesting success stories and gives it its edge is the connection it makes between these success stories and America's emerging national identity in the decades following the Revolution. The lives of these successful northern entrepreneurs, and nearly all of them were from the North, served as "models of innovation" for a society eager to forget the aristocratic past. These "individual stories of striving and succeeding poured into one large narrative" and "supplied the empirical evidence to validate sanguine assertions about American destiny." "Because political union preceded the formation of a national identity, the first generation," says Appleby, "was forced to imagine the sentiments that might bind the nation together." Out of their repeated messages of effort and accomplishment, ordinary northern white men and women acquired a heightened appreciation of their worth and captured control of America's sense of nationhood. By the 1820s the South, which at the time of the Revolution had thought of itself as the heart and soul of the nation,

had become a bewildered and beleaguered slave-ridden minority out of touch with the tales of reform and free enterprise that now dominated the country.

This first generation, says Appleby, created "a powerful myth about America that metamorphosed ordinary labor into extraordinary acts of nation building"—a myth of American identity so powerful that succeeding generations had great difficulty questioning it. Indeed, she writes, "this first cohort promoted attitudes that still retain their vitality." So self-congratulatory were its themes of individual autonomy, prosperity, and progress that those who did not share the triumphal optimism of these themes were stifled and ignored, "culturally disfranchised."

But since the 1960s many historians have challenged this earlier sense of national identity. In a book written with two collaborators a half dozen years ago, *Telling the Truth About History,* Appleby described the great advances that have been made since the 1960s by social historians with "radically different perspectives on the American past" from those of previous historians. (Among the more prominent writing about early America have been John Demos, James H. Merrell, Philip D. Morgan, and Laurel Thatcher Ulrich.) These new social historians have ignored the lives of statesmen, generals, diplomats, and other elites and have concentrated on the lives of those who had remained in the shadows of American history, "the poor, the persecuted, and the foreign." From their research over the past several decades these social historians have discovered "tales of frustration and disappointment which cannot be easily assimilated to the monolithic story of American success." They have "lifted from obscurity the lives of those who had been swept to the sidelines in the metahistory of progress." Historians, she contended, have taken on "the role of social critic" and have placed themselves "on a collision course with the conventional accounts of the American past"; indeed, it is the very conventional accounts that were largely created by her first generation of independent Americans.

These recent social historians are, in fact, challenging the old myth of

a homogeneous national identity that celebrates individualism, free enterprise, and progress. That, according to Appleby and her coauthors, is largely what multiculturalism is all about. In its most extreme form, multiculturalism contends that "national identity . . . is a chimera created by the elite to indoctrinate other groups in society with its self-serving conception of the country's purposes." But even in its milder forms, wrote Appleby, multicultural historians, "struggling . . . for control of the nation's memory," have fragmented the history of the United States, "not in comparison to the actuality of an earlier simplicity, but in reference to the simplified story that was told about the nation's past." In her earlier book Appleby admitted that the price of this multicultural fragmentation might be high. She even raised "the disturbing possibility that the study of history does not strengthen an attachment to one's country"; indeed, the new social history may even "weaken the ties of citizenship."

Appleby seems to believe that by showing, as she has done in this new book, that America's traditional sense of identity created by the first generation was not natural, not God-given but rather a myth, an imagined social construction based on the experience of some successful northern white men, then somehow or other we can shed that identity and adopt something new, something multicultural, something more in accord with the changing nature of America's social reality. But myths of national identity are not so easily shed or manipulated if they bear some accurate relation to the social reality. America's original ideology, however much of an artifact it was, however socially constructed, would never have lasted as long as it has if it did not largely reflect the hopes and the reality of more than just a few white men. The so-called myths of national identity are not just figments of a few people's imagination, or devices concocted by tiny elites to overawe the masses.

Appleby's new book if anything shows that. In the remarkable series of stories that make up much of her book she has shown us where America's optimistic and enterprising sense of itself really came from. And she has done it in the manner of a new social historian. She has not written about

presidents or generals but about common ordinary people. But instead of tales of frustration and disappointment, she has discovered tales of opportunity and enterprise out of which emerged an unbelievably robust and successful commercial society. Ironically her own vividly detailed evidence reveals that the conception of America as a nation dedicated to "innovation, enterprise, and reform" was not a "simplified story" without foundation in the social reality but rather a complicated one firmly rooted in the lives of many ordinary Americans.

It seems quite possible that this conception has persisted as long as it has because for large numbers of these common Americans—not for all, of course, but for many—it has continued to be a meaningful depiction of reality. Which is why Tocqueville's account of America, which Appleby strangely ignores, still today makes a remarkable degree of sense. When that reality of innovation, enterprise, and reform changes for the bulk of the American people—and we seem to be a long way from that—then and only then will the nation's idea of itself change as well. Historians can never do it all by themselves.

## AFTERWORD

It is fascinating that Tocqueville's account of America of the early 1830s should have had such resonance for Americans through the subsequent decades and still have resonance for us at the beginning of the twenty-first century. If historians are correct in their belief that theories of government cannot really transcend particular times and circumstances, why do Tocqueville's ideas of American democracy created in the 1830s continue to seem so meaningful nearly two centuries later? The answer lies in the point of Appleby's book: that the generation of Americans that Tocqueville observed has had an inordinate influence on American identity and American values.

This first generation to come of age following the Revolution created

a myth of American identity—the America of enterprising, innovative and equality-loving Americans—a myth of identity that, as Appleby shows, was so powerful that succeeding generations could scarcely question it. Indeed, Jacksonian America has always seemed to be the most American of all eras. It seems to be the central point in the trajectory of American history, the point toward which all previous American history was developing and the point from which all subsequent American history seems to be receding. The Jacksonian era was the period that defined the basic elements of America's individualistic and egalitarian get-up-and-go materialistic culture. Tocqueville came to America at the very moment when Americans were constructing their sense of nationhood—a sense of America as the land of enterprise and opportunity, as the place where anybody who works hard can make it, as the nation of free and scrambling money-making individuals pursuing their happiness. This conception of the liberal American dream is alive and well even today, if not for many academics, then at least for many other Americans, including most recent immigrants. This is why Tocqueville's great work of political theory, even though it grew out of the peculiar circumstances of Jacksonian America, still retains its power for us today.

# 19.

# HISTORY AS CULTURAL CRITICISM

*On Hallowed Ground: Abraham Lincoln and the Foundations of American History* by John Patrick Diggins

(New Haven: Yale University Press, 2000)

*The New Republic,* October 30, 2000

OR THE PAST thirty years or so, John Patrick Diggins has carried out a relentless intellectual campaign against New Left historians and all those who he thinks have foolishly promised to deliver us from our modern liberal predicament. In response he has been booed and scorned and called many names. Some have called him "a closet Catholic," others "some kind of Calvinist" or even "a conservative." Still others have labeled him "a troublemaker," or someone who spends his time "throwing cold water" on new schools of thought in American history writing.

This last charge seems to have clarified things for Diggins. Finally, he says, he is coming to accept his "peculiar situation in the field of intellectual history" as "a cold water historian." He now sees his role as one of dousing all the isms of recent times that seek to use history to destroy all that is central and exceptional about America—its persistent and deeply rooted liberal tradition.

Marxism was the first of these isms to challenge liberalism, and it had an enormous influence on history writing in the 1960s. So in the 1970s,

Diggins felt compelled to write several articles and two books criticizing the new social history with its Marxist categories of thought and its futile desire to rid the world of private property. As Marxism began to fade in the 1980s, a second ism arose to take its place: classical republicanism, which promised to subordinate private interests to the spirit of civic virtue. Like Marxism, this republicanism seemed to offer radical scholars an ideological alternative to liberal capitalism, but one that was homegrown and endorsed by the Founding Fathers. Once again Diggins felt challenged by what he saw as a misinterpretation of American history. And so he wrote *The Lost Soul of American Politics* (1984), in which he denied the applicability of classical republicanism to American history.

Then, in the 1990s, other scholars such as Richard Rorty tried to revive the older tradition of American pragmatism in an attempt to solve the problems created by a cruel and selfish liberalism. Pragmatism promised a world beyond competition, a world of cooperation and community governed by "intelligence." And again Diggins responded by writing and editing several works exposing the inability of pragmatism to move American liberalism beyond its own limitations. Now, more recently, two new isms have risen to challenge the dominance of liberalism in American thought: multiculturalism and poststructuralism. *On Hallowed Ground* is Diggins's retort to these latest attempts to distort our understanding of America's past by masking the reality of America's liberal tradition.

America, Diggins wants us to understand, is liberal through and through. After all the masks, all the isms, are peeled away, there remains liberalism and only liberalism at the core of American culture. And any attempt to deny this elementary fact of American life is only a snare and a delusion. America's liberalism "cannot imagine a possibility beyond itself." It "has no second act in history because it cannot liberate itself from itself."

By liberalism, Diggins means "a body of ideas that regards matter and property, comprehended by mind and conscience, as elementary and irreducible realities and views liberty and natural rights as the means by

which happiness is pursued and freedom protected." This body of liberal
ideas, he says, can be traced largely to the seventeenth-century philosopher John Locke, who first included in the meaning of property the value
of the labor that went into creating that property. Locke is everywhere
in Diggins's book, usually as a metonym for liberalism, but often as an
authentic historical figure personally influencing American thought.
(Since Locke attacked patriarchy, he calls him "the first male feminist.")
Diggins suggests that the seventeenth-century Locke spoke more directly
to Abraham Lincoln and the nineteenth century than did Thomas
Jefferson.

Although this Lockean liberalism requires a constitutional representative government based on majority rule, it is not necessarily identified
with particular methods of governing or particular political policies. It is
certainly not identical to the liberalism that is used in current political
discourse, as the opposite of American conservatism. Indeed, Diggins's
liberalism embraces the main ideas of both present-day political parties;
some might even say that it has more in common today with the Republican
Party than with the Democratic Party.

Although Diggins has often been called a conservative, or a neocon-
servative, he disavows these titles. He is a realistic and reluctant liberal
who has come to accept ambition, competition, and the pursuit of self-
interest as ineluctable facts of life. Indeed, Diggins's Lockean liberal
world sometimes seems little different from that of Thomas Hobbes. It is
a world of self-aggrandizement and an endless struggle for power, which
Diggins associates with the acquisition of wealth and the promotion of
self-interest. Since "democracy and power are mutually exclusive concepts," democracy does not have much to do with this kind of power. But
freedom does: "freedom is inseparable from power—the power to acquire
and exclude, but also the power to rise up and participate."

Diggins seems to think of democracy as the passive and formal expression of public opinion in contrast to the informal use of liberal power in
the back rooms where the real action is. That is why, he says, the women's

movement that concentrated on simply gaining the suffrage was so ineffectual. It chose democracy instead of power and self-interest. The lesson for blacks and other excluded groups, he says, is the same. In liberal America, interest groups "have to circumvent democracy to realize some measure of power."

Diggins's Lockean liberalism is a doctrine of ambition, hard work, respect for property, and freedom from political, social, and ecclesiastical authority. Diggins is especially interested in liberalism's defiance of authority. He suggests that "perhaps Walter Lippmann gave the best definition of liberalism when he described it as the overthrow of authority and the endless search for its surrogate." Diggins himself certainly has been searching throughout his adult life for something solid to believe in.

Ever since he lost his faith in Roman Catholicism in the 1950s, he has been engaged in a tireless search for authority in a world where no authority seems to exist. His uncompromising attacks on the isms of our time are attacks on false gods that would set themselves up as authorities. After years of looking for authority, he says, all he could find was power, and thus he has given up searching.

In his earlier book *The Lost Soul of American Politics,* Diggins seemed utterly pessimistic about the desolate and alienated world that he uncovered in liberal America. The only solution that he could imagine was some kind of religious redemption that would come from our acknowledging the selfishness and the power that lie at the heart of our liberalism. In this book, however, he seems less pessimistic and more accepting of the stark and power-laden liberalism that constitutes our culture, largely through the influence of his hero Lincoln. Even today, he says, Lincoln retains a marvelous authority among Americans. "Consider the contrast between him and recent occupants of the White House: on the one side homeliness, humility, self-doubt, magnanimity, and the need to know the right; on the other, slickness, hubris, self-righteousness, and the need to know the ratings."

With the brooding presence of Lincoln at his side, Diggins seems to

have come to terms with the terrifying liberal reality of America. If Lincoln, "the most profound president in American history," could accept, indeed, endorse, the liberal world of ambition, interests, and power, then why cannot we all? Like Lincoln, however, we must ground our acceptance in a sense of our own guilt and sinfulness and in a common moral foundation perhaps best expressed in the Declaration of Independence and the timeless ideals of the American Revolution.

As a politician, says Diggins, Lincoln may have been a pragmatist willing to adjust his policies to different circumstances. "As a philosopher, however, he was a moralist, and even an absolutist, unswerving in his belief that... [the] meaning of right and wrong is not relative and dependent on time and place." Without such a belief in an absolute and timeless moral foundation, all politics, Lincoln realized, would become simply a struggle for power, and America would be unable even to recognize the goals it was failing to achieve. Many present-day scholars dismiss America's liberal consensus as merely a product of the supposedly complacent and conservative decade of the 1950s, but Lincoln knew that the liberal oneness of America was deeply rooted in its history. "A Lockean liberal with a Calvinist conscience, Lincoln believed that the Republic could be both explained and guided by a unifying principle."

Lincoln, in Diggins's account, had a vision of America as a whole, and saw unanimity coming out of the many conflicts of American life. Unlike modern radical historians who mock patriotism and any attempt to see American values as exceptional, Lincoln believed in patriotism, in America's exceptionalism, and in the unifying consensus of its liberal values. "In his patriotic nationalism, in his liberal dedication to work and opportunity for all, and in his religious devotion to justice, charity, and magnanimity," Diggins writes, "American history reached its most sublime synthesis."

Diggins thinks of himself as an intellectual historian, but in fact he is not a historian at all. He is, rather, a cultural critic who uses history to make his points about our contemporary culture. The fact that he dedi-

cated his book to Louis Hartz and Christopher Lasch, fellow cultural critics who also used history to challenge Americans to come to terms with the nature of their society, is significant. Diggins seems to feel a special kinship with what he calls "the pilgrimage of Louis Hartz," and he spends a lot of time discussing and praising Hartz and his book *The Liberal Tradition in America* (1955). This is not surprising, for he has the same reductionist conception of Lockean liberalism as Hartz.

Hartz argued, following Alexis de Tocqueville, that Americans did not have to experience a European-type revolution. With the seventeenth-century migrations from the Old World, the colonists left feudalism and aristocracy behind. Thus because they were born equal, they did not have to become so. The result was that America was saddled with a liberal ideology of individualistic and private-property-loving capitalism that could not be shaken off and that limited its ability to understand the world. Hartz was not endorsing this consensus of Lockean liberalism, as is sometimes thought; he was simply telling Americans that that is what they thought and there was not much anyone could do about it. In the end, Hartz could only flee from this suffocating liberal consensus; he became a seeker, wandering throughout the non-Western world until his death in 1986.

Rather than flee this liberal consensus, Diggins wants to fight on its behalf against its many enemies, most of whom are now on the left. Thus the bulk of his angry and agitated book deals with the mistaken ways many contemporary historians have interpreted American history. Seeing everything through the matrix of a Hartz-like Lockean liberalism, Diggins finds most of recent history writing severely wanting. Because he jumps about from the Revolution to America's identity, from exceptionalism to citizenship, from the purpose of history writing to Tocqueville, from the Frankfurt School to Cold War intellectuals, his book is really much more a collection of short, desultory, and often repetitive discussions than a cohesive whole. Still, Diggins's honesty and earnestness hold it together.

Perhaps nothing that New Left historians have recently done to ma-

nipulate the past has irritated Diggins more than the *National Standards for History*, a controversial document produced in 1996 by the National Center for History in the Schools at UCLA and designed as a guideline for state education departments in the teaching of history. In their strenuous effort to de-emphasize the influence of all the white male leaders and capture the nation's diversity of race, ethnicity, class, and gender, the authors of the history standards, according to Diggins, have distorted the story of America and have sought to undermine its liberal foundations.

Diggins presumes that the reader has read Lynne Cheney's assault on the *Standards*, and, consequently, he offers us very few examples of the distortions. Indeed, throughout the book he assumes that the reader is already familiar with much of the political correctness in historical interpretation that he is railing against, whether it is the controversy over the *Enola Gay* exhibit or the flourishing of postcolonial studies. He gives us some examples from the writings of Gary Nash, Sean Wilentz, Eric Foner, and Joan Scott, but not as many as would be needed to convince a lay reader. More telling, perhaps, are some of his personal anecdotes: one from a history conference where he was hissed for endorsing patriotism; another from a visit to an eleventh-grade classroom in San Francisco where the walls were covered with images of foreign revolutionaries, black leaders, anarchists, Native Americans, and Cesar Chavez and Eugene Debs, but not George Washington, Thomas Jefferson, or Abraham Lincoln.

Everywhere Diggins sees the influence of a generation of scholars who not only deny that America has a distinct historical identity with a consensus of political values, but also are uneasy with any expression of old-fashioned patriotism. "In certain parts of the contemporary academic world, to oppose multiculturalism in support of national unity is tantamount to advocating oppression and domination." Not that Diggins has any brief for conservative flag-waving patriots who distort the past for their own political purposes. Like many radical scholars, conservatives, he

says, have concocted an equally imagined golden age where community and virtue thrived. Still, in his call for a history that teaches the development of human freedom instead of one that teaches only ethnic, racial, or gender identity and self-esteem, he is clearly on the side of the conservatives in the culture war.

Since Diggins is not really a historian, he does not have a historian's feel for the complexity, the nuances, the contexts, and the differentness of the past. He thinks of history as a social scientist might think of it: as a source for generalizations about human behavior that transcend time and place. "To study history," he says, "is to study events in order to understand how similar conditions lead to similar effects." But in reality, historians seek to study past events not to make transhistorical generalizations about human behavior but to understand those events as they actually were, in all their peculiar contexts and circumstances.

Diggins is so eager to counter what he sees as the moral relativity and skepticism of the present that he cannot accept the historian's instinctive assumption that all human thought and action are the products of particular historical circumstances. Instead, like many conservative political theorists, he dismisses the radical contextualism of most historians. He wants to telescope time and lump things together and reduce complexities to simple absolutisms. Above all, he seeks to hold on to some transhistorical truths, some eternal or universal judgments, that defy time and place. Otherwise, he fears, we will cut loose from Lincoln's moral absolutisms and fall into the modern abyss of skepticism and nihilism.

Since Lincoln was preoccupied with the American Revolution, Diggins is preoccupied with it too, and he writes at length about it. Like Hartz, Diggins assumes that America had a liberal consensus from its beginnings in the seventeenth century, and so he necessarily believes that the Revolution could not have changed much. The America of 1760 could not have been very different from the America of 1820. Convinced that the

Revolution was a conservative movement, he dismisses out of hand any evidence suggesting that it might have been a radical break from the colonial past. Even "the depictions of the many ways the colonists struggled to free themselves from all dependency relations, structures of authority, positions of subordination, and other modes of submission," he claims, "can hardly be described as revolutionary."

Apparently, the only revolutions that Diggins recognizes as truly revolutionary are those like the French and Russian revolutions, in which all order and property and religion are violently overthrown. "If America had a radical revolution, where are its traces?" he asks. He does not consider the replacement of "the rule of monarchy" by "the rule of money" to be revolutionary, when in fact that was just what was revolutionary about the Revolution, as Joyce Appleby recently demonstrated in *Inheriting the Revolution* (2000). Like many New Left historians, but not Marx himself, Diggins cannot imagine that a revolution that creates a liberal, middle-class, egalitarian, rights-obsessed society could ever be a radical event.

Since America's Lockean liberalism has always been with us, even the radical idea of the Declaration that Lincoln emphasized—that all men are created equal—had to be part of American history from the beginning. Because Locke offered a labor theory of value in the seventeenth century, Diggins assumes that everyone in the eighteenth century must have valued work in a modern liberal way. But, in fact, one of the consequences of the Revolution was a new conception of work that helped to separate the North from the South in the decades following the Declaration of Independence. Diggins concedes that the Southern slaveholding planters were a real leisured aristocracy, but he cannot explain where they came from ("Aristocrats don't migrate," he says) or why they became a beleaguered slave-ridden minority by the 1820s. In 1776, after all, the South, despite its slaveholders, correctly saw itself as the heart and soul of the new nation. But by the 1820s, it had already lost control of the nation and

the nation's identity to the rapidly developing democratic, liberal, egalitarian, and work-obsessed North. Diggins is unable to see that most of the antebellum South was still living culturally in the eighteenth century and did not share the newly created liberalism of the North, and for this reason he cannot explain the Civil War any more than Louis Hartz could explain it.

Diggins is not alone, of course, in his belief that the American Revolution was little more than a colonial rebellion. Other historians share many of his interpretations of early American history. But what about his passionate criticisms of what the New Left historians have been doing? How seriously should we take them? He is certainly correct in indicting much of the New Left writing that sees American history as simply a tale of domination and genocide. Such overstatements only convince the public that academics are even more ridiculous than it thought they were.

No doubt Diggins is correct too in criticizing the fashionable multicultural emphasis on ethnic, racial, and gender identities at the expense of people's identities as American citizens. Such multicultural emphases not only fragment our understanding of America's past, they also make that past irrelevant for everyone whose ancestors were not personally part of it—a serious problem for a nation of immigrants. Although Martin Luther King, Jr., and the great black singer Marian Anderson could easily and emotionally relate to "My Country 'Tis of Thee," with its celebration of the "land of the pilgrim's pride," Donna E. Shalala, secretary of Health and Human Services and former professor and university president, cannot. "My grandparents came from Lebanon," Shalala has said. "I don't identify with the pilgrims at the personal level."

Still, despite these kinds of multicultural perversions of our historical understanding, no American historian would want to eliminate all the superb works of history of the past generation that have resulted from the influence of the New Left historians—works that have forever illumi-

nated our understanding of slavery, African American life, women, Indians, and ordinary working people of all sorts. It is true that these histories have often come at the expense of Washington, Jefferson, Lincoln, and other great white men of our past; but surely these illustrious figures will continue to command the attention of both historians and the general public. There have also been many foolish excesses and a great deal of dross in the new social and cultural history of the past generation that will soon mercifully be forgotten, but there also has been much good work for others to build upon.

Diggins is no doubt correct as well in charging that many New Left scholars are contemptuous of present-day American society and attempt to use their history writing to reform it. What he fails to note is that they seldom achieve the effects they desire. Often their efforts are overwhelmed by the very powerful liberal consensus that Diggins has taken such pains to describe. Indeed, it is hard to see why Diggins is so anxious about all the various isms that presumably threaten America's liberal consensus. If liberalism is as strong and resilient as he says it is, it should have nothing to fear from all these threats.

And in fact, Diggins says as much—more than once. None of the many challenges, he writes, has "made a dent on the omnipresence of liberalism in American history and American life." New Left historians believe that recovering the stories of those left out of history—workers, blacks, women, Indians—will somehow subvert the old liberal consensus; but as Diggins points out, this falsely assumes "that those who had been excluded from the synthesis represented a challenge to it." To the dismay of many New Left scholars, it turns out that most of these hitherto marginalized groups want only to participate in the great liberal bonanza and are eager to use liberal power to do so. "Multiculturalists, feminists, Marxists, and other radical activists may see themselves in conflict with the values of liberalism, but are they not actually steeped in it in their common ambition for power and position in the name of 'rights'?" As

Diggins concludes in one of his many aphorisms, "Few live for liberalism, but many live off of it."

Despite all of his fears that we have "lost the culture war to the forces of multiculturalism," Diggins seems to be flogging a dying if not dead horse. Except for its use in the race problem, which seems beyond solution in the way it is presently construed, multiculturalism is fading, if not in academia, at least among the population as a whole. Recent Asian and Hispanic immigrants seem to have accepted and endorsed the liberal American dream even more readily than immigrants of the early twentieth century. As Orlando Patterson recently pointed out, "America continues to absorb vast numbers of newcomers from everywhere, and contrary to what multiculturalists imagine, they stay for the sheer liberation of living where they can get any job if they have the skills, can marry across any ethnic or cultural boundary and can live pretty nearly anywhere they want if they can afford to."

What this suggests is that history is not as weak a foundation for morality as Diggins and others who fear the relativism of a historical attitude believe. The pragmatic view that there is no knowledge outside experience does not imply that anything goes. Lincoln did not have to believe that the Declaration of Independence was God-given in order to ground its moral messages of liberty and equality in firm foundations. The history of the American Revolution and the experience of Americans during the decades leading up to the Civil War would have been, in fact, were, sufficiently strong foundations for Lincoln's beliefs.

The historical experience of a whole people is much tougher, much more tenacious, and much more resistant to the fashions and fads of intellectuals and historians than Diggins sometimes imagines. No doubt interpretations of America's past have changed and will continue to change; but no one is really free to interpret that past as he or she would like. In their choice of interpretations, historians are limited by the past itself, not only by the raw experience of the past but also by the conventions, values,

and meanings it has passed on. Despite a generation of writing, as Diggins himself has conceded, the New Left historians have not been able to change the basic contours of our liberal faith as much as they had hoped. History is much more powerful than the historians who would reform it.

## AFTERWORD

Diggins was angered by my review and resented being thought to be something other than a real historian. I had originally written "not primarily a historian," which the editor subsequently changed to "not really a historian"—no doubt for dramatic effect. I considered Diggins to be something other than a full-fledged historian because his purpose in writing his book was not to elucidate the past but to change the present. In my opinion, not everyone who writes about the past is a historian. Sociologists, anthropologists, political scientists, and economists frequently work in the past without really thinking historically. Diggins is one of the many scholars who are deeply involved in the past without being devoted to an accurate reconstruction of it. Instead, Diggins is primarily interested in using history to criticize our present-day culture. Diggins is a prolific and powerful cultural critic and one of our most distinguished public intellectuals—in the same league with Louis Hartz and Christopher Lasch, which is not bad company. It is perhaps gratifying that he would rather be known as a historian.

## 20.

# RACE, CLASS, GENDER AND HISTORY WRITING

*The Unknown American Revolution: The Unruly Birth of
Democracy and the Struggle to Create America*
by Gary B. Nash (New York: Viking, 2005)

*The New Republic,* June 6 and 13, 2005

G ARY B. NASH has had a long and distinguished career writing
about the various oppressed and downtrodden peoples in early
America. Almost from the beginning of his career in the mid-1960s Nash
has been preoccupied with issues of inequality, class conflict, and cultural
interaction in early America. In *Red, White and Black: The Peoples of Early
America,* in 1974, he was one of the first historians to call for the integration
of Indians and Africans into the story of the settlement of colonial
America—not as victims but as peoples who actively influenced the character of the colonial past. Giving the Indians and Africans a more prominent role meant that the older white-dominated success story of early
America would have to change, ideally to be replaced by a more complicated story of cultural conflict and cultural intermingling.

Nash next turned to the origins of the American Revolution, and in
his *Urban Crucible,* in 1979, he argued that the tensions arising from poverty
and other underlying social and economic inequalities in the cities led to
a radical lower-class politics that helps account for the Revolution. Over

the past several decades Nash has devoted himself to the study of African American slavery and African American antislave movements, subjects on which he has written his best work. At the same time, together with Charlotte Crabtree at UCLA, Nash launched the National History Standards Project with funds supplied by the National Endowment for the Humanities (NEH). The published work, *National Standards for United States History: Exploring the American Experience,* which appeared in 1994, was repudiated by Lynne Cheney, former head of the NEH, which had funded it, and disowned by the U.S. Senate, ninety-nine to one, though few senators had actually read the standards.

Through all the controversies and attacks—from the left as well as from the right—Nash never lost his faith that a fairer, more just, and more equitable America could be created by a more "inclusive" historiography, by historians uncovering all the inequities and brutalities of early America, especially those inflicted on Native Americans, African slaves, and poor lower-class whites. Although Nash did not write extensively on women in early America, inevitably he has been sympathetic to their cause as well. Throughout his career Nash has always sought to project his political vision into his history writing.

As much as anyone, therefore, Nash seems to represent the best of the "race, class, gender" historians of the past generation who have succeeded remarkably in transforming the kind of history taught in many colleges and universities. His role as one of the leaders of this major historiographical transformation makes his new book on the American Revolution all the more significant. Here he applies the "race, class, gender" formula to what is arguably the most important event in American history.

Although Nash has titled his book *The Unknown American Revolution,* his interpretation of the Revolution may not be as unknown, at least to historians, as he makes out, owing to the revisionist work of many academic historians over the past four decades. As a result of this work, many people now know who Crispus Attucks is. (But can anyone name the four other victims of the Boston Massacre?) Of course, if polls of seniors from

leading colleges and universities are to be believed, many events of the Revolution appear to be unknown to even the best-educated Americans. Only 34 percent of college seniors were able to identify George Washington as an American general at the battle of Yorktown. Only 23 percent knew that James Madison was the Father of the Constitution. So when Nash laments the "historical amnesia" of Americans, he doesn't appreciate the half of it.

Nash intends his book to be "a history of inclusion," an effort to bring into the story of the Revolution those who have been long forgotten: poor whites, Indians, African Americans, and women. Compared to the likes of Washington and Madison, these people may have been lowly and insignificant, but they "did not see themselves as puppets dancing on the strings of the supposed leaders." They were instead "agents of change" in a "people's revolution," which was "an upheaval among the most heterogeneous people to be found anywhere along the Atlantic littoral in the eighteenth century."

By concentrating on these forgotten people, Nash's account, or so he believes, will capture "the true radicalism of the American Revolution." It will demonstrate the Revolution's "highly diverse and fragmented character" and put to rest once and for all the comfortable notion of "united colonists rising up as a unified body to get the British lion's paw off the backs of their necks."

It's not clear who believes anymore that the colonists rose up against the British as a unified body. Certainly no reputable historian of the Revolution believes that. But Nash seems to need such straw men—"a unified story of the nation's birth"—that he sets up throughout his book in order to more easily knock them down.

In fact, beneath all Nash's multicultural inclusions exists a rather old-fashioned interpretation of the Revolution. Nash's book is an updated version of the old Progressive interpretation of the Revolution made famous a century ago by such historians as Carl Becker, Charles Beard, and Arthur Schlesinger, Sr. Becker is the historian who made the well-known

quip that the Revolution was not only about home rule, it was also about who was to rule at home. Nash accepts this dual nature of the Revolution— "It was a civil war at home as well as a military struggle for national liberation"—and refers to it throughout his book. Like the older Progressive historians, he sees two fairly coherent groups—the radicals made up of ordinary laboring people and the conservatives dominated by rich exploitative elites—struggling for control throughout the period.

Nash has divided his chapters into chronological units: 1761–1766, 1766– 1774, 1774–1776, and so on to his final chapter, 1781–1785. In each of these chronologically organized chapters he describes one after the other the actions of the oppressed and abused peoples with whom he is concerned. In Virginia they were "the driving force for Independence," and in no place were they ever a minority. "In reality," he says, these downtrodden people in "the nether strata of colonial society and . . . outside 'respectable' society were *most* of the people of revolutionary society." For these forgotten people, "for the people whom this book has featured, the Revolution was visionary and experimental." And again: "Without their ideas, dreams, and blood sacrifice, the American Revolution would never have occurred, would never have followed the course that we can now comprehend, and would never have reverberated around the world among oppressed people down to the present day."

So much for the ringing statements of Patrick Henry, John Adams, Thomas Jefferson, and the other great white males. In Nash's view, these elite leaders of the Revolution—these much-celebrated founders—were "reluctant revolutionaries" who had to be dragged into revolution by all those forgotten people below them. The problem is that many if not most of Nash's forgotten and oppressed people either fought on the side of the British or wanted to, so it is hard to know what to make of his claims.

Those ordinary people who did support the Revolution may not be as forgotten as Nash assumes. We now have many social histories of common people in the era (for example, in the work of Howard Zinn). Moreover, no respectable historian, even those who write big popular biographies of

George Washington and John Adams, has ever denied that the Revolution's success depended upon the participation of masses of ordinary people. But gaining recognition of the participation of ordinary people in the Revolution is not really Nash's point. He wants to show that those lowly people "*not* in positions of power and privilege" had their own agendas and, as the fashionable phrase goes, their own "agency" in bringing on the Revolution. His "lower-class and enslaved people, whom colonial leaders had always hoped to keep in the wings, if not off stage altogether," were now determined to assert themselves. These oppressed people were the popular radicals who carried on the Revolution in the face of opposition from elite conservatives who "tried to squash the popular movements of the early war years." Since Nash holds a quasi-Marxian view of American society, his "laboring-class people" necessarily become the "poor" who "suffered" from exploitation from "the wealthy." In the end, it was this exploitation that made these "laboring classes" rise up against their rich rulers.

Although the white colonists in British North America enjoyed the highest standard of living of any people in the Western world, one would never know it from Nash's account. No common person seems to have been satisfied with his lot. "Most" people in Boston, for example, "had fared badly" in the eighteenth century; indeed, merchants and other rich people for more than a generation had "disdained humble Bostonians and totted up their profits while the poor suffered." According to Nash, poverty was everywhere, especially in the cities, where by the 1770s there were "men in great numbers who experienced class oppression firsthand and were learning to express themselves openly." Even more erroneous is his view of the Virginians. He says they lived in a "highly stratified society, where tenant farmers greatly outnumbered landowners." Tenancy certainly existed in Virginia, but in no way was it the normal form of landholding.

All the incidents of rural rioting and urban mobbing that took place in the decade or so leading up to the Revolution are Nash's evidence for

popular resistance to all this class exploitation. Mobbing and rioting are exceedingly familiar to historians who have written a great deal about them. Unfortunately, however, these phenomena do not support Nash's argument. Not only did the rural rioting have little or nothing to do with the Revolution, but the urban mobs, which were indeed directed at British authority, did not represent the class upheaval that Nash assumes.

The rural riots all arose out of peculiar local circumstances and were hardly expressions of some sort of coherent class warfare. In New York in the 1760s, farmers, mostly immigrants from New England, where fee-simple landholding was the rule, rose in protest against what they believed were the archaic tenancy schemes of their New York landlords. In western North Carolina and in western Pennsylvania, rioters protested not only against unequal representation in the remote eastern assemblies, but in the case of North Carolina, against local fee gouging by carpetbagging officials, and in the case of Pennsylvania, against the Quaker-dominated assembly's pacifist unwillingness to aid the mostly Scots-Irish westerners in their fights against Indians. Contrary to Nash's contention, most of these rural rioters were anything but representative of most of the Revolutionaries. In North Carolina, indeed, the westerners, angry at the eastern patriot government, often remained loyal to the British Crown and fought against the Revolutionary cause. The same was true of many of the rioting tenants in New York.

Because Pennsylvania experienced the most radical change in 1776, largely through the efforts of Scots-Irish farmers and urban artisans, Nash gives its new state constitution a good deal of attention. The Revolutionary constitution provided for a unicameral legislature, term limits, a broad suffrage, and a plural executive. The constitution also stipulated that the assembly be reapportioned every seven years. "This commitment to proportional representation," Nash says, "was followed by no other state." This is a strange statement, since four other states—New Jersey, New York, Vermont, and South Carolina—wrote into their constitutions specific plans for periodic adjustments of their representation, so that, as the

New York constitution stated, it "shall for ever remain proportionate and adequate." This error is only one of many that Nash makes throughout his book. He mistakes Horace Walpole for his father, Robert Walpole, as prime minister of England. He writes that "American colonists, with rare exceptions, agreed that Parliament was entitled to pass external taxes meant to control the flow of trade"—even though Edmund S. Morgan and Helen M. Morgan decisively refuted this point more than fifty years ago. He refers to Edmund Randolph as Jefferson's son-in-law, confusing him with Thomas Mann Randolph. He says that Richard Henry Lee was "destined to be one of Washington's generals," mixing him up with his cousin Harry Lee. Small matters, perhaps, but cumulatively they tend to undermine a reader's confidence in Nash's knowledge of the period.

Nash greatly admires the radical Pennsylvania constitution of 1776. He thinks that of all the state constitutions, with its decentralized government and broad suffrage, it came closest to achieving a more democratic and equitable society. Of course, the fact that all the elites of Pennsylvania and elsewhere hated it makes it especially appealing to Nash. No leader disliked the Pennsylvania constitution more than John Adams. This gives Nash the opportunity to bash this famous Revolutionary whose own constitutional achievement—the Massachusetts constitution of 1780—protected the rich and offended "those who stared at poverty." Adams, Nash says, "loved liberty but not equality, and from this position he would not budge through the entire course of the long Revolution." This is an odd claim to make about someone who wrote ten years before the Declaration of Independence that "all men are created equal" and who worried about the power of aristocracy his entire life. As the distinguished historian R. R. Palmer wrote many years ago, "It seems hardly possible that anyone could read the *Defense of the Constitutions of the United States* without seeing that aristocracy was Adams' principal bugaboo."

Not only does Nash misunderstand the rural riots, but he misreads the urban mobbing of the 1760s and 1770s as well. Although these urban mobs were directed at various royal officials and could be very disorderly,

they were not unusual. Indeed, they were characteristic of eighteenth-century Anglo-American crowd behavior on both sides of the Atlantic—common protests by various groups against a perceived communal wrong—from the harsh impressment of sailors to temporary shortages of food. But Nash sees them very differently. He depicts them as direct challenges by the lower classes against the exploitative upper classes. In Boston, he writes, "the mobbish attackers were those who had suffered economic hardship while others fattened their purses." Because the mobs were a form of class warfare, he says, "the 'mob' has been feared throughout history by upper-class power holders, and historians have not been immune from this fear."

I don't know what historians he is thinking about, but he certainly writes as if he has never heard of the work on eighteenth-century American mobs by Pauline Maier and Paul Gilje, who have no fear of mobs. As these scholars have superbly demonstrated, the premodern mobs, far from being the preludes to Revolutionary class warfare, were often testimonies to the paternal and hierarchal organization of the society. Effigy hangings and status reversals in which the lowly acted the part of their betters (making the village idiot king for a day, for example) were protests, to be sure, and they could get out of hand, but generally they worked to emphasize the existing hierarchy of the society. Often they grew out of, and had much in common with, traditional Saturnalian festivals and popular rites. Far from fearing such mobs, many of the elite participated in them. Even the arch-Tory Thomas Hutchinson admitted in 1768 that "Mobs, a sort of them at least, are constitutional."

But what of all the rhetoric about the laboring people contesting the aristocratic few that Nash draws on to make his case for class warfare? There was, indeed, a serious division in eighteenth-century American society that reverberated through the northern states over the succeeding decades, but it was not the one that Nash describes. Instead of being divided between a rich upper class and a poor working class, as Nash sees it, anachronistically anticipating a later nineteenth-century division be-

tween employers and employees, eighteenth-century American society was still divided between a leisured gentry and the mass of artisans and other laborers who worked with their hands, many of them the businessmen of the future.

Since Aristotle's day, leisured elites had held those who worked, especially those who worked with their hands, in great contempt, as mean and despicable beings; such contempt for work was what justified slavery for thousands of years. But since the seventeenth century, if not earlier, ever-growing numbers of these laboring people had increased in wealth and self-consciousness to the point where these artisans, tradesmen, and others began calling themselves "middling sorts," caught between the gentry and those below them. Since the gentry continued to hold in contempt these middling men who worked with their hands or who ran shops with many employees where such work went on, it was inevitable that these middling sorts, angry and resentful at being so long denigrated, would mount increasing protests against arrogant leisured elites, including landed gentry, big merchants, and professionals, who unlike today's professionals did not put in many billable hours. To be thought vile and inferior because they worked became more and more insufferable to the growing numbers of artisans, tradesmen, and market farmers in the North, especially since they were sometimes wealthier than the aristocratic elites who looked down on them. So there was social conflict in the Revolution, but it was not quite the kind of class conflict that Nash presumes.

Nash is quite correct when he says that "all politics takes place within social and economic contexts." If we need a social force to explain the Revolution as it worked itself out in the northern states, we can do no better than to focus on these middling sorts who used the egalitarian rhetoric of the Revolution to justify their cause, an often exaggerated rhetoric that Nash usually reads literally. If all these middling people were suffering oppression, it was largely psychological or cultural oppression, for many of them were quite economically well off. By the early nineteenth century these middling people had destroyed the leisured pretensions of

would-be aristocrats in the northern states and had made work a badge of honor to a degree not duplicated in any other Western nation. Not that they made the society's distribution of wealth more equal; indeed, as Nash knows only too well, because he was one of the first to document it, wealth in northern society was more unequally distributed after the Revolution than before. Still, people felt more equal, wealth being the least humiliating form of asserting superiority over another; and this paradox can be explained only by the decline in the older idea of aristocracy and a radical change in the meaning of work.

Nash is so bound up in the modern Marxian categories of class warfare that he can make little sense of what happened. Since wealth alone was not the source of the social division, Nash has trouble understanding how the gentry could look down upon a very wealthy tradesman like Benjamin Franklin as long as he still ran his printing firm. As far as the gentry were concerned, a printer businessman, no matter how rich, no matter how many employees he had, was still a laborer. (If one wants to explain the Revolution in Marxian class terms, it probably is best seen as a bourgeois revolution, at least in the North.)

Since for Nash only actual economic oppression and real poverty can account for a revolution, he has to exaggerate the deplorable conditions under which the laboring people suffered. Thus he writes that "urban poverty challenged the governing modes of thought, shook confidence in the internal economic system, and intensified class feeling." Getting rich in America was "an illusion." Debtors were always poor with their backs to the wall. "Nagging poverty at the bottom of society and the crumbling of economic security in the middle gave rise to the most intense concern about the future." The Revolution became a response to all these class tensions and split the society into two coherent groups of poor radicals and rich conservatives. "It was the new vigor of urban laboring people in defining and pursuing their goals that raised the specter, in the minds of many upper-class townsmen, of a radicalized form of politics and radically changed society."

In his description of eighteenth-century white society Nash has inverted everything, changed the proportions of things. Instead of being the wealthiest and most equitable society in the eighteenth-century Western world, at least for whites, in Nash's account American society becomes a poverty-stricken, class-ridden place where rich and poor were at each other's throats. Nash never quite reconciles this woeful view of American society with the one that (as he admits) had the broadest ownership of farm land of any place in the Western world.

Locked into his Marxian categories, Nash inevitably misinterprets what was happening in the society, especially in the crucial decade of the 1780s. Although the war against Britain was winding down after Yorktown, he writes, "the war against poverty and the yawning gap between rich and poor was far from over." For most farmers, he says, the end of the Revolution "did not bring equality or enhanced economic opportunities." Instead, poverty, increasing debt, and "less than rosy prospects" characterized the years following the Revolution.

This seriously misreads the decade. No doubt debtors did get hurt during economic downswings, especially when the Massachusetts government in the 1780s increased taxes and tried to amortize its debt too quickly. But to see debtors as the poor is to misunderstand what was happening in the economy. Borrowing money, as we of any generation in American history ought to appreciate, was a sign not of poverty but of heightened expectations. People wanted to trade and exchange goods with one another. To do so they needed money, lots of it, and because gold and silver (real money) were scarce, they pressured their governments to print paper money. Commercial activity, democracy, and paper money went together, as the experience of the most commercial and democratic colony and state in the country, Rhode Island, demonstrates: it was the colony and state that printed by far the most paper money.

Despite economic fluctuations and political disorder, the 1780s were anything but wretched. As the British demographer Jim Potter long ago pointed out, the 1780s were the fastest growing decade demographically

in the whole of American history. This growth was owed not to immigration, which was negligible, but to the fact that people had high expectations and were marrying earlier and having more children. Many Americans were actively pursuing the promise of happiness that Jefferson had held out to them, something that Joyce Appleby has brilliantly documented in her work. The "unrestrained capitalism" that Nash scornfully talks about emerging in the 1780s was the product not, as he thinks, of a few mandarins, such as Robert Morris and Alexander Hamilton, but rather of the emerging middling multitudes of small producers, craftsmen entrepreneurs, and market farmers—his "laboring people"—who hitherto have been the oppressed heroes of his story.

In dealing with the participation of women in the Revolution, Nash pretty much follows the latest historical literature, except he goes too far in turning Abigail Adams into a protofeminist, taking literally all her teasing of her husband and emphasizing that she seriously believed the point "about men enslaving women." In order to demonstrate women as "agents of change" in the Revolution, he rather patronizingly lists all the contributions they made—from boycotting British goods, ostracizing loyalists, and leading food riots to making homespun and becoming camp followers of the Continental Army. "The army, in fact," he says, "could not do without women." Since this is true of armies from time immemorial, it hardly seems something to celebrate as peculiarly American or as an assertion of women's agency. And most radical feminists presumably would regard camp following as patriarchal oppression run wild.

Unlike many earlier studies of women and the Revolution, Nash's account does see real progress for women coming out of the Revolution: in education, in literacy, and in participation in civic and benevolent activities. By the 1790s with more and more talk of the equality of women, the Revolution had begun to erode the patriarchal world of the ancien régime. But Nash has much more difficulty relating his other "agents of change" to the Revolution: the Indians and African American slaves. His difficulty does not come from his excellent accounts of the experiences of Native

Americans and the free and enslaved blacks during the Revolution; rather, his difficulty comes from his attempts to relate these accounts to his understanding of the Revolution as an upheaval of forgotten people.

Perhaps Nash should have simply written off the Revolution as a failure, as some younger historians have. They consider the Revolution a failure because, as one of them puts it, it "failed to free the slaves, failed to offer full political equality to women, . . . failed to grant citizenship to Indians, [and] failed to create an economic world in which all could compete on equal terms."* If Nash shared that belief, he would have an easier time dealing with the fate of the Indians and black slaves. To his credit he does not believe the Revolution was a failure, "even for those with the most expansive ideas about a truly free, just, and equal society." It was, like all other revolutions, simply "incomplete."

But how could it have been made more complete for the Indians and the black slaves? For the Indians the Revolution was a catastrophe. Many of the Indian nations allied themselves with the British, rightly assuming that the British Crown could better protect their hunting grounds than the land-hungry Americans. Then the British government, in the peace treaty of 1783, ceded sovereignty over all Indian lands up to the Mississippi to the United States. And because so many Indians had fought on the side of the British, Americans tended to regard as enemies even those Indians who had been their allies.

Trying to extract some kind of worthwhile significance for the Indians out of the Revolution is not easy. If the Revolution was "rooted in a kind of dream life of a better future imagined by those who felt most dissatisfied with conditions they experienced as the quarrel with Great Britain unfolded," then it did not have much to offer the native peoples. It is difficult to see how their "ideas, dreams, and blood sacrifice" contributed to a Revolution that has "reverberated around the world among oppressed

---

* Peter C. Mancall, *Valley of Opportunity: Economic Culture Along the Upper Susquehanna, 1700–1800* (Ithaca, NY: Cornell University Press, 1991), 232.

people down to the present day." Indeed, it seems obvious that the Indians would have been much better off if the Revolution had failed. Once the Americans gained independence, it is hard to see any alternative to the tragedy that occurred.

Does Nash believe that anyone could have stopped the land-hungry white farmers from spilling over the Appalachians into Indian territory? Although the eastern elites that Nash most dislikes tried, at least in their rhetoric, to protect the Indian's culture, their few voices of compassion meant nothing to the hordes of white settlers on the ground. The very local popular democracy coming out of the Revolution that Nash so much praises made any federal resistance to the westward movement of the white settlers impossible. Nash never seems to appreciate that the "genocidal . . . land-crazed frontiersmen" he condemns were some of the very same people that he celebrates throughout as the poor, pugnacious Scots-Irish westerners standing up to all those rich, effete easterners.

For the black slaves and the Revolution the irony is equally powerful. For slaves in the North the Revolution was beneficial, for it set slavery on the road to abolition, often from pressure from blacks themselves. But southern slaves would have been far better off with a British victory. They might have been freed in 1834, when Britain abolished slavery in its empire, instead of having to wait for the Civil War. During the course of the Revolution, as Nash superbly shows, tens of thousands of southern slaves (these numbers are now contested) flocked to the British lines in search of freedom. In fact, before the Civil War the British army was the greatest instrument of emancipation in American history.

Nash is especially angry that the Revolutionaries let slip the best opportunity to eliminate slavery entirely from the country. He admits that the obstacles were formidable, but he insists that "inspired leadership" from the "national heroes" could have overcome them—a rather ironic statement in light of Nash's habitual contempt for the possibility of such national heroes doing anything positive. He mentions in particular the lack of leadership by Washington and Franklin, which is surprising since

both men actually did try to end slavery. Washington's experience in freeing his slaves in his will shows us how difficult such action was in the South in the late 1790s. He had to keep the will secret, for by 1799 his desire to free his slaves flew in the face of everyone around him, including apparently even his wife.

Historians these days are emphasizing the centrality of slavery to the early Republic, perhaps too much so. The Revolutionaries did not pay as much attention to slavery as we understandably wish they would have. They put a lot of confidence in the elimination of the slave trade promised for 1808 and lived with the illusion that slavery would naturally die away. As Oliver Ellsworth, the third chief justice of the Supreme Court, declared, "As population increases, poor labourers will be so plenty as to render slaves useless. Slavery in time will not be a speck in our country."

Many of the leading opponents of slavery, such as the wealthy southern gentleman John Laurens and the New England Federalist Theodore Sedgwick, were exactly the sorts of aristocratic upper-class types whom Nash dislikes. Those supporting slavery in Pennsylvania were precisely those Scots-Irish Presbyterian radicals whom Nash had earlier praised for writing such a popular constitution. He does not seem to realize that democracy and local popular control were not good for the causes of antislavery and the decent treatment of the native peoples.

Someone once said that all history is ironic, except when it is tragic. But Nash has no appreciation of these wise words; it is not in his temperament. He has no sense of irony or tragedy; he is all anger and indignation. Strangely, he stops his book in 1785 and does not apply his neo-Progressive scheme to the writing of the Constitution of 1787, the subject that in 1913 established the reputation of Charles Beard, the best known of the Progressive historians. By not discussing the origins of the Constitution, Nash avoids the embarrassment of having to deal with the modern multicultural claim that the Iroquois Indians made key contributions to the idea of federalism and the making of the Constitution. Maybe Nash sensed that his interpretation of his "unknown Revolution" was al-

ready so overloaded with modern multicultural politics that adding this outlandish claim would finally sink it.

## AFTERWORD

Present-day graduate students of history are well aware that "race, class, gender" is the mantra they must repeat as they proceed through their studies and write their dissertations. Of course, this emphasis on the themes of race, class, and gender has led to many excellent studies of women and slavery in early America (but not so many good studies of class). Yet so suffocating has been the stress on "race, class, gender" issues that sometimes beginning graduate students hesitate to write about anything else. A female historian who wanted to study the eighteenth-century founders told me that she was criticized by other female scholars for wasting her time working on those "dead white males."

# 21.

# PRESENTISM IN HISTORY

*Dark Bargain: Slavery, Profits, and the Struggle for the Constitution*
by Lawrence Goldstone (New York: Walker, 2005)
*American Taxation, American Slavery* by Robin L. Einhorn
(Chicago: University of Chicago Press, 2006)

*The New York Review of Books,* June 28, 2007

I T IS A TRUISM that history writing tends to reflect the times in which it is written. All history is "contemporary history," wrote the Italian historian Benedetto Croce, by which he meant that history is seen mainly through the eyes of the present and in relation to its problems. The distinguished American historian Bernard Bailyn agrees that history writing is not mere antiquarianism; he is keenly aware of the present's need to relate to the past and the power of that need in stimulating historical inquiry and writing. "There is always," he writes, "a need to extract from the past some kind of bearing on contemporary problems, some message, commentary, or instruction to the writer's age, and to see reflected in the past familiar aspects of the present." But without "critical control," this need, says Bailyn, "generates an obvious kind of presentism, which at worst becomes indoctrination by historical example."

Thus at the beginning of the twentieth century when class conflict was rife—poor versus rich, western farmers versus eastern merchants, soft

money versus hard money—it was not surprising that history writing about the American Revolution and the formation of the Constitution tended to express these turbulent social circumstances. Historians like Carl Becker and Arthur Schlesinger, Sr., wrote about class conflict in the Revolution, and Charles Beard attempted to show that the Constitution grew out of a struggle between different kinds of property interests.

Since our greatest domestic issue over the past half century has been race relations, it was inevitable that historians would look back at the sources of our race problem and write the fullest and richest accounts of slavery in America that we have ever seen. It was inevitable too that our recent accounts of the Revolution and the founding of the nation would reflect our increased understanding of the importance of slavery to the history of America. Indeed, there is hardly a book now written about the founding of the nation that does not place the problem of slavery at its center. So in recent years we have had Leonard L. Richards's *The Slave Power* (2000); Don E. Fehrenbacher's *The Slaveholding Republic* (2001); Paul Finkelman's *Slavery and the Founders* (2001); Garry Wills's *"Negro President": Jefferson and the Slave Power* (2003); Alfred W. Blumrosen and Ruth G. Blumrosen's *Slave Nation: How Slavery United the Colonies and Sparked the American Revolution* (2005); and Gary Nash's *The Forgotten Fifth: African Americans in the Age of Revolution* (2006). Now we have these additional two books under review to help satisfy the seemingly insatiable desire of many historians today to place slavery at the heart of America's origins.

Thanks to the works of these historians and many others, we now know more about slavery and the founding of the nation than previous generations of historians ever thought possible. But is all this new historical knowledge true to the reality of the past? Have the historians who have written these works exercised Bailyn's "critical control" and avoided distorting the past with their present-minded concerns?

No one can deny the importance of slavery to the development of early America. Of the total American population of two and a half million

on the eve of independence, one fifth—a half million men, women, and children—was enslaved. The most populous colony, Virginia, had the most slaves—two hundred thousand, or 40 percent of its population. Although most slaves lived in the southern colonies, slavery was not inconsequential in the North. Fourteen percent of New York's population was enslaved. New Jersey held 8 percent and Rhode Island held 6 percent of their populations in lifetime hereditary bondage. Northerners, especially Rhode Islanders, were also deeply involved in the international slave trade. Slavery existed throughout the colonies, and nearly every white American colonist directly or indirectly benefited from it.

It is also important, however, to provide some historical context for understanding the omnipresence of slavery in colonial America. We need to know just how cruel and brutal the eighteenth-century ancien régime was in the years before the Revolution—cruel and brutal in a multitude of ways. Not only was there black slavery, but many whites were denied freedom and kept in various degrees of dependency. Indeed, the ubiquity of servitude in that patriarchal age tended to blur the conspicuousness of black slavery, especially in the North. Many masters regarded their white servants as "filth and scum," "miserable wretches," "insolent young Scoundrels," and sometimes treated them as harshly as masters treated their African slaves. A drunken and abusive servant being transported by ship to Virginia in the 1770s, for example, was horse-whipped, put in irons and thumbscrewed, and then gagged for a night and handcuffed for nine days.

Of course, such harsh treatment of white servants was rare compared to the ferocity with which some eighteenth-century masters treated their slaves. Regarding the African slaves as little more than animals, the slaveholders bought them at market, branded them, sometimes gave them names ordinarily reserved for dogs and horses, and bridled, haltered, and punished them as if they were domesticated livestock. Still, "the similarities in the treatment of slaves and servants, and in attitudes toward slaves

and the poor," writes Philip D. Morgan, the distinguished historian of early American slavery, "help explain how the overwhelming majority of Anglo-Americans took slavery for granted."*

Indeed, the fact that slavery had been taken for granted for thousands of years prior to the mid-eighteenth century must be the starting point in any assessment of its influence on early American politics and nationhood. With the exception of some isolated people with strong principles, especially Quakers, few Americans prior to the Revolutionary era seriously questioned the institution of slavery. It was the Revolution and its emphasis on liberty that made slavery a problem for Americans in the Revolutionary era.

Lawrence Goldstone, who is the author (with his wife, Nancy) of several works of history on subjects other than early America, begins his book *Dark Bargain* with a brief overview of the ways the interpretations of the origins of the Constitution have changed over the past two hundred years; he writes, without much self-reflection, that "the manner in which Americans have viewed the document is to a great extent a parallel of the manner in which the nation has viewed both itself and the role of slavery in its history."

Few historians of the Constitution, he says, have paid proper attention to the importance of slavery. Instead of describing the politics of slavery in the Convention, most present-day constitutional scholars, he complains, have been too caught up in philosophical abstractions. Recent accounts of the framing of the Constitution, he writes, have focused so exclusively on ideas that they have turned the document into nothing more than "a product of theory." By concentrating on the thinking of "a small number of cerebral delegates—Madison, Hamilton, Franklin, or even the recently resurrected Gouverneur Morris"—present-day histo-

---

* Philip D. Morgan, *Slave Counterpoint: Black Culture in the Eighteenth-Century Chesapeake and Lowcountry* (Chapel Hill: University of North Carolina Press, 1998), 271.

rians and political theorists have concluded that these few men "produced virtually the entire document among themselves."

Goldstone wants to correct this mistaken emphasis on ideas and theories in the making of the Constitution by describing it as the consequence of pragmatic politics, most of it involving slavery. "The story of the forging of the Constitution is as much a study of the forces and factors that comprised American life as it is a stringing together of the political theories of Madison, Hamilton, and Franklin." Slavery was at the heart of the making of the Constitution. "Of all the issues that would arise in Philadelphia," he says, "the one that evoked the most passion, the one that left the least possibility of compromise, the one that would most pit morality against pragmatism, was the question of slavery."

To concentrate our attention on the issue of slavery, Goldstone introduces several characters who he thinks have been relatively ignored in the story of the Convention, including Oliver Ellsworth and Roger Sherman of Connecticut and especially John Rutledge of South Carolina. Indeed, Rutledge is Goldstone's real hero. "If one man can truly be deemed Father of the Constitution, at least at the convention," he writes, "it is Rutledge." Rutledge, says Goldstone, made the Constitution a pro-slavery document.

Rutledge was the crucial person in bringing together the slaveholders of the Upper South with those of the Deep South in order to persuade the northern delegates to agree that slaves would be counted as three-fifths of a person for purposes of representation in the House of Representatives and the electoral college. He was also the central figure in fashioning a compromise with northerners, principally Ellsworth and Sherman, on protecting the slave trade for twenty years and on the regulation and taxing of overseas trade. It was Rutledge, Goldstone claims, who "put South Carolina on the winning side of both contests."

Most historians consider July 16 the decisive day in the Convention. That was the day on which the Connecticut Compromise was adopted,

which gave each state, however large or small, equal representation in the Senate. But Goldstone wants us instead to concentrate on July 12, which he considers of equal if not of greater importance. That was the day in which the three-fifths compromise was adopted—a victory, he suggests, for the South and South Carolina in particular. This counting of slaves as three-fifths of free persons for apportioning direct taxes and representation in the Congress and electoral college was part of the reason William Lloyd Garrison and other later abolitionists called the Constitution a "covenant with death and an agreement with hell."

Yet, as Goldstone admits, many southern delegates, including the entire South Carolina delegation, "had continually urged that slaves be counted in full" In other words, many southern delegates wanted slaves counted as five-fifths for purposes of representation, which would have substantially increased the power of the South in the House of Representatives and the electoral college. By contrast, the northern delegates preferred not to have the slaves represented at all. But South Carolina's motion to count the slaves as five-fifths of free persons was defeated seven states to three. So the three-fifths compromise might be seen as a defeat for the Carolinians if not a victory for the northern states.

If Goldstone is to establish Rutledge as the real father of the Constitution, he has to diminish James Madison's role in the Convention. Madison was the author of the Virginia Plan, which became the working model for the Convention. Crucial to Madison's plan was a veto power given to the Congress over all state laws and the proportional representation for each state of its people or its financial contributions or some combination in both houses of Congress. Any kind of proportional representation, Madison believed, was preferable to representation of the states as states. Since states represented as states was what was wrong with the Articles of Confederation, Madison was convinced that retaining any semblance of state sovereignty in the new national government would vitiate it and ultimately destroy it. That's why the Convention's rejection of his proposal for proportionate representation in both houses of the

Congress and the adoption of the Connecticut Compromise on July 16 so deeply depressed him and other national-minded delegates. So alarmed were they by what they correctly saw as their defeat (it was no "compromise" for them), they caucused the next day to decide whether or not to withdraw from the Convention.

Madison's passion on this issue of proportional representation in both houses of Congress helps explain his several arguments made prior to his defeat on July 16. Goldstone, like many other historians, takes these arguments out of context to demonstrate the importance of slavery to the Convention. Since the principal support for equal representation in the Congress came from the small states, who feared their interests would be swallowed up by the more populous states in a system of proportional representation, Madison desperately needed to get the delegates to think of their divisions in terms different from small versus large states. This is why he argued in the days preceding the Connecticut Compromise that it was "pretty well understood that the real difference of interests, lay not between the large & small but between the N. & Southn States," and that it was "the institution of slavery & its consequences formed the line of discrimination."

Once these statements are put in context, we can begin to understand why Madison was willing to go so far as to throw into the debate the specter of a sectional split in order to get his colleagues back to thinking about proportional representation in both houses of Congress. Of course, at that point he did not imagine the Civil War and had little inkling of how potentially explosive his statements were.

Giving a sense of surrounding circumstances, which is the essence of historical explanation, is not Goldstone's strong point. His account of the 1780s, for example, lacks such historical background. Although Virginians in that decade were actually relaxing their black codes that governed the slaves' lives, forming antislave societies, and manumitting their slaves by the thousands, Goldstone pictures the South in the 1780s gripped by an overriding fear of slave insurrections. (He could never account, for ex-

ample, for the College of William and Mary's conferring in 1791 an honorary degree on the celebrated British abolitionist Granville Sharp.) Goldstone turns this "ongoing fear of slave revolts" into "the lever" that Madison and the other nationalists "needed to generate interest in a meeting of all the states" in the summer of 1787. For Goldstone, Shays' Rebellion of debtor farmers in western Massachusetts in the winter of 1786–87 was simply an unnerving reminder to the slaveholding southerners of what their black slaves might do to them. Even more alarming in the 1780s, he claims, was the fear of forced emancipation. "As northerners either outlawed slavery or phased it out, southerners were convinced that their northern neighbors intended to compel them, either by financial pressure or force, to do the same. . . . Or," he suggests, "perhaps foreigners might free the slaves." Despite Goldstone's claims, we have little or no evidence that many southerners in the 1780s were possessed by these kinds of fears or that fears like these lay behind their willingness to create a stronger national government.

If we are to understand properly the role of slavery in the making of the Constitution, we have to try to rid ourselves of our knowledge of what happened in the succeeding decades. The founders did not know the future, any more than we do, and most of them at the outset lived with the illusion that slavery in the United States was dying away and would somehow eventually disappear, especially with the ending of the slave trade. Of course, they could not have been more wrong, but that mistaken confidence in the future, reinforced by misleading developments in the Upper South, including thousands of manumissions, the explosion of "freedom suits" in the courts, and the initial antislave sentiments of evangelical Protestant groups, made both northerners and Virginians willing to compromise on the issues of the three-fifths clause and the slave trade.

By 1820, following the crisis over whether Missouri could be admitted to the Union as a slave state, those illusions and that optimism were gone: from that moment the North and South saw themselves heading for a

cataclysmic confrontation. But it is anachronistic to read back into 1787 knowledge of that confrontation. Slavery was undoubtedly important in the making of the Constitution, but unfortunately it was not as important to most of the delegates as we today think it ought to have been.

Robin L. Einhorn has no problem reading the present back into the past or, for that matter, reading the past forward into the present. In her book, Einhorn, who is professor of history at the University of California, Berkeley, has no doubts about the manifest and latent effects of slavery on America. For her, slavery did not merely shape the making of the Constitution; it shaped as well the capacity of the South to become truly democratic, which led not only to the Civil War but to a profound American misunderstanding of the role of strong government that affects us even today. She has George W. Bush's red-state America very much on her mind and makes no effort whatsoever to hide her present-minded agenda.

At the outset, she rejects what she believes are several conventional narratives of American history. She dismisses the story that pits a liberty-loving, tax-averse people against an ever-encroaching federal government. With the income tax amendment and the emergence of the welfare state, this story, she writes, "has been a downhill slide ever since: government growing, tax burdens skyrocketing, and our liberty in more danger than George III ever posed." But equally false in her opinion is the "liberal" story that the growth of the federal government in the twentieth century came in response to the problems of industrialization and urbanization. The crucial weakness of this story, she claims, is that it is dated. It simply assumes that "the New Deal represented a progressive step toward a more democratic society and that Franklin Delano Roosevelt's four freedoms (of speech and religion, from want and fear) outlined a political program that everyone except a few crazy extremists supported." But, says Einhorn, these assumptions are no longer warranted. "Today, the former extremists run the country, championing 'creationism,' attacking regulation, and pledging to cut taxes no matter what the cuts do to the ability of our

governments to provide the services people want, from law enforcement to social security and environmental protection (meanwhile running budget deficits)."

But since "the former extremists" who still control the presidency and until recently the Congress as well were democratically elected, there has to be something fundamentally wrong with the way American democracy now works. We the people have been hoodwinked by elites, and this, Einhorn argues, is all because of the way American taxation and American slavery became intertwined and influenced Americans' attitude toward government. By investigating the various ways Americans, right from the beginning of their history, dealt with taxation at the colony, state, and federal levels, Einhorn finds that democracy and liberty in the North created confidence in strong government; slavery created the opposite. In other words, says Einhorn, "the antigovernment rhetoric that continues to saturate our political life is rooted in slavery rather than liberty. The American mistrust of government is not part of our democratic heritage. It comes from slaveholding elites who had no experience with democratic governments where they lived and knew only one thing about democracy: that it threatened slavery." It is not at all clear how a nonslaveholding radical like Thomas Paine, who favored democracy and yet fully shared Jefferson's mistrust of government, fits into Einhorn's argument.

With or without Paine, however, Einhorn's account is certainly revisionism with a vengeance. She clearly realizes the radical implications of her argument. Jefferson as a southern slaveholder has to be not merely brought down a peg (which historians have been doing for decades) but kicked right out of the story of the development of liberty and democracy in America. "The Jeffersonian story is wrong," she says. The slaveholding founders, especially Jefferson and Madison, worked out a "brilliant" narrative, "in which, not coincidentally, they were the heroes," that has deceptively dominated American culture for over two hundred years. Jefferson and Madison told this story "in the romantic idiom" borrowed from radical British opposition thinking that historians have called the

"republican ideology." This ideology, which Einhorn dismisses as a mere cover for slavery, not only idealized independent yeoman farmers and country life, but rested on a profound fear of bloated monarchlike governments, high taxes, large public debts, and standing armies. When Hamilton and the Federalists tried in the 1790s to impose just such a monarchlike government on the new United States, Jefferson resisted, "retailed the [republican] ideology with all the trappings," and led the opposition against these native tyrants just as Americans had resisted the British tyrants in the 1770s.

Einhorn mocks this conventional Jeffersonian story that hides the reality of slavery and southern class conflict behind popular talk of liberty. "The Jeffersonian 'Revolution of 1800' had nothing to do with slaveholders taking over the federal government," she writes sarcastically. "It brought 'the people' to power."

How, she asks, could historians be taken in by such a fatuous story? One reason they have been deluded, she claims, is that some of the people who told the story in the North actually were poor farmers and artisans. Precisely because the North was more democratic than the South, it contained more "'plebeian' writers" who could teach the lower orders how to organize against "commercial elites" much more effectively than the yeoman farmers of the South could organize against the slaveholding elites. Consequently, wealthy southern slaveholders like Jefferson and Madison did not have to defend their superior status or denounce democracy in the ways the northern Federalist elites, such as Gouverneur Morris, had to do. "As a result," Einhorn writes, "they left behind fewer elitist statements for us to use against them." If the southern yeoman farmers had only contested their elites as northern farmers and artisans did, Jefferson and Madison might have been forced to expose themselves as the hypocritical slaveholding aristocrats they really were.

It is high time, says Einhorn, that we junk this fraudulent Jeffersonian narrative of the origins of America and put a more accurate story in its place, one that puts slavery and taxation front and center where they

belong. Unless we expose the reality of slavery in the past and the power of the slaveholders in keeping government weak and taxes low, we are apt to lose confidence in our present-day democracy. Indeed, she says, "our invocations of 'democracy' are coming to sound fatuous once again." And this is because the heirs of the slaveholding founders who so perverted our attitudes toward government are "back" in control of our government, still claiming to be vulnerable elites needing protection from taxation and government. To save our democracy, concludes Einhorn, "we must purge the legacies of the slaveholders and their demands for 'security' from our public life."

To retell the story of America, which means filling in "the gulf between this Jeffersonian story and the truth," Einhorn has chosen "to use the history of tax policies and tax debates as a lens to focus in on when, where, and with what kinds of results democratic governments existed in the United States." Einhorn begins her analysis by comparing the tax policies of Virginia and Massachusetts going back to the colonial period. She has very little sympathy with the difficulties premodern governments had in extracting money from their people. With her modern idea of progressive taxation in mind, she repeatedly faults the tax systems of these early governments for being regressive and for not favoring equity over simplicity. Since her purpose is to show the insidious influence of slavery, she has to play down the fact that Virginia's dispersed and corrupt county governments and its poll tax on tithables were established in the seventeenth century well before slaves in any numbers were introduced into the colony. Instead, she implies that Virginia's corrupt county politics, which "was far from democratic," and its primitive tax system flowed from slavery and compares them to the less corrupt, more democratic politics and more sophisticated tax structure of relatively slave-free Massachusetts. She even questions the view of Edmund S. Morgan and other historians that by the mid-eighteenth century Virginia had developed a system of responsible aristocratic government that served the public reasonably well. Instead, she contends that slaveholding Virginia created an oligar-

chic system in which "clever members of a privileged gentry class" simply milked the public for their own benefit. "Corruption," she says, "... lay at the heart of gentry rule." No wonder "Virginians did not trust their officials," and no wonder they came to believe in minimal government.

In contrast with Virginia the "remarkably democratic" government of Massachusetts could do no wrong. Even when Massachusetts town officials flouted provincial tax laws, they did so in ways that illustrated their "competence and sophistication." Even though Massachusetts's taxes were "as regressive as Virginia's," they were administered more fairly and with less corruption. Since slavery was not involved in the tax politics of Massachusetts, the history of taxation in the colony and state was "recognizably modern"; it was a history "in which various groups competed over the distribution of tax burdens"—something not experienced by Virginians.

Einhorn continues with a detailed and desultory discussion of the differing tax systems of several other colonies and states, focusing on those of Pennsylvania and South Carolina. Surprisingly, slaveholding South Carolina created as sophisticated a tax system as that of democratic Pennsylvania and one that was "the most progressive on the continent." Lest this claim damage her thesis, Einhorn is quick to explain that South Carolina did not really have any tax politics in which ordinary settlers pooled their tax revenues to buy roads, schools, and courthouses. Instead, the history of taxation in South Carolina is "a story about how elites distributed burdens among themselves." Amid all the diverse tax systems, the essential point, Einhorn maintains, is that the northern colonies and states "generally taxed wider ranges of objects in more sophisticated ways" than the southern slaveholding colonies and states. Because of the relative absence of slaves, governments were also "more democratic in the North than in the South." Einhorn's lesson for us today is obvious: sophisticated high-tax systems fairly and competently administered are a measure of real democracy.

In the second part of her book, Einhorn moves to taxation at the fed-

eral level during the early decades of the new Republic. At this level, taxation was generally confined to customs duties or tariffs levied on imported goods; when tried, other sorts of taxes—direct taxes and excise taxes—did not last long. The reason the early Congresses focused exclusively on the tariff, she says, was that it was "the only tax Congress could adopt without talking about slavery." She doesn't make much of the simplicity and indirectness of the tariff and never mentions President Jefferson's reason for favoring it: as he told the Congress in 1806, "the great mass of the articles on which impost is paid is foreign luxuries, purchased by those only who are rich enough to afford themselves the use of them."

Throughout her book Einhorn has many serious and substantial discussions of tax policies and tax politics, and one wishes she had done more of that, especially since early American taxation is a much-neglected subject. We can all agree that slavery was the crucial element separating the South from the North, that the antebellum South was less democratic than the North, and that the tax systems of the northern states tended to be more sophisticated than those of the southern states. But Einhorn is not satisfied to establish these important points. So interested is she in showing the influence of slavery persisting into our own day that she sometimes seems to exaggerate its reach.

Take, for example, her discussion of the various "uniformity clauses" adopted by many of the new northern and western states in their antebellum constitutions, which consumes a large part of the third section of her book. These constitutional uniformity clauses required that different forms of property be treated "uniformly"—that is, that they be assessed in the same way and taxed at the same rate. No one kind of property—farmland, for example—could be taxed at a higher rate than any other kind of property of equal value—financial assets, for example. Many of the new northern and western states adopted such clauses out of a Jacksonian democratic desire to ensure that their legislatures would be bound by a rule that would secure equal taxation and thus would not tax majorities more heavily than minorities. In their desire for equality these

Jacksonian states, according to Einhorn, misunderstood the real source of such uniformity clauses. She is sure that the idea behind the uniformity clauses originated in the desire of southern slaveholders to protect themselves from oppressive taxation on one of their most valuable properties—their slaves—by nonslaveholding majorities, even though none of the constitutions of the states of the Deep South actually contained any such uniformity clause. The framers in the states of the North and Northwest that adopted such clauses, including the later states of California and Oregon, Einhorn says, simply didn't know what they were doing; they mistook a defense of slavery as a defense of equality. "Because they did not realize that these constitutional restraints on majority rule were elitist restraints on 'the people,'" she writes, "they turned concessions to slaveholders into shelters for other elites." Thus by protecting the property rights of minority elites, slavery stretched its terrible political tentacles into the free states of the North and Northwest, and by extension even into our own time.

Too much of Einhorn's book follows this pattern of argument. Slavery was "the elephant in the room" that no one wanted to notice; yet she assumes it was everywhere influencing events, even when the evidence for such influences is hard to come by. The evidence is scarce because the southern political leaders hid their real motives—to defend slavery—beneath their "romantic idiom" of republicanism. Inevitably, her account has no place for idealism. Although all the leading founders condemned slavery as inconsistent with everything the Revolution was about, Einhorn is sure that "they had no intention of taking any steps toward abolishing it."

Her picture of the seventy-eight-year-old Madison in the Virginia constitutional convention of 1829–30 as an inveterate and deceitful defender of slavery with nearly fifty years of experience to draw upon is a caricature. "He had mastered the manipulation of the terms 'persons' and 'property'—to defend whatever concessions slaveholders were demanding at any particular moment—in his struggles with northerners in the

1780s." Although "nobody had ever guilt-tripped Madison successfully," he was finally ready, she says, to come clean on what she believes was always his hidden desire to defend slavery. Unfortunately, she totally misunderstands the conciliatory role Madison was trying to play in a convention deeply divided over the representation of eastern slaveholders. Madison initially favored the cause of the state's western nonslaveholders who wanted representation in the legislature based on white population alone, but out of fear that the convention would collapse and the state would break apart he eventually came to side with the eastern slaveholders and to favor some representation in the legislature of their "peculiar" interest in their slaves. By ignoring Madison's desperate efforts at compromise, Einhorn's account has none of the contextual complexity that makes, for example, historian Drew McCoy's description of Madison in the Virginia convention, in his book *The Last of the Fathers* (1989), so sensitive and compelling. Perhaps what she needed in this account of Madison, and throughout her book, was not merely more of what Bernard Bailyn calls the historian's "critical control" but also some sense of the tragedy of the past.

## AFTERWORD

I suppose the most flagrant examples of present-mindedness in history writing come from trying to inject politics into history books. I am reminded of Rebecca West's wise observation that when politics comes in the door, truth flies out the window. Historians who want to influence politics with their history writing have missed the point of the craft; they ought to run for office.

# INDEX

# CREDITS

# THE PURPOSE OF THE PAST